DISPUTE PREVENTION THROUGH COMMUNITY ENGAGEMENT IN INFRASTRUCTURE DEVELOPMENT IN THE ASIA PACIFIC

SHAHLA F. ALI
University of Hong Kong

CAMBRIDGE
UNIVERSITY PRESS

CAMBRIDGE
UNIVERSITY PRESS

Shaftesbury Road, Cambridge CB2 8EA, United Kingdom

One Liberty Plaza, 20th Floor, New York, NY 10006, USA

477 Williamstown Road, Port Melbourne, VIC 3207, Australia

314–321, 3rd Floor, Plot 3, Splendor Forum, Jasola District Centre,
New Delhi – 110025, India

Cambridge University Press is part of Cambridge University Press & Assessment,
a department of the University of Cambridge.

We share the University's mission to contribute to society through the pursuit of
education, learning and research at the highest international levels of excellence.

www.cambridge.org
Information on this title: www.cambridge.org/9781009497664

DOI: 10.1017/9781009497688

When citing this work, please include a reference to the DOI 10.1017/9781009497688

First published 2026

Cover image: zonadearte / DigitalVision Vectors via Getty Images.

A catalogue record for this publication is available from the British Library

A Cataloging-in-Publication data record for this book is available from the Library of Congress

ISBN 978-1-009-49766-4 Hardback
ISBN 978-1-009-49765-7 Paperback

DISPUTE PREVENTION THROUGH COMMUNITY ENGAGEMENT IN INFRASTRUCTURE DEVELOPMENT IN THE ASIA PACIFIC

This book explores the emerging development of community–investor dispute prevention and facilitation mechanisms employed by multilateral and national development banks in the Asia Pacific region. In the decades since the development of the first accountability mechanisms were introduced, much has been learned about public consultation, community engagement and dispute prevention during the early stages of major infrastructure development programs. Drawing on case studies, project statistics and survey data, this book explores the achievements, challenges and lessons learned in community–investor dispute prevention and resolution in infrastructure projects in twelve states in the Asia Pacific region. Given the widescale impact of such projects, understanding how to advance consultation practices with local communities is necessary to realise the benefits of sustainable growth. This book allows readers to understand that localised decision-making channels, far from aggregating disputes, conversely provide a conduit to incorporate joint aspirations into project design such that disputes are avoided.

SHAHLA F. ALI is a professor of law at the University of Hong Kong, where her teaching and research focus on arbitration, governance and law, and sustainable development in a comparative context. She serves as a bilingual arbitrator and advises on mediation systems design and training with US Agency for International Development, International Finance Corporation/World Bank, Asian Development Bank, Asian Infrastructure Investment Bank and the United Nations.

When an effort is participatory, in the sense that it seeks to involve the people themselves in the generation and application of knowledge . . . all forge together a path of progress.

Universal House of Justice, letter dated 26 November 2012

CONTENTS

FIGURES

TABLES

ACKNOWLEDGMENTS

The research for this book has been made possible by funds from the government of Hong Kong's Research Grants Council HKU 17610921 and CRF C7030-24 G. Without the valuable observations from dispute resolution and mitigation practitioners in the Asia Pacific, including members of the Asian Development Bank, Asian Infrastructure Investment Bank, European Bank of Reconstruction and Development and the World Bank, the practical insights in this book would not be possible.

Many people have helped with this book. Special thanks to the Cambridge University Press publishing team, including Joe Ng who expertly oversaw the review and publication of this book. Anonymous reviewers provided extremely valuable input at the early stages of the project. Special thanks go to an outstanding team of research assistants including Fan Ziwei, Hayley Chan, Lily Li, Bonnie Lai, Bill Sun, Faith Lee, Angel, Fiona Zhang, Prakritree Yonzon, Abdullah Bin, Claudia, Siddharth, Nathan Tsang, Stephanie, Matt, Geoff, Gao YueYang and John Tseung.

Numerous colleagues have provided valuable insights that have improved this book. I am grateful for fruitful exchanges with Kevin Davis, Mathew Erie, Hiro Aragaki, Eric Feldman, Susan Franck, Jean Oi, Hui Li, May Farid, Lori Noguchi, David Palmer, Ma Jun and Fan ZiWei. I am also thankful to our law faculty dean Fu Hualing, associate deans for research Simon Young and Michael Ng, and department heads Zhao Yun and Michael Jackson for providing a supportive research environment at the University of Hong Kong. I am also grateful to participants who shared valuable feedback at the following conferences: Asian Law and Society Association Conference (Seoul, Hanoi); International Association of Comparative Law (Paris); CASS International Law Conference (Beijing); ABS (Association for Borderlands Studies) Annual Conference (Atlanta); IACM (International Association for Conflict Management, Singapore); Law and Society Association Conference (Denver, Puerto Rico); Singapore Convention Week; ICCA (International Council for Commercial

Arbitration, Hong Kong); American Society of International Law (Washington, DC); American Society of Comparative Law Conference (Miami); Asian Law Scholars Conference (University of Washington); Comparative Procedural Law and Justice (CPLJ) Max Planck Institute (Luxembourg); International Association of Procedural Law (Brescia); and the American Bar Association (ABA) Section on Dispute Resolution Spring Conference.

This book is dedicated to my parents, Charleen and Nasrollah Maghzi, and after my father's passing, my mom's husband Steve. All that is positive in this book reflects the support and generosity of family, including my two beautiful girls, husband, siblings, colleagues, research participants, family, friends and associates. All errors and omissions are my own.

ABBREVIATIONS

ADB	Asian Development Bank
ADC	Amaravati Development Corporation
ADGM	Abu Dhabi Global Market
AfDB	African Development Bank
AGL	Adjaristsqali Georgia LLC
AIIB	Asian Infrastructure Investment Bank
ALU	Awami Labor Union
AM	accountability mechanism
AMAN	Association for Mass Advancement Network
APCRDA	Andhra Pradesh Capital Region Development Authority
AS	advisory services
ASCCDP	Amaravati Sustainable Capital City Development Project
ASM	artisanal and small-scale mining
BAC	Beijing Arbitration Commission
BCRM	compliance review and mediation unit
BCS	broad community support
BIT	bilateral investment treaty
Blue Book	dispute resolution mechanism for the Belt and Road
BOT	build, operate, transfer
BP	British Petroleum (Shah Deniz) Limited
BRG	Bismark Ramu Group
BRI	Belt and Road Initiative
BSDA	Benban Solar Developers Association
BSL	Benban Solar Labour
BSP	Benban Solar Park
BT	build, transfer
BUC	Beijing Urban Construction
CABEI	Central American Bank for Economic Integration
CAD	Canadian dollars
CAO	Compliance Advisor Ombudsman
CBA	collective bargaining agreement
CCCMC	China Chamber of Commerce of Metals, Minerals and Chemicals Importers and Exporters

CCPIT	China Council for the Promotion of International Trade
CEIU	Complaints-resolution, Evaluation and Integrity Unit
CERC	Committee on the Elimination of Racial Discrimination
CICT	China Information and Communication Technologies Group Corporation
CJSC	closed joint-stock company
CPEC	China–Pakistan Economic Corridor
CPPA	Central Power Purchasing Agency
CRO	complaint receiving officer
CRP	Office of the Compliance Review Panel
CSO	civil society organisation
CSR	corporate social responsibility
CTWG	community technical working group
DCI	Department of Commerce and Industry
DEG	Deutsche Investitions and Entwicklungesellschaft MBH
DMC	developing member country
DSO	direct shipping of ore
E&S	environmental and social
EA	environmental assessment
EBRD	European Bank of Reconstruction and Development
EHT	Elected Herders Team
EIA	environmental impact assessments
EIB	European investment bank
EMP	environmental management plan
EOT	Erdenes Oyu Tolgoi, LLC
EPC	engineering, procurement and construction
EPFT	Equator Principles financial institution
EPs	Equator Principles
ESF	Environmental and Social Framework
ESG	environment, sustainability and governance
ESIA	environmental and social impact assessment
ESMF	Environmental and Social Management Framework
ESP	environmental and social policy
ESS	environmental and social standards
EU	European Union
FPIC	free, prior and informed consultation
FPP	Forest Peoples Programme
GMs	grievance mechanisms
GoPNG	government of Papua New Guinea
GRM	grievance redress mechanism
GRS	grievance redress service
H&SH	health and safety home

HCR	Herders' Complaint Resolution Agreements #1 and #2
HKIAC	Hong Kong International Arbitration Centre
HPP	hydropower project
HUMA	Humanitarian Medical Assistance
IBA	International Bar Association
ICC	International Chamber of Commerce
ICEL	International Council of Environmental Law
ICP	informed consultation and participation
ICSID	International Centre for Settlement of Investment Disputes
IDB	Inter-American Development Bank
IDF	International Development Finance
IEE	initial environmental examination
IEP	independent expert panel
IFC	international finance corporation
ILO	international labour organisation
IPAM	Independent Project Accountability Mechanism
IRC	Inter-ministerial Resettlement Commission
IsDB	Islamic Development Bank
ISDS	investor–state dispute settlement
JATAM	mining advocacy network
KAU	anti-debt coalition
KHPP	Karot hydropower project
KIARA	People's Coalition for Fisheries Justice
KPCL	Karot Power Company Limited
KSG	Khanbogd Soum government
LAC	land acquisition committee
LARR	Land Acquisition, Rehabilitation and Resettlement
LATIN	Lembaga Alam Tropika Indonesia
LCIA	London Court of International Arbitration
LMMPL	Lum Maushun Minerals Private Ltd
LPSs	land pooling schemes
LSC	Lafarge Surma Cement Ltd
LUMPL	Lafarge Umium Mining Private Ltd
LUOs	local umbrella organisations
MA&UD	Department of Municipal Administration and Urban Development
MDB	multilateral development bank
MDT	multi-disciplinary team
MICI	independent consultation and investigation mechanism
MIGA	multilateral investment guarantee agency
MOU	memorandum of understanding
MPSA	agata mineral production sharing agreement
MRL	Mindoro Resources Ltd

MUB	municipality of Ulaanbaatar City
NAP	national action plan
NCIP	National Commission of Indigenous Peoples
NDB	National Development Bank
NGO	non-governmental organisation
NTDC	National Transmission and Despatch Company Limited
OECD	Organisation for Economic Co-operation and Development
OED	Operations Evaluation Department
OED SES	Operations Evaluation Department Special Evaluation Study
OSPF	Office of the Special Project Facilitator
PCA	Permanent Court of International Arbitration
PCDP	public consultation and disclosure plan
PCM	project complaint mechanism
PIC	project information center
PMIZ	Pacific Marine Industrial Zone
PMO	project management office
PNG	Papua New Guinea
PPI	policy on public information
PPM	project-affected people's mechanism
PPQs	project processing queries
PRI	principles for responsible investment
PS	performance standard
RCI	Responsible Critical Mineral Initiative
RCR	requests for compliance review
RDR	requests for dispute resolution
RGC	Royal Government of Cambodia
RPF	resettlement policy framework
RTU	registrar of trade unions
SARS	severe acute respiratory syndrome
SCA	Societe Concessionaire de l'Aeroport
SCC	Arbitration Institute of the Stockholm Chamber of Commerce in Sweden
SCPX	South Caucasus pipeline expansion
SDGs	Sustainable Development Goals
SESA-ESMF	Strategic Environmental and Social Assessment and Environmental and Social Management Framework
SEZ	special economic zone
SHU	Social Hydro Labour Union
SIA	Sihanoukville international airport
SOE	state-owned enterprise
SPF	special project facilitator
SPS	safeguard policy statement

SSTA	small-scale technical assistance
TANAP	Trans-Anatolian Natural Gas Pipeline Project
THR	Turquoise Hills Resources
TPC	Tri-partite Council
UN	United Nations
UNCITRAL	United Nations Commission on International Trade Law
UNCTAD	United Nations Trade and Development
UNDRIP	United Nations Declaration on the Rights of Indigenous Peoples
UNGC	United Nations Global Compact
UNGP	United Nations Guiding Principles
USA	United States of America
USD	United States dollars
WALHI	Wahana Lingkungan Hidup Indonesia (Friends of the Earth)
Washington Convention	Convention on the Settlement of Investment Disputes between States and Nationals of Other States
WB	World Bank
WBG	World Bank Group
WBN	PT Weda Bay Nickel
WWF	World Wildlife Fund

PART I

Global Principles of Community Engagement in Infrastructure Development

1

Introduction

Is an Ounce of Prevention Worth a Pound of Cure? Assessing the Development of Dispute Prevention Mechanisms in Infrastructure Financing

While infrastructure development has long been associated with social progress, economic development and advanced living standards, it has likewise given rise to challenges including disruption, environmental harm and inequity. On the one hand, infrastructure development has been described as presenting both 'immaterial ideals and material notions necessary to change the world'.[1] It speaks to both 'physical forms and social supports'[2] that are necessary to the functioning of an orderly and healthy society. On the other hand, 'ill-conceived infrastructure stifles and suppresses human development and produces inequitable social and economic systems'.[3]

Much of how infrastructure is viewed, the aspirations it fulfils and the values it reflects are determined by the processes that give rise to its conceptualisation and implementation. Whether it is established through corruption, greed and indifference or through a process that responds to the aspirations of those for whom the infrastructure serves determines the extent to which it advances social good. A key element of responsive infrastructure development is driven by the attention placed on pre-project community–investor consultation and communication channels.

This book explores the emergent development and challenges in implementing community–investor consultation, dispute prevention and facilitation mechanisms amongst multilateral and national development banks operating in the Asia Pacific region. In the several decades since the

[1] Mahmoudi, H., Roe, J., & Seaman, K. (Eds.). (2022). *Infrastructure, Wellbeing and the Measurement of Happiness*. Abingdon: Taylor & Francis, p. 1.

[2] Ibid, p. 1.

[3] Ibid, p. 1.

development of the first multilateral community–investor dispute resolution and accountability mechanisms (AMs), much has been learned about public facilitation, community engagement and dispute prevention during the early stages of major infrastructure development programs.

Drawing on a qualitative triangulating approach that compares public facilitation policy design with case-based practice, the book analyses the International Finance Corporation (IFC), Asian Development Bank (ADB) and Asian Infrastructure Investment Bank (AIIB) community–investor dispute resolution policy design. Case studies, surveys and interviews of select private non-state actors in the Asia Pacific region address the question of whether, and if so how, multi-stakeholder community–investor public facilitation methods contribute to the prevention and early resolution of infrastructure disputes and advance sustainable development objectives.

When considering this question, it is important to ask what is meant by prevention. Does prevention imply the minimisation, diminishment and abatement of community concerns in order to advance project implementation, or rather does it imply genuine consultative design of project aims in a way that benefits community and project stakeholders? The aim of the book is to examine mechanisms that support the latter objective.

Public Facilitation for Major Infrastructure Projects

With the passage of several decades since the introduction of AMs, including the first Compliance Advisor Ombudsman (CAO) office at the IFC/World Bank (WB), significant learning has been gained regarding community facilitation mechanisms.

As a general matter, community–investor public facilitation mechanisms are formal, legal or non-legal processes that can be used by parties affected by investment activities and operations. The approaches include pre-project consultation and post-project grievance mechanisms as well as mediation, recommendations or impact studies.[4] These mechanisms that have been developed in response to a global learning process following challenges and identification of shared norms includes the United Nations (UN) Guiding Principles on Business and Human Rights, which expects companies to establish 'operational-level . . . mechanisms for individuals and communities'

[4] Centre for Research on Multinational Corporations (SOMO). (n.d.). What are grievance mechanisms? https://shorturl.at/c99cS.

to arrive at shared understanding and agreement (Guiding Principle 29) regarding resolution of community–investor issues.[5] The Organisation for Economic Co-operation and Development's (OECD's) 'Due Diligence Guidance for Meaningful Stakeholder Engagement in the Extractive Sector' provides for principles of engagement in the context of mining, and oil and gas enterprises. It calls for multinational enterprises to carry out risk-based due diligence to identify, prevent and mitigate actual and potential adverse impacts, and to engage in decision-making with stakeholders regarding project impacts.[6]

Amongst the earliest established multilateral community–investor public facilitation mechanism was the CAO, established under the IFC and Multilateral Investment Guarantee Agency (MIGA) of the WB Group in 1999. The CAO engages project-affected communities in dialogue on the social and environmental impacts of IFC/MIGA projects and helps affected parties identify alternatives for resolving issues of concern, which may include multi-stakeholder problem solving. The CAO is an independent office[7] that reports directly to the President of the WB Group.[8]

Research Approach

In examining the question under study – namely whether, and if so how, multi-stakeholder community–investor public facilitation contributes to the prevention of disputes and advancement of sustainable development objectives in the Asia Pacific region – the research methodology relies on a qualitative, triangulating approach to analyse public facilitation policy design alongside case-based implementation in order to answer the overarching question of whether 'an ounce of prevention is worth a pound of cure' in community–investor dispute resolution.

[5] United Nations. (2011). *Guiding Principles on Business and Human Rights*. Geneva: United Nations. www.ohchr.org/sites/default/files/documents/publications/guidingprinciplesbusinesshr_en.pdf.

[6] OECD. (2017). *OECD Due Diligence Guidance for Meaningful Stakeholder Engagement in the Extractive Sector*. Paris: OECD Publishing. https://doi.org/10.1787/9789264252462-en.

[7] Balaton-Chrimes, S., & Haines, F. (2015). The depoliticisation of accountability processes for land-based grievances, and the IFC CAO. *Global Policy*, *6*(4), 446–454. https://doi.org/10.1111/1758-5899.12275.

[8] Office of the Compliance Advisor Ombudsman. (2016). *Annual Report 2016*. www.cao-ombudsman.org/publications/documents/CAOAnnualReport2016_English_web.pdf.

The book draws on a comparative and socio-legal policy-oriented approach[9] through an inductive review of secondary sources and analysis of ADB, AIIB and IFC community–investor dispute resolution policy 'in the books'. Followed by surveys of select dispute resolution actors, neutrals and legal professionals working with project-affected communities in key Belt and Road Initiative (BRI) 'legal hubs'[10] 'in action' in order to identify conditions for successful community engagement and assess potential relevance for project implementation.[11]

The key principles underlying the selected methodology include a participatory framework and triangulating approach,[12] ensuring that those directly affected by the study's potential outcomes are given a voice in refining the questions under study.[13] The use of multiple techniques can help compensate for deficiencies of a single method.[14]

In recent times, growing outbound financing, particularly from major Asia Pacific economies including China, are increasingly understood as having not only significant economic but also governance, geopolitical and environmental implications. In relation to environmental impacts, efforts are underway to develop more robust frameworks for sustainable development and community facilitation mechanisms. While progress has been made in introducing accountability and consultation mechanisms in some sectors, challenges remain in some cases pertaining to land use rights, water and air pollution, deforestation and Indigenous cultural preservation.[15] Given the wide-scale impact of multi-jurisdictional development initiatives with

[9] See e.g. Feldman, E. A. (2015). Compensating the victims of Japan's 3-11 Fukushima disaster. *Asian-Pacific Law & Policy, 16*, 127.

[10] Erie, M. (2018). Dispute resolution, law and development, and legal elites in China's outbound investment. Law and Society Association talk on Panel 'China, International Law, and Development', CRN 33.

[11] Ali, S. (2023). Advancing research and practice in the governance of dispute resolution institutions through inclusive devolved reflection. In S. Ali (Ed.). *Comparative and Transnational Dispute Resolution* (pp. 59–79). Abingdon: Routledge.

[12] Denzin, N. K. (1978). *The Research Act: A Theoretical Introduction to Sociological Methods*. New York: McGraw-Hill.

[13] Diessner, R. (2020). Action research. *Converging Realities, 1*(1). Retrieved from https://bahai-library.com/diessner_action_research.

[14] Shaffer, G., & Ginsburg, T. (2012). The empirical turn in international legal scholarship. *American, 106*(1), 1–46.

[15] Bloomberg News. (2020, 21 December). What it's like living next to a Belt and Road project. *Bloomberg*. www.bloomberg.com/news/articles/2020-12-21/what-it-s-like-living-next-to-a-belt-and-road-project?embedded-checkout=true.

outbound financing within the greater Asia Pacific region, understanding how best to coordinate with local communities is necessary in order to realise the benefits of sustainable growth.

Public Facilitation Process

Research concerning best practices in public facilitation highlights the importance of early intervention, substantive engagement and training.[16] Early engagement with affected groups[17] in balancing health, environmental and financial priorities and interests[18] has been identified as key to the prevention of lawsuits, project relocation, indefinite postponement, price escalation, cost overruns and even cancellation of projects.[19] Stakeholder engagement was critical to a water supply project in Guwahati, India,[20] a public–private partnership scheme in Hong Kong[21] and pollution remediation in Guangdong Province.[22]

Substantive engagement is likewise a critical factor in meaningful outcomes. Avoiding tokenistic passive engagement[23] while supporting functional interactive participation leads to long-term socio-economic success.[24] Successive steps beginning with education and advancing to feedback, consultation, joint planning, mediation, litigation and finally

[16] Ali, S. F. (2016). *Governing Disasters: Engaging Local Populations in Humanitarian Relief.* Cambridge: Cambridge University Press.

[17] Ibid.

[18] Min, J. H., Jang, W., Han, S. H., Kim, D., & Kwak, Y. H. (2018). How conflict occurs and what causes conflict: Conflict analysis framework for public infrastructure projects. *Journal of Management in Engineering, 34*(4). https://doi.org/10.1061/(ASCE)ME.1943-5479.0000625; Ng, S. T., Wong, J. M. W., & Wong, K. K. W. (2010). Public participation in public private partnership projects: The way forward. *WIT Transactions on Ecology and the Environment, 142*, 79–87. https://doi.org.10.2495/SW100081.

[19] Das, R., Laishram, B., & Mohammad, J. (2019). Public participation in urban water supply projects: The case of south-west Guwahati, India. *Water Research, 165*, 114989. https://doi.org/10.1016/j.watres.2019.114989.

[20] Ibid. See also Cuppen, E., Bosch-Rekveldt, M. G., Pikaar, E., & Mehos, D. C. (2016). Stakeholder engagement in large scale energy infrastructure projects: Revealing perspectives using Q methodology. *International Journal of Project Management, 34*(7), 1347–1359.

[21] Ng et al., Public participation in public private partnership projects.

[22] Lo, C. W., & Tang, S. (2014). *Institutions, Regulatory Styles, Society, and Environmental Governance in China.* Abingdon: Routledge.

[23] Pretty, J. N., Guijt, I., Thompson, J., & Scoones, I. (1995). *Participatory Learning and Action: A Trainer's Guide.* London: International Institute for Environment and Development.

[24] See Ali, *Governing Disasters.*

resolution[25] are envisioned in the context of a multidimensional process involving planning, action, reflection, learning and change.[26] Facilitators work to find agreement between stakeholders and decision makers with diverse backgrounds, values, beliefs and needs.[27]

Conversely, predetermined decisions are antithetical to the spirit of the facilitation process.[28] During early phases of project development, communities should have access to relevant information regarding proposed plans and a commitment should be in place to address concerns and identify interests.[29] A concept of 'shared infrastructure', which involves acknowledging the social value derived from infrastructure including both associated rights and obligations, has been recommended.[30] Training of community members in consultation skills has contributed to building trust and cohesion, overcoming power asymmetries and fostering participatory dialogue.[31] Participatory learning and action, characterised by a process of dialogue, action, analysis and change,[32] and participatory mapping and modelling have facilitated the bridging of interests.[33] Likewise, supporting the development of spaces for joint

25 Connor, D. M. (1988). A new ladder of citizen participation. *National Civic Review*, *77*(3), 249–257. https://doi.org/10.1002/ncr.4100770309; Constitutional and Mainland Affairs Bureau. (25 November 2011). 深圳市人民政府 香港特別行政區律政司法律合作安排 [Shenzhen Municipal People's Government and the Department of Justice of the Hong Kong Special Administrative Region Legal Cooperation Arrangement]. chrome-extension://efaidnbmnnnibpcajpcglclefindmkaj/https://www.doj.gov.hk/tc/mainland_and_macao/pdf/HK_SZ_Coop_Agt_tc.pdf.

26 Chambers, R. (2002). *Participatory Workshops: A Sourcebook of 21 Sets of Ideas and Activities*. London: Earthscan.

27 Nandago, M. (2007). Training and facilitation: The propellers of participatory methodologies. In K. Brock & J. Pettit (Eds.). *Springs of Participation: Creating and Evolving Methods for Participatory Development* (pp. 29–39). Brighton: Institute of Development Studies, as cited in Sirajuddin, Z., & Grudens-Schuck, N. (2017). Public participation in agriculture and natural resource management projects in south and southeast Asia: A literature review. *Asian Journal of Agriculture and Development*, *14*(1), 107–118.

28 Buckley, A. (2012). Best practice community engagement for infrastructure projects: Building community ties that dig deeper. *Public Infrastructure Bulletin*, *1*(8), 1–2.

29 Erkul, M., Yitmen, I., & Çelik, T. (2016). Stakeholder engagement in mega transport infrastructure projects. *Procedia Engineering*, *161*, 704–710. https://doi.org/10.1016/j.proeng.2016.08.745.

30 Dialogue by Design and UCL Transport Institute. (2015). *Infrastructure and the Citizen* (pp. 1–19). Thornton Heath: Dialogue by Design.

31 Ali, S., Davis, W. E., & Lee, J. (2011). Multi-stakeholder dispute resolution: Building social capital through access to justice at the community level. *Pepperdine Dispute Resolution Law Journal*, *11*(2), 181–206.

32 See Pretty et al., *Participatory Learning and Action*.

33 Sirajuddin & Grudens-Schuck, Public participation in agriculture.

knowledge generation at the community level has been found essential for systematic learning.[34]

While public facilitation literature has provided important insights into community engagement for major infrastructure projects in Western development banks, this book extends findings to include examination of contributions by banking institutions operating in the Asia Pacific.

Devolved Collaboration

Beginning in the early 1990s, international declarations have increasingly encouraged the use of consultative 'devolved collaboration' as a means of regulation of public resources.[35] This encouragement largely arises from a view that public resource decision-making is 'best handled with the participation of all concerned citizens, at the relevant level'.[36] In many respects, this emphasis on localised decision-making reflects an aspiration towards 'develop[ing] new institutional methods for gauging social needs and devise[ing] sensible, politically feasible, and socially acceptable legal remedies'.[37]

Devolved collaboration can be described as a method of localised decision-making that encourages 'widespread, independent participation by local groups to craft comprehensive solutions to difficult [resource] concerns on a geographically-focused scale'.[38] On the basis of this approach, 'public and private stakeholders collaborate to identify concerns, establish priorities, and design and implement holistic solutions' to a broad spectrum of natural resource problems within a specific community.[39] Successful collaboration identifies 'common interests and values . . . and social capital among its participants'.[40]

[34] Ali, S. (2018). The power of reflection: Advancing governance and dispute resolution systems through devolved reflection and shared knowledge generation. *The Journal of Baha'i Studies, 28*(4), 23–89.

[35] *Agenda 21: Programme of Action for Sustainable Development; Rio Declaration on Environment and Development; Statement of Forest Principles: The Final Text of Agreements Negotiated by Governments at the United Nations Conference on Environment and Development (UNCED), 3–14 June 1992, Rio de Janeiro, Brazil.* Geneva: United Nations.

[36] Ibid.

[37] Nonet, P., & Selznick, P. (1978). *Law and Society in Transition: Toward Responsive Law* (1st ed.). Piscataway, NJ: Transaction Publishers.

[38] Foster, S. R. (2002). Environmental justice in an era of devolved collaboration. *The Harvard Environmental Law Review, 26*, 459–498.

[39] Ibid.

[40] Nickelsburg, S. M. (1998). Mere volunteers? The promise and limits of community-based environmental protection. *Virginia Law Review, 84*(7), 1371–1409. https://doi.org/10.2307/1073675.

When successful, devolved community-based resource management efforts respond to the aspiration for broad-based input into policies and decision-making.[41] Yet, when implemented without regard to issues of universal representation and disparate access to resources, the process has the potential of replicating and possibly exacerbating existing representation problems.[42] Therefore examining the gap between public facilitation policy as written and as practiced is imperative for continued progress.

At the outset, it is useful to distinguish between approaches to devolved collaboration as developed within multilateral development banks (MDBs) including stakeholder engagement, grievance mechanisms, post-conflict mediation, arbitration and litigation.

Stakeholder engagement generally refers to a process of group decision-making conducted throughout a project life cycle. Where properly designed and implemented, it supports the development of constructive and responsive relationships that are important for the management of a project's environmental and social risks. Stakeholder engagement is most effective when initiated at an early stage of the project development process,[43] and is an important component of early-stage decision-making, assessment, management and monitoring of a project's environmental and social risks and impacts.[44]

Project-level grievance mechanisms provide avenues for borrowers to respond to concerns and grievances of project-affected parties in relation to the environmental and social performance of a project. Grievance mechanisms are expected to address concerns promptly and effectively, in a transparent manner that is culturally appropriate and readily accessible to all project-affected parties, at no cost and without retribution and should not prevent access to judicial or administrative remedies.[45] When disputes cannot be addressed through grievance processes, or compliance review, mediation, arbitration and litigation are available to parties.

[41] See Nonet & Selznick, *Law and Society in Transition.*

[42] See Foster, Environmental justice in an era of devolved collaboration.

[43] See Ali et al., Multi-stakeholder dispute resolution.

[44] World Bank. (2016). *Environmental and Social Framework: Setting Environmental and Social Standards for Investment Project Financing* (p. 131). Washington, DC: World Bank. https://consultations.worldbank.org/content/dam/sites/consultations/doc/migration/the_esf_clean_final_for_public_disclosure_post_board_august_4.pdf.

[45] Ibid, p. 136.

Key Findings of the Study

Drawing on a mixed-method triangulating approach that compares public facilitation policy with case-based practice, the book draws on project statistics, case studies, interviews with and surveys of dispute resolution professionals to better understand the dynamics of community investor dispute prevention and resolution in practice and conditions for successful community engagement, leading to both empirical and theoretical insights.

The key empirical findings of this study confirm the adage that an ounce of prevention is in fact worth a pound of cure in the context of infrastructure development. At the same time, challenges remain in facilitating effective preventative measures. Project data, survey findings and comparative case studies suggest that the introduction of increasingly rigorous pre-project community consultation and grievance mechanisms within global MDBs in the mid 2010–2020s have corresponded with a drop in the percentage of grievances per project from 15.4% in 2019 to 7.1% in 2021.[46] While this downward trend has been followed by a slight resurgence,[47] after 2021, the lack of consultation, disclosure or due diligence was no longer the single most cited cause of grievances amongst project-affected communities.[48] Greater attention to pre-project due diligence and community awareness of grievance channels appear to account for these findings. Survey findings of fifty-five practitioners engaged in infrastructure-related dispute prevention in the Asia Pacific region likewise found that prior community consultation was considered the most effective approach to preventing infrastructure disputes, and that overall, most disputes arose because of lack of adequate consultation with members of the community. Similarly, the twelve community–investor dispute case studies show that in circumstances of increasingly heightened standards for community consultation compared with ad hoc discretionary consultation practices, the number of stalled/cancelled and litigated cases declined by 33%, the percentages of cases referred to local courts declined by 16%, and the number of cases pursuing party agreement through mediation or negotiation increased by 50%. Overall, these findings provide measured evidence supporting the

[46] Ali, S. (2024). The seeming paradox of prevention: Dispute mitigation by multilateral development banks. *Civil Justice Quarterly*, *43*, 142–168.

[47] See Araabi, S. (n.d.). A new decade of complaints. *Accountability Console*. www.accountabilityconsole.com/newsletter/articles/a-new-decade-of-complaints/.

[48] Ibid.

development of increasingly robust community consultative engagement channels, particularly for multilateral and national banks that have not yet implemented such policies. Such engagement channels, far from aggregating complaints, conversely correlate with a reduction in the overall proportion of project disputes.

The findings of this study have theoretical significance demonstrating the importance of community consultation in the Asia Pacific infrastructure development context. While infrastructure development theory has largely moved beyond an emphasis on top down approaches to planning and implementation with growing recognition of the importance of community engagement in decision-making for project sustainability, legitimacy and responsiveness,[49] limited evidence of impacts of community-based consultation in dispute prevention is available in the Asia Pacific region.[50] This study demonstrates that where attention to consultation, information sharing, grievance mechanisms and accountability are robust, a higher rate of project completion and dispute avoidance is reported. These findings confirm prior research the efficiency gains of cohesive, inclusive and meaningful local co-ownership in project design.[51]

In addition, the findings demonstrate the important role of independent accountability professionals within multilateral and national banking institutions, non-governmental organisations (NGOs) and community groups in contributing to increasingly harmonised legal and policy innovations for expanded community access and accountability.[52]

Structure of the Book

The book is divided into three parts. Following an introduction outlining the global context and development of community engagement practices in infrastructure development in Part I, Part II explores community engagement case studies and survey findings in the Asia Pacific region before 2013 when pre-project community engagement practices were

[49] Ali, S. (2023). Decentralized global legal ordering. *Michigan State Law Review, 2023*(2), 319–376. https://ssrn.com/abstract=4047456.

[50] Ali, S. (2024). Comparative international arbitration law. In *Cambridge Handbook of Comparative Law* (pp. 610–624). Cambridge: Cambridge University Press.

[51] See Ali, *Governing Disasters.*

[52] Ali, S. (2021). *Forming Transnational Dispute Settlement Norms: Soft Law and the Role of UNCITRAL's Regional Centre for Asia and the Pacific.* Cheltenham and Northampton, MA: Edward Elgar Publishing.

largely discretionary to post-2013, when more robust mandatory procedures were introduced. Part III then examines the unique developments regarding community engagement in the BRI region. Finally, it concludes with lessons learned and policy recommendations regarding inclusive approaches to sustainable infrastructure development. Historically, in the several decades since the first multilateral community–investor dispute resolution and AMs were introduced, much has been learned about public facilitation, community engagement and dispute prevention during the early stages of major infrastructure development programs. Part I of this book examines these historical developments. Knowledge sharing between banks has supported a robust process of collective norm development. This has emerged out of crises, decentralised knowledge generation[53] amongst multilateral banking institutions, NGOs and community groups resulting in legal and policy innovations ultimately providing for expanded community protections and accountability on the part of funding institutions. The creation of shared learning spaces such as the International Financial Institution Meetings, hosted by the world's MDBs on a rotating basis on themes such as information disclosure and stakeholder engagement, has resulted in growing agreement on the relevance of underlying principles and good practices in community engagement in the context of infrastructure planning including open communication, accountability, redress and information disclosure.

Building on early learnings, Chapter 2 explores the emergence of global principles of community engagement in infrastructure development through a process of global norm development. Growing agreement regarding the parameters of community engagement have been crystalised in global policy documents including the Equator Principles, the UN Guiding Principles of Business and Human Rights, the OECD Due Diligence Guidelines for Meaningful Stakeholder Engagement in the Extractive Sector, the Principles for Responsible Investment, and the International Labour Organisation Convention advancing the need for consultation between project finance institutions and host communities to arrive at shared understanding and agreement on matters that affecting community well-being and prosperity.

Part II of the book presents multilateral bank-funded project data, survey research and case studies on the achievements, challenges and lessons learned in community–investor dispute prevention and resolution mechanisms amongst MDBs operating in the Asia Pacific

[53] Ibid.

region. Chapter 3 explores aggregate comparative data tracking the development and impact of dispute prevention mechanisms in MDBs on subsequent claims. It finds that prior to the mid 2010s, MDB's investor–community consultation was largely conducted on an ad hoc basis, usually after grievances occurred. Since then, greater attention has been placed on facilitating early-stage consultation, information disclosure and grievance mechanisms.[54] Internal bank policies have likewise converged towards requiring increasingly higher levels of accountability and responsiveness for project-affected communities including transparent disclosure of prior complaints and outcomes. In some cases, broad community support is required for project initiation while for projects in the highest risk categories, community consent is necessary.

The aim of the survey and follow-up conversations is to provide insights into the dynamics, challenges and lessons learned in engaging with communities to prevent and manage disputes in the context of infrastructure projects. Respondents offered suggestions on how community–investor dispute resolution systems might be improved, including the need for more public education regarding community consultation and grievance mechanisms, a clear framework for the consultation process to encourage clarity of process and more efforts to educate the community so that they 'understand ... the risk of investment'. Follow-up conversations between 2021 and 2023 with practitioners working in dispute mitigation offered additional insights regarding the emerging duty of consultation and social license to operate, the development of hybrid forms of resolution and an emphasis on long-term contracting models and multi-tiered approaches to resolution. Given the small size of the survey sample, the findings cannot be considered generalisable. Likewise self-reported perceptions are subject to bias so statements may not always reflect actual practice.[55] However, the survey findings, together with the statistical analysis in Chapter 3 and subsequent case studies point to a common finding underscoring the significance of prior community consultation and effective grievance mechanisms in mitigating infrastructure disputes.

[54] See Ali et al., Multi-stakeholder dispute resolution, pp. 181–206.

[55] Wall, J., & Kressel, K. (2012). Research on mediator style: A summary and some research suggestions. *Negotiation and Conflict Management Research*, 5(4), 403–421. https://doi.org/10.1111/j.1750-4716.2012.00117.x.

Chapters 5 and 6 present twelve case studies of community–investor dispute cases arising from projects either solely financed by the WB/IFC or collaboratively financed with the ADB, AIIB and European Investment Bank in the Asia Pacific region in the transport, extractive and special economic zone development sectors. The first six cases presented in Chapter 5 were selected from disputes occurring prior to 2013 when pre-project consultation processes were largely discretionary. The second set of six cases presented in Chapter 6 occurred after 2013, when consultation processes became increasingly mandated and a higher threshold for ascertaining community consent was introduced. During the first discretionary consultation phase prior to 2013, of the six cases, four were cancelled or stalled, one proceeded to court litigation and one was closed. For the second, post-2013 phase characterised by heightened consultation standards, of the six cases, two were stalled/cancelled, zero proceeded to litigation, one was closed and three underwent a process of mediation or negotiation. The key comparative finding of the cases is that in circumstances of increasingly heightened standards requiring community consultation with higher thresholds for ascertaining community consent, the number of stalled/cancelled or litigated cases declined by 33%, the percentages of cases proceeding to court declined by 16% and the number of cases pursuing party agreement through mediation or negotiation increased by 50% compared with ad hoc discretionary consultation practices prior to 2013.

The case studies highlight the risks of insufficient attention to community consultation. The necessity of maintaining relationships with decision-makers that emerge over the course of a project life cycle, the need for genuine multi-directional rather than 'uni-directional' consultation and the importance of thorough prior environmental and social impact assessment are highlighted. As noted, prior to 2013, standards regarding pre-project community engagement were relatively lax. The primary issues raised in project complaints included insufficient community consultation, lack of environmental planning, inadequate compensation for relocation, damage to local resources including water and farmland, economic harm, forced land transfer, undue influence, lack of consent and limited external monitoring.

Chapter 6 examines cases arising after increasingly robust community engagement practices emerged starting in 2013, and underscores a number of continuities and advancements. The six case studies arising after standards for pre-project community consultation were raised demonstrate a number of key improvements including greater rigour in consultation and diligence mechanisms, heightened precision in identification of issues of community concern, higher pre-project diligence and screening standards, ongoing environmental and technical monitoring, the presence of locally trained mediators, skill development for consultation participants, a longer-term view of community welfare and responsive grievance remedies. Challenges persisted in some cases, including instances of duress, lack of information disclosure, fraud, limited access to consultation mechanisms and environmental harm leading to project cessation in two cases. On the whole, however, corresponding with an overall trend towards more rigorous community consultation and diligence standards, during this phase, the number of stalled/cancelled and litigated case declined by 33%, the percentages of cases referred to local courts declined by 16%, and the number of cases pursuing party agreement through mediation or negotiation increased by 50%.

The last part of the book examines community engagement developments in the BRI region and beyond. Chapter 7 explores the contributions and challenges in advancing sustainable development along the BRI and efforts at strengthening engagement with local communities. Through analysis of a select number of case studies, it finds that when project funders reference relatively robust host-country environmental, social and governance standards with higher pre-project diligence and accountability requirements, disputes tend to be avoided, while conversely when referencing lax host country standards, gaps in diligence often give rise to disputes. A number of approaches and proposals have emerged to address resulting claims. These include both formal and informal dispute mitigation and resolution mechanisms, including the introduction of China's mediation and consultation mechanism for the mining industry, as well as post-dispute mediation[56] and arbitration.[57] Conversations with

[56] Ali, S. F. (2024). Conciliation beyond the courts: Aspirations and limits of mandated and voluntary court mediation programmes from a multi-jurisdictional perspective. *Comparative Procedural Law and Justice*, Part XV (Ch 2). https://doi.org/10.2139/ssrn.5095024

[57] Ali, S. F., & Ginsburg, T. B. (2013). *International Commercial Arbitration in Asia* (3rd ed.). Huntington, NY: Juris Publishers.

project coordinators highlight the importance of neutrality and relationship preservation in the selection of resolution forums.

Future Directions and Recommendations

Drawing on case studies and survey data, this book has explored the achievements, challenges and lessons learned in community–investor dispute prevention and resolution in infrastructure projects. Given the widescale impact of multi-jurisdictional infrastructure development initiatives in the Asia Pacific region, understanding how to advance a practice of shared ownership in localised decision-making with local communities is necessary in order to realise the benefits of sustainable growth.

The key finding of the book, that community consultation channels, far from aggregating complaints, conversely are correlated with a reduction in the overall proportion of project disputes, support the exploration of a number of relevant recommendations as follows.

First, given that the majority of funding support for infrastructure development projects in the Asia Pacific region come from national banks, advancing effective pre-project due diligence policy in the region is recommended. This may be achieved through supporting national banks and relevant NGOs to advance joint knowledge generation with MDBs to develop increasingly robust transparency, accountability and pre-project consultation standards. Systematic and regular shared learning spaces between independent AMs and national banking institutions to explore best practices will be helpful in supporting this effort.

Second, within the context of UN Commission on International Trade Law's (UNCITRAL's) Working Group III and relevant global bodies, specialised learning spaces can be arranged to advance shared understanding regarding the interface between policies advancing sustainability and the resolution of cross border infrastructure investment disputes to ensure that such mechanisms account for both public welfare and private interests.

Third, the development of shared screening standards equipped to filter out projects that present unjustifiable risks to communities in terms of social and environmental impact will be useful. Ongoing monitoring and evaluation of project selection will further reinforce sustainable outcomes.

Fourth, while attention to the necessity and reach of community consultation has expanded over time, advancing the quality of consultation can be further strengthened through deeper exploration of relevant consultative principles that can guide the processes in diverse cultural settings including accountability and truthfulness, diversity, gender equity and justice.[58] The forms of community representation that result in manageably sized groups to advance high-quality consultative decision-making;[59] the type of preparation necessary to ensure that individuals have the requisite skills and capabilities to constructively engage in the consultation process; the safeguards needed to protect the integrity and objectivity of the consultation process from coercive practices and examining the type of systems that can track effective follow-up implementation of decisions. Ongoing learning amongst members of the infrastructure development community to advance genuine consultative engagement for community prosperity will reinforce the beneficial impact of such projects.

[58] Ali, S. (2010). Measuring success in devolved collaboration. *Journal of Land Use & Environmental Law 26*(1), 93–112.

[59] See Soraya, G. (2024, 16 March). Indonesia: Turning to unity for rebuilding communities after natural disasters. *World Bank Blogs*. https://blogs.worldbank.org/en/eastasiapacific/indonesia-turning-unity-rebuilding-communities-after-natural-disasters.

2

Emerging Global Principles of Community Engagement in Infrastructure Projects

Norms governing community engagement in infrastructure projects have emerged out of crises and shared learning between multilateral banking institutions resulting in legal innovations.[1] This process has accelerated in the context of cross-border infrastructure development projects that often involve coordination between national and multilateral standards. A learning orientation, accompanied by the creation of shared learning spaces such as the International Financial Institution Meetings – which are hosted by the world's multilateral development banks (MDBs) on a rotating basis on themes such as information disclosure and stakeholder engagement – have resulted in growing agreement on relevant underlying principles and good practices in community engagement in the context of infrastructure planning.

Transnational legal innovations have historically been examined from a number of perspectives, with the earliest literature focusing on transplantation and diffusion of legal norms. This has advanced to include exploration of how public norms are developed by global private actors[2] through corporate codes[3] and soft law[4] and vernacularised through replication and hybridisation in legal ordering.[5] Recent developments in infrastructure governance demonstrate the important role of shared

[1] Ali, Davis & Lee, Multi-stakeholder dispute resolution.

[2] Zumbansen, P. (2023). Law as critical cartography: Global value chains, borders, and the spatialisation of vulnerability. *Transnational Legal Theory*, *14*(1), 1–45. https://doi.org/10.1080/20414005.2023.2206760.

[3] Teubner, G. (2002). Hybrid laws: Constitutionalizing private governance networks. In P. Selznick, R. A. Kagan, M. Krygier & K. I. Winston (Eds.). *Legality and Community: On the Intellectual Legacy of Philip Selznick* (pp. 311–331). Lanham, MD: Rowman & Littlefield.

[4] Ali, S. (2021). *Forming Transnational Dispute Settlement Norms: Soft Law and the Role of UNCITRAL's Regional Centre for Asia and the Pacific*. Cheltenham: Edward Elgar Publishing; Merry, S. E., Davis, K., & Kingsbury, B. (2015). *The Quiet Power of Indicators: Measuring Governance, Corruption, and Rule of Law*. Cambridge: Cambridge University Press. https://doi.org/10.1017/cbo9781139871532.

[5] Halliday, T. C., & Carruthers, B. G. (2007). The recursivity of law: Global norm making and national lawmaking in the globalization of corporate insolvency regimes. *American*

learning between nations, reflection on experience in light of relevant global norms and policy innovation.

The concept of networked transnational legal ordering[6] and 'decentralised transnational law making'[7] characterised by expanded representation and engagement in global soft law making drawing from the rich diversity of legal traditions[8] provides a helpful lens to understand an emerging process of advancing infrastructure development standards through a mutual learning process amongst nations drawing from shared challenges, insights and experience.

A growing body of work has examined the development of MDB public engagement in project-affected communities. As a general matter, community–investor public facilitation mechanisms are formal, legal or non-legal processes that are used by parties affected by investment activities and operations. The approach taken by such mechanisms varies, including mediation, recommendations or impact studies.[9] The core elements of such engagement includes (1) pre-project due diligence, consultation and free, prior and informed consent in appropriate cases; (2) information disclosure on potential impacts and (3) grievance mechanisms.

These innovations have emerged out of reflection on shared challenges arising in the context of infrastructure development in light of emerging norms including the United Nations (UN) Guiding Principles (UNGPs), which expect companies to establish 'operational-level . . . mechanisms for individuals and communities' to arrive at shared understanding and agreement (Guiding Principle 29) regarding resolution of community–investor issues and the Organisation for Economic Co-operation and Development's (OECD) Due Diligence Guidance for Meaningful Stakeholder Engagement in the Extractive Sector.[10]

Journal of Sociology, *112*(4), 1135–1202; Halliday, T. C., & Shaffer, G. (Eds.). (2015). *Transnational Legal Orders*. Cambridge: Cambridge University Press.

[6] Ibid; Li, J., & Shaffer, G. (2024). China and the international legal order: Introduction to the symposium. *UC Irvine Journal of International, Transnational, and Comparative Law*, *9*(1). https://escholarship.org/uc/item/3mq3p93m; Shaffer, G. (2016). Theorizing transnational legal ordering. *Annual Review of Law and Social Science*, *12*(1), 231–253. https://doi.org/10.1146/annurev-lawsocsci-110615-085128.

[7] Ali, Forming Transnational Dispute Settlement Norms.

[8] Ibid.

[9] Centre for Research on Multinational Corporations (SOMO). (n.d.). What are grievance mechanisms? www.somo.nl/hrgm/what-are-grievance-mechanisms/#:~:text=A%20grievance%20mechanism%20 is%20a,certain%20business%20activities%20and%20operations.

[10] OECD. (2017). *OECD Due Diligence Guidance for Meaningful Stakeholder Engagement in the Extractive Sector*. Paris: OECD Publishing. https://doi.org/10.1787/9789264252462-en.

Forging MDB Accountability through Crises in the 1980s

The first formal MDB's public facilitation mechanisms including the International Finance Corporation's (IFC) Compliance Advisor Ombudsman's (CAO) office emerged following a series of significant accountability challenges in the 1980s. In 1982, after several years of preparatory work, the World Bank furnished its first policy on development of Indigenous and tribal peoples' territories.[11] This policy followed several project-/region-specific movements against World Bank-financed projects that simmered around the world and ultimately resulted in the need for comprehensive guidelines, such as the resistance of the Cordillera people of the Philippines to a hydroelectric project in the Chico River Basin, the Polonoroeste project in the Brazilian Amazon and the transmigration of Indonesians from overcrowded inner islands to the outer islands of Indonesia.[12]

Shortly after the first policy, the protests against hydropower projects in the Narmada valley in India proved to be the longest of all campaigns against the World Bank, which led to its withdrawal from the project in 1993 at the request of the Government of India.[13]

Up until the 1980s, the position of the World Bank in respect of 'problem projects' was that it was primarily the responsibility of the borrower government to manage domestic conflict, citing the need to avoid political interference in a country's internal affairs. The Bank's usage of terms such as consultation and participation was required to be construed as voluntary/elective means for project-affected persons to engage with the proposed development rather than a mandatory or supervised processes enforced by a legal or financial body.[14]

A review of the initial permissive policy was conducted, and a 1986 revised policy was implemented. This revised policy included remedial actions, recommendations for additional staff and expansive guidelines requiring the arrangement of an alternative productive base for resettlers.

[11] Fox, J. A., & Brown, L. D. (1998). *The Struggle for Accountability: The World Bank, NGOs, and Grassroots Movements*. Cambridge, MA: The MIT Press.

[12] Gray, A. (1998). Development policy–development protest: The World Bank, Indigenous peoples, and NGOs. In J. A. Fox & L. D. Brown (Eds.). *The Struggle for Accountability: The World Bank, NGOs, and Grassroots Movements* (pp. 268–281). Cambridge, MA: The MIT Press.

[13] Ibid, p. 287.

[14] Ibid, p. 294.

However, the 1994 review proved that revisions in policy did not directly translate to improvements.[15]

After reviewing assessment reports from various operating divisions primarily responsible for project design and implementation, the Resettlement and Development report was published by the Bank's task force in 1993. The report received funds and political support to carry out field assessments to support independent verification of events that were reported in project documents.[16]

Resettlement and Development Report

The report found that there was a direct association between large projects resulting in displacement of people and regions with overall poor political representation of displaced people. Between the years of 1986 and 1993, involuntary resettlement occurred in 192 projects, displacing a total of 2.5 million people.[17]

The report listed key factors to ensure resettlement 'success'. They included political commitment by the borrower, systematic implementation of established guidelines and procedures by the bank and borrower, sound social analysis, accurate cost assessments and commensurate financing, effective executing organisations and public participation in setting resettlement objectives, and identifying reestablishment solutions and their implementation.[18]

The Bank's resettlement policy required that pre-project preparation includes four requirements: (1) baseline planning surveys of affected populations; (2) resettlement timetables coordinated with civil works construction; (3) resettlement plans to restore lost incomes; and (4) a resettlement budget. The report claimed that there was significant improvement in these four areas since 1992, while noting that recurrent failures in project preparation and appraisal remained the root cause of problematic resettlement.[19]

[15] Fox, J. A. (1998). When does reform policy influence practice? Lessons from the bankwide resettlement review. In J. A. Fox & L. D. Brown (Eds.). *The Struggle for Accountability: The World Bank, NGOs, and Grassroots Movements* (p. 309). Cambridge, MA: The MIT Press.

[16] Ibid, p. 311.

[17] Ibid, p. 313.

[18] Ibid, p. 314.

[19] Ibid, p. 318.

Water Resources Management Policy

Water projects and large-scale dams in particular have been part of many MDB's portfolio, including the World Bank since its inception. Between 1980 and 1990, the World Bank contributed to one-third of the total global investment, approximately 100 billion USD, in the global water sector, of which rural water supply projects received 3%. The majority of the funds were diverted to irrigation and hydropower projects with limited focus on water supply and sanitation.[20]

The Bank's first effort to host a consultative policy-making process was in 1991, when it invited various non-governmental organisations (NGOs) to discuss its draft forestry policy less than a month before it was scheduled to be presented before its executive directors for approval. It was during this meeting that the Bank first publicly announced its intention to develop a new water resources management policy.[21]

To establish a formal consultative process, NGOs and international organisations rallied for the adoption of several requirements. These included NGO involvement in early stages of policy formulation, funding for staff time to critique and respond to policy documents and travel expenses to participate in the consultation process, holding of consultative meetings in the region of the project, and allowance of adequate time between provision of policy documents, along with translations, and clarity by the Bank on how NGO contributions would be considered and incorporated into policy.[22]

The Bank's water resources management policy was released in 1993. Despite extensive efforts by NGOs to introduce more robust accountability mechanisms (AMs) and safeguards, most of the operational guidelines in the policy were broadly defined and lacked enforcement mechanisms. The only item that came close to a loan condition was the limitation of lending for potable water for countries that were not making progress in meeting their priorities for reform; although, the criteria for evaluating whether a country was 'making progress' was not well defined.[23]

[20] Moore, D., & Sklar, L. (1998). Reforming the World Bank's lending for water: The process and outcome of developing a water resources management policy. In J. A. Fox & L. D. Brown (Eds.). *The Struggle for Accountability: The World Bank, NGOs, and Grassroots Movements* (p. 347). Cambridge, MA: The MIT Press.

[21] Ibid, p. 359.

[22] Ibid, p. 358.

[23] Ibid, p. 373–374.

The overall campaign by NGOs for greater participation and enhanced criteria for the selection of water projects for financing demonstrated that unless rules for access to information and the consultative process were clearly defined and enforced, the Bank–NGO consultation process would not be constructive.

Public Accountability

Prior to the early 1990s, projects financed by the World Bank were planned and designed with little public input or scrutiny. Local communities in borrowing countries were denied access to the most basic project information at the project planning and design stage, which resulted in limited or non-existent local consultation and public participation, ill-conceived and poorly planned projects, and deteriorating project quality.[24]

Owing to intense public international pressure and the threat of reduced or halted funding by the US Congress, an independent appeals panel and revisions to the Bank's information policy supporting the release of relevant project information was approved by the World Bank in 1993. It was envisaged that these changes would allow citizens adversely affected by the Bank's policies to file claims.[25] Grassroots groups and NGOs hoped that by increasing transparency through greater access to information, problematic projects may be caught, halted or restructured relatively early in the pipeline through citizen input.[26]

The US Congress ultimately cut the Treasury's previous pledge to the World Bank by 200 million USD and the pledge to the International Bank for Reconstruction and Development by 15 million USD following continued opposition from various NGOs that claimed that the Bank's efforts to strengthen public accountability provisions were inadequate and unacceptable.

In 1994, an Inspection Panel was established by the Bank. The Panel was empowered to investigate complaints submitted by project-affected communities regarding violations of policy, procedures and loan agreements.[27]

[24] Udall, L. (1998). The World Bank and public accountability: Has anything changed. In J. A. Fox & L. D. Brown (Eds.). *The Struggle for Accountability: The World Bank, NGOs, and Grassroots Movements* (pp. 391–392). Cambridge, MA: The MIT Press.

[25] World Bank, 'The World Bank Inspection Panel', resolution no. 93-10, resolution no. IDA 93-6 (Washington, DC: World Bank, September 1993), 'The World Bank Policy on Disclosure of Information' (March 1994), 'Disclosure of Operational Information', *Bank Procedures*, BP 17.50 (September 1993).

[26] Udall, The World Bank and public accountability, p. 393.

[27] Ibid, p. 414.

Although the information policy and establishment of an inspection panel were important steps in moving towards public accountability, transparency and improved project quality at the World Bank, discussions on how to effectively achieve these objectives continue to be a focus of NGOs and donor governments.[28]

These crises ultimately led to the development of independent AMs first within the World Bank and later within many of the leading MDBs, as will be explored in more depth in Chapter 3. These crises also led to global exploration of the relevant standards and principles necessary to regulate bank–community relationships in the context of infrastructure development, as will be discussed later.

Emergence of Global Principles of Community Engagement

A degree of consensus is emerging among MDBs regarding principles of community–investor governance and decision making. This is reflected in the evolution of global principles crystalising the centrality of localised consultation in infrastructure planning including: the Equator Principles (EPs), the UNGPs of Business and Human Rights (2011), the OECD's Due Diligence Guidance for Meaningful Stakeholder Engagement in the Extractive Sector, the Principles for Responsible Investment (PRIs), and the International Labour Organisation (ILO) Convention outlined later.[29]

Equator Principles

The EPs are a set of ten voluntary standards incorporating World Bank practices and guidelines developed by a group of financial institutions in 2003. These principles aim to ensure socially responsible development of projects and sound environmental management practices. A total of ninety-six EP financial institutions in developed

[28] Ibid, p. 426.

[29] Ali, S. (2016). *Governing Disasters: Engaging Local Populations in Humanitarian Relief*, Cambridge: Cambridge University Press. These principles mirror similar norms in the post-disaster context of requiring the participation of relief beneficiaries 'in the design, management and implementation of assistance'. *See* United Nations & Inter-Agency Standing Committee. (2008). *Civil-Military Guidelines and Reference for Complex Emergencies*. New York: United Nations. www.unocha.org/sites/unocha/files/dms/Documents/02.%20Civil%20Military%20Guidelines%20and%20Reference%20for%20Complex%20Emergencies.pdf.

and emerging markets worldwide have adopted the EPs. Stakeholder engagement and grievance mechanisms are central to the EPs, respectively providing that the client should carry out effective consultations with affected communities and have mechanisms in place to facilitate resolution of concerns relating to the project's environmental and social performance.

Due Diligence Guidance for Meaningful Stakeholder Engagement in the Extractive Sector

The OECD's Due Diligence Guidance for Meaningful Stakeholder Engagement in the Extractive Sector provides principles of engagement in the context of mining, oil and gas enterprises, and calls for multinational enterprises to carry out risk-based due diligence to identify, prevent and mitigate actual and potential adverse impacts, and engage in decision making with stakeholders regarding project impacts. The OECD Guidelines for Multinational Enterprises are currently implemented by forty-eight states.[30]

The UNGPs on Business and Human Rights

The UNGPs expects companies to establish 'operational-level . . . mechanisms for individuals and communities' to arrive at shared understanding and agreement (Guiding Principle 29) regarding resolution of community–investor issues. The third pillar of the UNGP[31] incorporates both judicial and non-judicial recourse for communities impacted by investment projects.[32] Within the East Asian region, similar to other global jurisdictions, states have been adopting national action plans in line with the UNGP, implementing the three pillars including the right to remedy.[33]

[30] Ali, *Governing Disasters*, 207.

[31] Deva, S. (2021). The UN Guiding Principles on Business and Human Rights and its predecessors. In I. Bantekas, M. A. Stein & F. Seatzu (Eds.). *The Cambridge Companion to Business and Human Rights Law* (pp. 159–164). Cambridge: Cambridge University Press.

[32] Ibid.

[33] White, M. (2021). Does the slipper fit? National action plans on business and human rights in South East Asia. In R. Ramcharan & J. Gomez (Eds.). *Business and Human Rights in Asia: Duty of the State to Protect* (pp. 21–34). Singapore: Palgrave Macmillan.

The UN Global Compact

The UN Global Compact is an initiative supported by the UN to engage the private sector.[34] The PRIs (2006–2022) consist of six voluntary investment principles supported by the UN,[35] garnering over 1,800 investor and financial institution signatories worldwide. The PRIs mandate signatories to, inter alia, incorporate environmental, social and governance (ESG) issues into their decision-making, investment and progress reporting, with a goal of facilitating investors in understanding the implications of sustainable investment.

ILO Convention No. 169

In relation to the special rights of Indigenous populations affected by infrastructure activity, the ILO Convention no. 169 (1989) establishes the right of Indigenous communities to be consulted in measures affecting them, and in some cases, provides them with a veto right over proposed plans that do not align with community aspirations.[36] Article 32 of the Declaration on the Rights of Indigenous Peoples also puts such development initiatives to the approval of the communities.[37] Further, the Committee on the Elimination of Racial Discrimination general recommendation 23 calls for governments to establish effective participation mechanisms for Indigenous communities.[38]

IFC Sustainability Framework

The IFC Framework approved in 2009 originates out of the World Bank's Environmental Sustainability Framework, with specific modifications

[34] Rasche, A. (2021). The UN Global Compact and the OECD Guidelines for Multinational Enterprises and their enforcement mechanisms. In I. Bantekas, M. A. Stein & F. Seatzu (Eds.). *The Cambridge Companion to Business and Human Rights Law* (p. 201). Cambridge: Cambridge University Press.

[35] Principles for Responsible Investment. (n.d.). What are the Principles for Responsible Investment? www.unpri.org/pri/what-are-the-principles-for-responsible-investment.

[36] Suárez Santos, R. (2019). Three decades since the ILO's Convention 169: Reflections in light of the experience of the private sector with prior consultation. *The International Journal of Human Rights*, *24*(2–3), 272–278. https://doi.org/10.1080/13642987.2019.1677618.

[37] Kanosue, Y. (2015). When land is taken away: States' obligations under international human rights law concerning large-scale projects impacting local communities. *Human Rights Law Review*, *15*(4), 643–667. https://doi.org/10.1093/hrlr/ngv026.

[38] Ibid.

catered towards the IFC's focus on the private sector. The Framework comprises IFC Performance Standards for Environmental and Social Sustainability, IFC Policy for Information Use and IFC Performance Standards.

The Performance Standards contained in the IFC Framework cover eight areas, including:[39] (1) assessment and management of environmental and social risks and impacts; (2) workforce and working conditions; (3) resources efficiency and pollution prevention; (4) community health, safety and security; (5) land acquisition and involuntary migration; (6) biodiversity conservation and sustainable management of biological natural resources; and (7) aboriginal and (8) cultural heritage.

Stakeholder engagement and grievance mechanisms are included in the environmental policies of MDBs, respectively providing that clients should carry out effective consultations with affected communities and have mechanisms in place to facilitate resolution of concerns relating to a project's environmental and social performance.

National Development Bank Standards

Some national development banks may reference these environmental and social frameworks or refer to host-country environmental regulations. Given the wide range of national standards, significant compliance gaps have led to heightened sustainability risks, resulting in ESG grievances, as will be discussed in later chapters.

Transnational Innovation of Investor–Community Dispute Resolution Principles

Global norm development in relation to community engagement in the context of infrastructure development has emerged out of crises and decentralised shared knowledge generation[40] amongst national and multilateral banking institutions, resulting in legal innovations. This process has accelerated in the context of cross-border infrastructure projects, which often involve coordination between national and multilateral standards. This learning orientation, including the creation of shared learning spaces such as the International Financial Institution

[39] International Finance Corporation. (n.d.). E&S performance standards. www.ifc.org/wps/wcm/connect/Topics_Ext_Content/IFC_External_Corporate_Site/Sustainability-At-IFC/Policies-Standards/Performance-Standards/.

[40] Ali, Forming Transnational Dispute Settlement Norms.

Meetings, which are hosted by the world's MDBs, has resulted in growing agreement on the relevant underlying principles and good practices in community engagement in the context of infrastructure planning.

Transnational legal innovations have historically been examined from a number of perspectives, with the earliest literature focusing on transplantation and diffusion of legal norms. Recent work has examined how public norms are developed by global private actors through corporate codes,[41] soft law,[42] cultural adaptation,[43] and vernacularised through replication and hybridisation in legal ordering.[44] Developments in infrastructure governance demonstrate the important role of shared learning between nations, reflection on experience in light of relevant global norms, and policy innovations to transform and mitigate global infrastructure disputes.

At present, greater emphasis has been placed on networked transnational legal ordering,[45] and increasingly 'decentralised transnational law making'[46] characterised by expanded representation and engagement in global soft law making.[47] Building on these insights, transnational legal innovation, including advancing sustainability and community consultation and engagement standards in relation to infrastructure development, can be characterised by a mutual learning process amongst nations drawing from shared challenges, insights and experience.

The rise of hybrid organisational structures[48] and other forms of vertical disaggregation are breaking down uni-directional law-making processes. Public law norms are no longer the sole purview of the State[49] but have increasingly extended to the public–private domain.[50] Corporate codes are increasingly taking on a constitutional character,

41 Teubner, Hybrid laws.

42 Merry, Davis & Kingsbury, The Quiet Power of Indicators; Ali, *Forming Transnational Dispute Settlement Norms.*

43 Ali, S. (2011). *Resolving Disputes in the Asia Pacific Region: International Mediation and Arbitration in East Asia and the West.* New York: Routledge.

44 Halliday & Shaffer, *Transnational Legal Orders*, see also Ali, *Forming Transnational Dispute Settlement Norms.*

45 Halliday & Shaffer, *Transnational Legal Orders*; Li & Shaffer, China and the International Legal Order; Shaffer, Theorizing transnational legal ordering.

46 Ali, *Forming Transnational Dispute Settlement Norms.*

47 Ibid.

48 Teubner, Hybrid laws.

49 Ibid.

50 Ibid. See also Ramraj, V. V., & Tengaumnuay, T. (2022). Privatization of constitutional law: Thailand. In *Constitutionalism in Context* (pp. 517–540). Cambridge: Cambridge University Press. https://doi.org/10.1017/9781108699068.024.

requiring courts to grapple with the nature of such codes,[51] particularly where such codes lay down fundamental principles of social order.[52] Most MDBs' minimum consultation standards are outlined in relevant safeguard policy statements. In the case of national bank-funded projects, in many cases, reference is made to national policy, which varies greatly in relation to requirements for community engagement (from no requirements at all, to requirements similar to those outlined in the MDB policy statements), as will be examined in Chapter 3.

Transnational infrastructure safeguard policies have increasingly come to be 'vernacularised' in each jurisdiction, including distinct public consultation standards that interface with diverse local norms of dialogue with implications for subsequent grievances, as will be explored in Chapter 3.

Contributions and Limits of Soft Law-Derived Community Grievance Mechanism

While significant progress has been achieved in reaching consensus on principles relevant to community–bank accountability standards, nevertheless, regulating MDBs' investor behaviour entirely on the basis of soft law regulatory norms is not without limits. For example, while the UNGPs represents an advancement of global norms of community engagement by establishing a standard for voluntary initiatives,[53] observers have expressed the concern that the UNGP fails to clearly articulate alternatives available for communities who are unable to hold corporations accountable,[54] given that such norms are not seen as hard obligations but rather aspirational 'responsibilities'.[55] The purported emphasis on non-judicial remedies in the UNGP, some argue, obscures the need for judicial remedies.[56]

[51] Teubner, G. (2012). *Constitutional Fragments: Societal Constitutionalism and Globalization* (G. Norbury, trans.). Oxford: Oxford University Press.

[52] Teubner, G. (2011). Self-constitutionalizing TNCs? On the linkage of 'private' and 'public' corporate codes of conduct. *Indiana Journal of Global Legal Studies*, *18*(2), 617. https://doi.org/10.2979/indjglolegstu.18.2.617.

[53] Ibid.

[54] Ibid.

[55] Jägers, N. (2011). UN Guiding Principles on Business and Human Rights: Making headway towards real corporate accountability? *Netherlands Quarterly of Human Rights*, *29*(2), 159–163. https://doi.org/10.1177/016934411102900201.

[56] Ibid.

While there is no doubt that national policies play an important role in mediating the efficacy of the UNGP,[57] particularly in regions where a government may prioritise business interests over those of a local community,[58] scholars have pointed out that 'soft laws' such as the UNGP and the OECD Guidelines have led to the adoption of increasingly robust national or regional 'hard laws', which have become directly binding,[59] including through the development of enforcement mechanisms implemented by national contact points under the OECD Guidelines.[60]

In relation to ILO Convention no. 169, significant progress has been made in relation to the protection of Indigenous peoples.[61] However, in some jurisdictions, given that many states have yet to introduce legislation ratifying the Convention,[62] the implementation of the right to prior consultation under Article 6 has likewise been limited.[63] Notwithstanding, the Convention has strengthened Indigenous rights, particularly in Latin America,[64] while some MDBs have incorporated this standard internally for funded projects. In the Asia Pacific region, the Convention has thus far only been ratified by Nepal.[65] Nevertheless, the Convention remains a key

[57] Siddiqui, J., & Uddin, S. (2016). Human rights disasters, corporate accountability and the state. *Accounting Auditing & Accountability Journal*, *29*(4), 679–704. https://doi.org/10.1108/aaaj-07-2015-2140.

[58] Ibid.

[59] Momsen, C., & Schwarze, M. (2018). The changing face of corporate liability: New hard law and the increasing influence of soft law. *Criminal Law Forum*, *29*(4), 567–593. https://doi.org/10.1007/s10609-018-9355-x.

[60] Seck, S. L. (2016). Indigenous rights, environmental rights, or stakeholder engagement? Comparing IFC and OECD approaches to the implementation of the business responsibility to respect human rights. *McGill International Journal of Sustainable Development Law and Policy*, *12*(1), 48–91.

[61] Larsen, P. B. (2019). Contextualising ratification and implementation: A critical appraisal of ILO Convention 169 from a social justice perspective. *The International Journal of Human Rights*, *24*(2–3), 94–111. https://doi.org/10.1080/13642987.2019.1677613.

[62] Santos, Three decades since the ILO's Convention 169.

[63] Ibid.

[64] Yupsanis, A. (2010). ILO Convention no. 169 concerning Indigenous and tribal peoples in independent countries 1989–2009: An overview. *Nordic Journal of International Law*, *79*(3), 433–456. https://doi.org/10.1163/157181010x512576.

[65] Errico, S. (2019). ILO Convention no. 169 in Asia: Progress and challenges. *The International Journal of Human Rights*, *24*(2–3), 156–169. https://doi.org/10.1080/13642987.2019.1677611.

guiding instrument,[66] and has informed the gradual development of consultative and participatory rights.[67]

As will be seen in Chapter 3, many of these principles have increasingly been incorporated into MDB policies, providing an important avenue for accountability.

Conclusion

Global norm development in relation to community engagement in the context of infrastructure development has emerged out of crises, decentralised shared knowledge generation[68] amongst national and multilateral banking institutions, NGOs and community groups, resulting in legal innovations that ultimately provide for stronger community protections and accountability on the part of funding institutions. This learning orientation, including the creation of shared learning spaces such as the International Financial Institution Meetings, has resulted in growing agreement on the relevant underlying principles and good practices in community engagement in the context of infrastructure planning. Such principles in recent years have included the EPs, the UNGPs of Business and Human Rights, the OECD's Due Diligence Guidance for Meaningful Stakeholder Engagement in the Extractive Sector, the PRIs, and the ILO Convention, advancing the need for consultation between project finance institutions and host communities to arrive at shared understanding and agreement on matters that affect community well-being and prosperity. While limitations persist in the implementation of meaningful consultation spaces, the process has accelerated in the context of cross-border infrastructure projects that often involve coordination between national and multilateral standards.

66 Ibid.

67 Tomaselli, A. (2019). Political participation, the International Labour Organization, and Indigenous peoples: Convention 169 'participatory' rights. *The International Journal of Human Rights*, *24*(2–3), 127–143. https://doi.org/10.1080/13642987.2019.1677612.

68 Ali, *Forming Transnational Dispute Settlement Norms.*

3

Dispute Mitigation in Global Multilateral Development Banks

This chapter examines the question of when expanded channels of community consultation and redress are made available in infrastructure project-affected communities, are grievances aggregated or reduced. To what extent do such mechanisms facilitate community participation and serve as a conduit to incorporate genuine community concerns into project design such that disputes are avoided?

To provide context for the nature and functioning of redress mechanisms and requirements for community consultation alongside other safeguard policies, including information disclosure and building on Chapter 2's exploration of the emergence of increasingly shared principles of accountability, this chapter examines the increasingly stringent application of such principles in the practices of a select number of global multilateral development banks (MDBs) supported by the Partnership for Global Infrastructure and Investment and Belt and Road initiative – including the World Bank, Asian Development Bank (ADB) and Asian Infrastructure Investment Bank (AIIB). The chapter explores how their environmental and social frameworks (ESFs), beginning in the early 2000s, were designed to mitigate negative social and environmental impacts of project investments. This is followed by a statistical comparison of the proportion of grievances per project raised prior to and after bank policy amendments between 2010 and 2020 expanded access to pre-project consultation, informed consent and formalised grievance mechanisms (GMs) amongst ten of the world's MDBs. In particular, it examines the number of disputes lodged in this time period, before and after these rule changes were made, in order to determine whether increasing channels of consultation and accountability lead to an increase or reduction in the number of project disputes.[1]

[1] Rule changes include the IFC Sustainability Framework (2009), the World Bank Environmental and Social Framework (October 2018), the IDB Environmental and Social Sustainability Policy (September 2013), the ADB Safeguards Policy Statement (January 2010), the European Bank for Reconstruction and Development Environmental and Social Policy

The findings indicate that the percentage of grievances per project peaks at 15.4% in 2019 then drops significantly in 2021 to 7.1%. This drop in percentage of grievances corresponds with the implementation of heightened MDB community engagement policies. This overall decline in the percentage of grievance cases could be due to a number of intervening factors including heightened environmental screening standards, Covid lockdowns and self-help. Overall, the findings provide measured evidence supporting the development of increasingly robust community engagement channels, particularly for MDBs and national development banks (NDBs), which have not yet implemented such policies. The findings of the chapter indicate that these engagement channels, far from aggregating complaints during the period examined, conversely appear to serve as a conduit to incorporate concerns into project design such that disputes are avoided.

While more recent data from 2022 have shown a slight uptick in filed complaints,[2] this corresponds with a 6% increase in total project funding, suggesting modest movement in overall percentage of grievances per project in recent years.[3] These data likewise reflect a growing awareness of the availability of GMs and the existence of a higher number of complaints passing the eligibility threshold amidst post-Covid revived infrastructure activity.

Significantly, new grievance data since 2021 show that the increased attention on the part of MDBs to pre-project consultation, disclosure and due diligence has been positively recognised by affected communities. This is demonstrated by the fact that before 2021, the lack of consultation, disclosure or due diligence was the single most cited cause of grievances amongst affected communities. After 2021, it was no longer the single most cited cause, but rather became the second issue cited after concerns regarding displacement became the primary concern amongst complainants.[4]

As was explored in Chapter 2, over the past twenty years, significant learning has been generated regarding the centrality of community engagement and the development of appropriate GMs oriented towards

(April 2019), the European Investment Banks Environmental and Social Standards (October 2018), and the AIIB Environmental and Social Framework (2016/amended 2019).

2 See Accountability Council Report, A new decade of complaints. www.accountabilityconsole.com/newsletter/articles/a-new-decade-of-complaints/.

3 Based on estimated total MDB infrastructure development funding comparison between 2021 and 2022.

4 See Accountability Council Report, A new decade of complaints.

the prevention of conflicts arising from major infrastructure projects. This emerges from a growing 'recogni[tion] [that] multi-stakeholder partnerships a[re] important vehicles for mobilizing and sharing knowledge, expertise, technologies and financial resources' in achieving sustainable development objectives' (United Nations (UN) Sustainable Development Goal 17).

Prior to the early 2000s, few if any, infrastructure projects financed by MDBs had early-stage consultation or post-project GMs in place prior to the initiation of a project. Community engagement, if at all, was conducted on an ad hoc basis, usually after a major grievance occurred. During the period between 2010 and 2019, ten out of twelve of the world's MDBs amended or introduced environmental and social policy (ESP) frameworks, requiring heightened (1) pre-project due diligence, consultation, and free, prior and informed consultation (FPIC) in appropriate cases; (2) information disclosure on potential impacts; and (3) GMs in internal bank policies.[5] Attention has increasingly focused on the quality and depth of the consultation process, and in more recent times, halting projects found not to be in compliance with increasingly robust standards.

With the passage of twenty years since the establishment of the first Compliance Advisor Ombudsman (CAO) office at the International Finance Corporation (IFC)/World Bank, significant learning has been gained regarding community consultation and GMs. As a general matter, community–investor public consultation mechanisms are formal, legal or non-legal processes implemented before project commencement and continuing through project implementation that offer a channel for parties to lodge or address grievances that result from MDB investment activities and operations. The approach taken to pre-project engagement includes consultation, mediation, recommendations or impact studies.

Emergence of Community–Investor Facilitation and Dispute Resolution Mechanisms

The following sections explore the early development of the Office of the CAO of the IFC/World Bank followed by the subsequent development of independent accountability mechanisms (AMs) within the ADB and

[5] Ali, Shahla F., Davis, William E., & Lee, Joanna (2010). Multi-stakeholder dispute resolution: Building social capital through access to justice at the community level. *Pepperdine Dispute Resolution Law Journal, 11*(2), 181–206.

AIIB operating in the Asia Pacific Region. A theme running through these examinations is the increasingly heightened stringency of environmental, social and governance safeguards over time, including requirements for consultation with affected communities, provision of GMs and project transparency.

CAO of the IFC/World Bank

As discussed in Chapter 2, following a series of internal reviews aimed at strengthening community engagement, in 1998, the IFC/World Bank formally established the Office of the CAO. Since this time, significant learning has been gained regarding community facilitation mechanisms.[6]

The CAO, as the designated recourse and AM for social and environmental concerns arising out of IFC/Multilateral Investment Guarantee Agency (MIGA) projects, is an independent office based in Washington, DC, reporting directly to the President of the World Bank Group.[7] It electively engages project-affected communities in dialogue with the stated aims of:

- addressing concerns of individuals and/communities affected by IFC/MIGA projects;
- enhancing social and environmental outcomes of IFC/MIGA projects; and
- fostering greater public accountability of IFC and MIGA.[8]

Since its establishment, the CAO's role and powers have expanded. The CAO's terms of reference (1998) stipulated that the scope of the CAO was, inter alia: providing advice and assistance to IFC/MIGA in respect of 'sensitive or controversial' projects at the request of the President of the World Bank or IFC/MIGA management; handling of complaints made by external stakeholders affected by IFC/MIGA projects with the aim of correcting project failures; in addition to supervisory and advisory roles over IFC/MIGA's environmental and social performance to ensure ex post facto compliance with environmental and social policies, procedures, guidelines, resources and systems.[9]

[6] Ibid.

[7] CAO (2016). Annual report 2016. www.cao-ombudsman.org/resources/cao-2016-annual-report. See also: CAO (2013). Terms of reference. https://aconsole-static.s3.amazonaws.com/media/public/cases/AviancaAuditTORApril2013.pdf.

[8] CAO (n.d.) About the CAO: Who we are. www.cao-ombudsman.org/about-us.

[9] CAO, Terms of reference, pp. 1–2.

Compared with the original terms of reference (1998), the CAO now carries out a larger role in managing relationships through its dispute resolution work not only among individuals and communities affected by IFC/MIGA projects and IFC/MIGA clientele, but civil society, non-governmental organisations (NGOs), governments and other relevant stakeholders.[10] The CAO is now specifically mandated to conduct independent investigations of IFC/MIGA project performance and compliance appraisals, not only pursuant to complaints or at the request of the President of the World Bank (or IFC/MIGA senior management) but at the discretion of the Vice President.[11] Notably, it is permitted a more proactive role in exercising its advisory function in respect of emerging social and environmental issues that may arise from IFC/MIGA projects.[12] In discharging its roles, the CAO further observes principles of independence and objectivity, as well as guiding principles geared at enhancing transparency, certainty and consistency.[13]

The CAO's terms of reference (2013) thus reflect the CAO's updated mandate, pursuant to which it exercises three functions, as reflected by its organisational structure reporting to the CAO Vice President.

(1) Dispute resolution: professional dispute resolution between IFC/MIGA clients and communities affected by IFC/MIGA projects;
(2) Compliance: oversight of social/environmental performance of IFC/MIGA projects;
(3) Advisory: independent advice to the President of the World Bank Group and senior management.[14]

In 2019, the CAO reported that it handled sixty cases in thirty-five countries, comprising twelve new eligible complaints and forty-eight cases in which CAO continued to conduct assessment, dispute resolution and compliance investigations.[15] The breakdowns provided indicate that the bulk of complaints related to IFC projects (89%) as opposed to IFC/MIGA projects (10%) or MIGA projects (1%). These were filed by individuals and communities (43%) or supported by civil society groups (52%), with a minority being initiated by CAO itself (5%).

[10] See also: Ibid, p. 2.
[11] Ibid.
[12] Ibid.
[13] Ibid.
[14] Ibid.
[15] CAO (2019). Annual report 2019, p. 2. www.cao-ombudsman.org/resources/cao-2019-annual-report.

Developments in the CAO/IFC's Community Engagement Standards: From Consultation to Informed Consent in Special Cases

The evolution of the CAO/IFC's role in effecting accountability and recourse for communities affected by IFC/MIGA projects and its development of standards for stakeholder engagement can be tracked over the past two decades with reference to IFC policies.[16]

Over the span of two decades, the IFC's approach to community engagement 'in the books' has tangibly shifted from passive community consultation towards greater project engagement based upon principles of broad community support (BCS), informed consultation and participation (ICP) and FPIC.[17] This formed the context for the External Review of IFC/MIGA Environmental and Social Accountability Review, to be further examined here.

Prior to 30 April 2006

Prior to 30 April 2006, the IFC's community engagement policies were formulated in terms of 'public consultation' requirements as comprehensively set out under the IFC's Procedure for Environmental and Social Review of Projects (1998) ('1998 Environmental and Social Review Procedure') and Policy on Disclosure of Information (1998) ('Disclosure Policy').[18] Notably, public consultation at this time was conducted with a view to solicit views on social and environmental impacts with community input simply taken into account.[19]

Projects were required to formulate a public consultation and disclosure plan (PCDP) including localised consultation and disclosure, identifying relevant stakeholder groups, establishing strategies and timetables for consultation, implementation plans for PCDP activities and reporting/documentation of relevant activities.[20] Key principles identified in the production of PCDPs included, inter alia, effective written and oral communications (including in local languages), accessibility to written information and consultation process by stakeholders, consultation of

[16] Ali, Davis & Lee, Multi-stakeholder dispute resolution.

[17] Ibid.

[18] IFC (December 1998). *Procedure for Environmental and Social Review of Projects*, p. 13. www.ifc.org/wps/wcm/connect/topics_ext_content/ifc_external_corporate_site/sustainability-at-ifc/policies-standards/es-proc-manual.

[19] Ibid, p. 13.

[20] Ibid, Guidance Note F, p. 50.

adequately representative groups (including ethnic, religious and other vulnerable minority groups).[21]

Minimum requirements for public consultation and public disclosure for projects included the responsibility of the project sponsor to consult project-affected groups and local NGOs in respect of the project's environmental aspects, albeit limited only to Category A (and certain Category B) projects, comprising those projects anticipated to engender significant adverse environmental impacts.[22] In general, the project sponsor was expected to consult with relevant groups to obtain and 'take into account' their views at least twice: (1) shortly after environmental screening; and (2) prior to finalisation of the terms of reference of the environmental assessment (EA), as well as during project implementation as necessary to address EA-related issues.[23] Project sponsors were further expected to ensure the provision of relevant materials (dependent on classification as a Category A or B project) such as proposed project objectives, description and potential impacts and/or draft EA reports in a form, language and location accessible and comprehensible by parties in good time prior to the consultation.[24]

Following the completion of the EA report for Category A projects, the IFC's Disclosure Policy required that a summary report, including details of public consultations (and comments thereon) made during EA preparation, be made publicly available at least sixty days prior to the proposed date for consideration by the Board of Directors for dissemination at the InfoShop, the World Bank's former non-profit bookstore and resource centre with a view to promoting accountability, transparency, openness and improved decision making.[25] A similar process was implemented for Category B projects, substituting a summary of key findings of environmental review and a deadline of thirty days prior to the proposed Board date, in the Disclosure Policy and the Environmental

21 Ibid.

22 IFC (October 1998). 'Environmental assessment', *Operational Policies* (OP 4.01). www.ifc.org/wps/wcm/connect/8fbad499-03f6-4903-a586-d180e34a73f0/OP401_EnvironmentalAssessment.pdf?MOD=AJPERES&CVID=jqeAUET.

23 Ibid, paras 12–13, p. 4. In cases where classification as a 'Category A' project has been completed prior to IFC involvement, the IFC reviews existing public consultation and disclosure and, as necessary, undertakes a supplemental consultation prior to proceeding with disclosure requirements.

24 Ibid, paras 14–16.

25 Ibid, para. 17. See also: IFC (September 1998). IFC's policy on disclosure of information. www.ifc.org/wps/wcm/connect/topics_ext_content/ifc_external_corporate_site/sustainability-at-ifc/policies-standards/safeguards-pre2006#safeguard.

and Social Review Procedures.[26] The local release of consultation information, in the local language and in a culturally appropriate manner, in advance of Board consideration was also provided for to facilitate community awareness.[27] More generally, information pertaining to specific projects, including Project Information (for ongoing projects) and Summary of Project Information (for projects pending consideration), was published on InfoShop with the aim of informing and eliciting responses from affected local communities, stakeholders and the public at large.[28]

Developments after 2006: FPIC

After 2006, adopting its Policy and Performance Standards on Social and Environmental Sustainability ('Sustainability Framework'),[29] the IFC expanded, refined and strengthened its community engagement strategies requiring engagement with project-affected communities.

The IFC's Performance Standards (governing social and environmental performance in the execution of projects) shifted course in establishing principles for disclosure of information, consultation and 'informed' participation of communities affected by IFC projects.[30] In particular, Performance Standard 1 expanded on the definition of informed participation in requiring consultation and incorporation of affected communities' views on matters directly affecting them (e.g. implementation issues, mitigation measures and sharing of opportunities created by project development).[31] The IFC, in its Sustainability Framework, likewise broke ground in committing to standards for local community engagement involving (1) FPIC enabling informed participation of affected local stakeholders and (2) generation of BCS for projects.[32] The importance of FPIC and BCS in IFC's Environmental and Social

[26] See Ibid, p. 3.
[27] Ibid, p. 4.
[28] Ibid.
[29] IFC (30 April 2006). *Policy and Performance Standards and Environmental Sustainability.* www.ifc.org/wps/wcm/connect/topics_ext_content/ifc_external_corporate_site/sustainability-at-ifc/policies-standards/ifcsustainabilityframework_2006.
[30] Ibid, paras 19–20, p. 4.
[31] Ibid. See also IFC (April 2006). *Procedure for Environmental and Social Review of Projects,* p. 27. www.ifc.org/wps/wcm/connect/topics_ext_content/ifc_external_corporate_site/sustainability-at-ifc/policies-standards/es-proc-manual.
[32] Ibid.

Review Procedure is evidenced in their integration as prerequisites to presentation of a project for approval by the IFC Board.[33]

The new focus on FPIC and BCS in community engagement standards was developed and elaborated upon in the IFC's revamped Environment and Social Review Procedure (2006) for IFC-financed projects.[34] At all project stages, procedures were put in place to review compliance with disclosure, FPIC obligations and determination of BCS.[35] A Procedural Note on Reviewing Free Prior Informed Consultation and Determining BCS outlined the relevant requirements within the Sustainability Framework and Performance Standards.[36] The IFC specifically recognised, in this regard, BCS as a 'collection of expressions by the affected communities ... in support of the project' while recognising that the presence of dissent does not negate BCS.[37] In this regard, recognising the inherent linkage between the process of FPIC and BCS, the IFC conceived of two review streams consisting of consideration of: (1) the process (i.e. whether the project client has conducted FPIC and enabled informed participation of affected communities); and (2) the outcome (i.e. the level of support, including whether BCS is reached as seen in the particular context, among affected communities for the project) and provides guidelines therefor.[38] These standards were maintained and expanded in subsequent updates to the IFC's Environmental and Social Review Procedure in 2007 and 2009.[39]

Developments after 2012: FPIC

In 2012, the IFC's Sustainability Framework was updated again and refined further to consist of an eighteen-month consultation process, further expanding the role of project-affected communities in pre-project participatory processes.[40]

While previous community engagement processes under the IFC's 2006 Sustainability Framework in respect of projects with potential for highly adverse impacts required 'free, prior and informed *consultation*'

[33] Ibid.
[34] Ibid.
[35] Ibid. See e.g. para. 3.2.12(d) and (e); 4.2.2; 6.1.1.
[36] Ibid, p. 27.
[37] Ibid, p. 27.
[38] Ibid.
[39] See: IFC (July 2007). *Procedure for Environmental and Social Review of Projects.* Also: IFC (August 2009). *Procedure for Environmental and Social Review of Projects.*
[40] IFC (2012). *Policy on Environmental and Social Sustainability.*

resulting in BCP, it is significant that the IFC's 2012 Sustainability Framework uses the vocabulary of 'free, prior and informed *consent*' as a higher standard building on ICP.[41] This is borne out by elaboration of a table of different levels of stakeholder engagement in IFC's 2012 Sustainability Framework, which connects increasing levels of risk and impact on project-affected communities with a sliding scale of client responsibilities ranging from:[42]

(1) External communication (investment activities generally)
(2) Consultation (moderate impact projects)
(3) ICP (significant impact projects, including those relating to Indigenous peoples and cultural heritage)
(4) FPIC (significant impact projects)

At every part of the environmental and social review process, BCP, ICP and FPIC characterise community engagement processes and compliance checks.

Role of the CAO in IFC-Financed Projects and Community Engagement

From 2006, the IFC specifically referred to the role of the CAO as an independent oversight authority in responding to complaints and grievances by people and communities affected by IFC-financed projects.[43]

The IFC's Environmental and Social Review Procedure provides for recourse mechanisms in the event of complaints filed and accepted by the CAO.[44] Clients of IFC-financed projects are expected to comply with CAO investigations. In this regard, the CAO supplements project-level procedures and established dispute resolution mechanisms in host countries.[45] Nonetheless, interactions between the CAO and the IFC in the discharge of their respective roles has come under scrutiny, recognised as meriting review in the recent External Review of IFC/MIGA Environmental and Social Accountability Report and Recommendations.[46]

[41] IFC (2012). *Sustainability Policy*, para. 30, p. 6.
[42] IFC (2012). *Procedure for Environmental and Social Review of Projects.*
[43] IFC, *Sustainability Policy*, paras 31–45, p. 7.
[44] IFC, *Procedure for Environmental and Social Review of Projects* (2006), p. 46.
[45] Ibid.
[46] IFC (June 2020). *External Review of IFC/MIGA E&S Accountability, Including CAO's Role and Effectiveness: Report and Recommendations.*

Efforts towards Increasing Responsiveness of the IFC's CAO Office

In June 2020, an External Review of IFC/MIGA's Environmental and Social Accountability[47] provided a range of observations and recommendations in respect of: (1) governance structures in the discharge of its dispute resolution, compliance and advisory functions; (2) the current role and effectiveness of the CAO; (3) IFC/MIGA's level of responsiveness to adverse environmental and social impacts; (4) the impact of current CAO processes on project stakeholders; and (5) possible adjustments to IFC/MIGA's own mechanisms for complaint response.[48] The Review Team notably made certain findings in relation to improvements relating to the engagement of project-affected communities and stakeholders.

One area of reform included addressing divergences and disagreements between IFC/MIGA and CAO in the context of IFC/MIGA's environmental and social requirements, as well as CAO compliance investigations and investigation findings (and lack of remedial actions arising therefrom), resulting in strained collaboration and interaction efforts.[49] In noting complaints and concerns by project clients of insufficient support and/or guidance on Environmental and Social Compliance by IFC/MIGA, as well as extended and cumbersome CAO processes by both clients and complainants, the Review Team largely proposed, in summary, adjustments to IFC/MIGA roles as well as CAO processes to forge a more collaborative relationship between IFC/MIGA to address disagreements and permit clarification of remedial actions.[50] Some of the suggestions relating to a greater role for direct community engagement and dialogue by IFC/MIGA in addressing environmental and social concerns in the context of complaints or concerns are examined here.

Attention has been required for IFC/MIGA (and by extension project clients) to strengthen capacities, systems and mindsets to address complaints and concerns raised by people and communities affected by IFC projects.[51] While the Review Team recognised CAO as an 'essential

[47] Ibid.

[48] The World Bank (12 August 2020). External review of IFC/MIGA environmental & social (E&S) accountability, including CAO's role and effectiveness. www.worldbank.org/en/about/leadership/brief/external-review-of-ifc-miga-es-accountability.

[49] IFC, External review, pp. vii–viii.

[50] Ibid.

[51] Ibid, p. xi.

component' of environmental and social accountability for IFC/MIGA, it took the view that the CAO ought not be the sole mechanism by which affected stakeholders are able to raise issues.[52] It was observed in this regard that while the IFC Performance Standards require project-level engagement processes and dispute resolution, supervision and evaluation records show that 'insufficient attention' is accorded by IFC/MIGA and clients to the proper establishment and facilitation of GMs for affected communities.[53] Further, where affected communities bypassed project-specific mechanisms for reasons of lack of confidence in clients (e.g. fear of retaliation) and lodged complaints with IFC/MIGA staff, there was no centralised register or mechanism for a standard response to such complaints by the IFC, such that organisational response depended on the initiative of individual officers.[54] Indeed, the Review Team found that groups of complaints subsequently sought redress from the CAO and used non-compliance findings to litigate alleged breach of duty of the IFC in national courts.[55]

In addressing such structural deficiencies, the Review Team suggested conducting detailed assessments of implementation of GMs in existing projects, and in so doing, consulting directly with both affected communities and clients.[56] Such consultation with all relevant stakeholders per the IFC's Performance Standards are not only necessary for ensuring the implementation of effective and project-specific recourse mechanisms, but further integral to facilitating trust and confidence between clients and affected communities in the creation of a trusted and efficient complaint response culture. The aim is that such strengthened mechanisms will, over time, assist in reducing the number of complaints filed at CAO due to the more efficient resolution of complaints at the project level.[57]

It was further recognised that a prerequisite for the proper functioning of AMs is knowledge of its existence by stakeholders, communities and civil society organisations (CSOs).[58] In this regard, the Review Team recommended that IFC/MIGA ensure that clients overseeing

52 Ibid, p. xi.
53 Ibid.
54 Ibid.
55 Ibid, p. 17.
56 Ibid, p. xi.
57 Ibid.
58 Ibid, p. 84.

projects requiring the establishment of GMs provide sufficient information in relation to: (1) the project client's GM; and (2) the CAO, with the IFC/MIGA to take a proactive role in ensuring that project clients discharge such responsibility.[59] It was subsequently concluded that GMs need to be rigorously supervised, with interviews of GM staff alongside members of affected communities to ensure that GM capacity is being properly developed and effective in addressing complaints.[60] In making such recommendations, the Review Team sought to ameliorate proper and sufficient involvement of affected communities as a principle of environmental and social, as well as in resolving disputes that had arisen.

A more active engagement culture and greater willingness to engage with both clients and complainants was a further recommendation.[61] In this regard, the Review Team noted the existence of attitudes within IFC/MIGA that the responsibility of implementation of environmental and social measures, including those relating to consultation with, receiving and addressing concerns from and general engagement with affected communities, fell upon project clients.[62] The Review Team emphasised the need for IFC/MIGA to 'embrace fully and without equivocation' their responsibility to engage with affect clients and clients to provide effective responses to concerns, irrespective of the IFC/MIGA's primary role as investor (and client's role as primary project implementer).[63] In recognising that a culture shift at the institutional level is necessary, the Review Team noted that direct engagement with affected people and communities is imperative: (1) for the proper comprehension of issues and options in the project context; (2) for the resolution of issues of concerns by being in a position to provide well-informed, contextualised advice to the project client; and (3) to be able to demonstrate IFC/MIGA commitment to affected communities.[64]

While the External Review did not create any binding obligations on IFC/MIGA and/or CAO, its recommendations are regarded as continuing.[65]

59 Ibid, p. 84.
60 Ibid, p. 87.
61 Ibid, p. xii.
62 Ibid.
63 Ibid.
64 Ibid.
65 The World Bank, External review.

Summary

In relation to the IFC's Office of the CAO[66] engagement mechanisms, while it has established an important model for other MDB's, it faces challenges,[67] including information asymmetry given that local communities may be unaware of IFC/World Bank's involvement in a project and, hence, the availability of the CAO as a recourse.[68] The timing of engagement is an additional challenge.[69] For example, the IFC's Glamis Gold project called for a community-wide referendum, resulting in the outright rejection by the community of the project;[70] however, the IFC funding had already been dispersed prior to the community referendum.[71] Finally, given that the CAO is not empowered to issue injunctions or require compensation for IFC violations of its internal guidelines, its accountability actions are limited.[72] Of significance, however, is the broad trend in the evolution of IFC performance standards over time to advance from a position of taking communities input 'into account' to increasingly requiring communities' 'free, prior and informed consent' in high-risk projects or those affecting Indigenous communities.

ADB Independent AMs

The ADB is an Asian MDB that aims to maximise the development impact of its assistance to its member states through facilitating policy dialogues, mobilising financial resources and offering advisory services via co-financing operations from different sources.[73]

In the early 1960s, the initial idea had arisen to develop a financial institution to foster economic growth and cooperation in Asia. The ADB's largest shareholders include Japan, the United States of America, Australia, Canada and Korea. In 1963, upon the passing of a resolution at the first Ministerial Conference on Asian Economic

66 Ibid, p. 78.

67 Saper, Benjamin M. (2012). The International Finance Corporation's Compliance Advisor/Ombudsman (CAO): An examination of accountability and effectiveness from a global administrative law perspective, *International Law and Politics 44*(1279).

68 Ibid, p. 1318.

69 Ibid.

70 Ibid, p. 1320.

71 Ibid.

72 Ibid, p. 1321.

73 ADB (25 May 2021). About ADB. www.adb.org/who-we-are/about.

Cooperation held by the UN Economic Commission for Asia and the Far East, the ADB was created. Manila, Philippines, was chosen as the host, and the bank was established on 19 December 1966 with thirty-one members to serve a predominantly agricultural region. During the early days of the ADB, the bank's main focus was on assistance on food production and rural development.[74]

The ADB currently envisions and aims to build a prosperous, inclusive, sustainable and resilient Asia and Pacific region, whilst attempting to eradicate extreme poverty within the region. It assists members in promoting social and economic development through the provision of loans, technical assistance, grants and equity investments.[75]

In the 1970s, the ADB increased its support for energy projects during the first global oil price shock. In particular, the ADB promoted the development of domestic energy sources amongst its member countries. The Bank's co-financing operations also began to provide additional resources for projects and programmes by the ADB. Another major landmark at the time included the establishment of the Asian Development Fund in 1974, which provided low-interest loans to the ADB's developing economy members. By the end of the decade, the ADB observed considerable improvement in the economies of many of its Asian member states, with several states no longer requiring the assistance of the ADB.[76]

In the 1980s, the ADB mainly continued to support its member states in infrastructure development and energy projects. The Bank increased its focus on social infrastructure, extending its projects to involve work related to microfinance, the environment, education, urban planning, gender equality and health issues.[77]

During the 1990s, the ADB became the first multilateral organisation to put in place a governance policy requiring board approval for loans, which served as a mechanism to ensure principled deployment of development assistance. Such policies included, notably, rules and regulations around involuntary resettlement and the protection of Indigenous people. Its list of members continued to expand until the 1997 financial crisis. By 1999, the ADB adopted poverty reduction as an overarching goal of the ADB.[78]

[74] Ibid.
[75] Ibid.
[76] Ibid.
[77] Ibid.
[78] Ibid.

In the 2000s, the ADB mainly focused on helping its member states achieve the Millennium Development Goals. With the spread of the SARS epidemic, the ADB also began supporting its member states in responding to the epidemic, influenza and other growing health threats such as HIV and AIDs. The ADB also supported its member states in facing unprecedented natural disasters and recovering from the aftermath of such events.[79]

In the 2010s, despite rapid growth in Asian economies and strong economic recovery, Asia still remained home to two-thirds of the world's lowest income countries. The widening wealth gap encouraged the ADB's shift in focus to promote inclusive growth in the region. The ADB also announced the combination of the lending operations of its two main funds – the Asian Development Fund and its ordinary capital resources to boost total annual lending and grant approvals.[80]

In recent years, the ADB has supported developing member states in addressing the Covid-19 pandemic and sustainable recovery, as well as longer-term development goals. To date, the ADB has grown significantly from its thirty-one members at its initial establishment in 1966, to a total of sixty-eight members – including forty-nine Asia Pacific and nineteen non-Asia Pacific member states respectively.[81]

Pre-project Finance Approval Community Consultation Requirements

The ADB's pre-project consultation process has evolved in recent years to require borrowers to actively engage with the public, communities, groups and affected populations through the disclosure of adequate and relevant information, as well as inviting consultation and informed participation commensurate with the risks and impact on the affected population.[82] Where the project involves significant adverse impacts on the environment, Indigenous peoples or involuntary resettlement, the project team must take additional care in its consultation activities to understand the concerns of the affected population, and ensure that

[79] Ibid.
[80] Ibid.
[81] Ibid.
[82] ADB. (2009). *Safeguard Policy Statement* (pp. 1–97, Policy Paper), pp. 20–21.

such considerations are addressed in the safeguard plans and project design.

In addition to ensuring appropriate information disclosure, public consultation and community participation is a key requirement.[83] The ADB aims to work with borrowers to facilitate meaningful consultation early in the preparatory stages of the project, and invites ongoing participation in the consultation process throughout the project cycle. Meaningful consultation includes the provision and timely disclosure of information that is readily accessible and easily understood by the affected population. Project consultation should be undertaken freely and voluntarily, without intimidation or coercion. It should be gender-inclusive, responsive and should be tailored to the needs of vulnerable groups. Invitations to participate should be extended to the affected population, and the ADB is required to incorporate all relevant views into the project's design, mitigation measures and development benefits and opportunities.

According to ADB's 2009 Safeguard Policy, informed consent in cases involving involuntary resettlement or significant impact on Indigenous populations must be ascertained through the consultation process.[84] This applies to projects involving the commercial development of cultural resources, physical relocation of Indigenous peoples from traditional or customary lands, the commercial development of natural resources within customary lands affecting local livelihoods, or the use of cultural, ceremonial or spiritual resources of Indigenous peoples.

Informed consent refers to consent by a collective expression of BCS by impacted individuals or recognised community representatives.[85] Such consent must be properly documented and reviewed by the ADB.

ADB's Pre-project Environmental and Social Safeguards

To facilitate and support inclusive economic growth and environmentally sustainable growth, the ADB developed certain key environmental and social safeguards to achieve these aims.[86]

[83] Ibid, pp. 20–21.
[84] Ibid, pp. 20–21.
[85] Ibid, pp. 20–21.
[86] ADB (3 September 2020). Overview: Safeguards. www.adb.org/site/safeguards/overview.

Historically, the ADB had separately adopted three different policies targeting its three main areas of environmental and social impact, namely its Involuntary Resettlement Policy (1995), Policy on Indigenous Peoples (1998) and its Environment Policy (2002).

More recently, the ADB has gradually advanced its pre-project approval mechanisms towards a more well-rounded and comprehensive policy.[87]

The ADB currently adopts the safeguard policy statement (SPS), a framework approved by its Board of Directors in July 2009 that builds upon the three key issues safeguarding the environment, involuntary resettlement and Indigenous peoples. The SPS focuses on helping its developing member countries (DMCs) in managing and addressing the environmental and social risks in development projects. It encourages DMCs to avoid, and if unable to avoid, to at least mitigate or minimise, any adverse impacts of its projects on the environment, people and their communities.

The current framework of the SPS draws on the safeguards included in the previous policies and replaces it with a single consolidated policy framework to enhance its effectiveness, relevance and coherence. The SPS also supersedes ADB's three separate former policies on involuntary resettlement, Indigenous peoples and the environment, as mentioned earlier. The SPS applies to all ADB-supported projects that are reviewed or approved by the management of ADB from 20 January 2010 onwards.

Environment Safeguards

Environmental management is crucial to preventing conflict through reduction or elimination of environmental harms.[88] Environmental safeguards targets aim to alleviate pressure on the region's natural resources, such as land, forests, wetlands, marine ecosystems and water systems, all of which remain critical resources for communities in the region.[89]

An initial EA was introduced into the ADB's pre-project assessment and lending operations in 1979. During the past two decades prior to adoption of the Environment Policy in 2002, the principles and scope of

87 Ibid.

88 ADB, *Safeguard Policy Statement*, p. 6.

89 ADB (22 March 2018). Environment safeguards. www.adb.org/site/safeguards/environment.

the EA has evolved from the original focus on technical assessment and mitigation, to an emphasis on developing a more comprehensive environmental management plan (EMP). The EMPs centre around the themes of mitigation, monitoring, cost-related estimates and budgets, and institutional arrangements. More significantly, the EA process highlights the importance of public consultation and the disclosure of information. Implementing recommendations in practice remains a challenge.

In 2006, a special evaluation study of the ADB's environmental safeguard policy was conducted by the Operations Evaluation Department (OED SES). The study found that the environmental safeguard policy was relevant and effective in avoiding major adverse environmental impacts arising from ADB-financed projects, despite reduced efficiency. The study also made further recommendations, including: (1) shifting focus from front-end loan processing to the delivery of results; (2) better integration of country standards with the EA policy; (3) extending the focus of policy application from the project itself to general capacity building; and (4) better integration of the ADB's environmental and social safeguards to advance sustainable development.

ADB's Current Environmental Safeguards: The 2018 SPS

A continuing focus of pre-project conflict mitigation is screening for environmental soundness and sustainability.[90] At the pre-project stages, the 2018 SPS requires borrowers to identify the impact of the project on the environment, assess the significance of its impacts, consider possible alternatives and prepare EMPs.

In assessing and measuring environmental impacts and risks of a potential project, as well as prescribing an appropriate EMP, the initial environmental examination (IEE) describes the environmental condition of a project, mitigation measures and the preparation of the monitoring needed in fulfilling institutional and environmental requirements.[91] The environmental impact assessments (EIAs) examines the environmental consequences of a project and provides comprehensive information to the public and decision-makers at the ADB to make informed decisions.

[90] Ibid.
[91] Ibid.

During the project, the ADB also requires the borrower to carefully implement and monitor its proposed EMPs.[92]

Involuntary Resettlement

Involuntary resettlement may give rise to critical economic, social and environmental risks.[93] If ill-managed, such development projects may lead to significant long-term hardship and impoverishment of the affected population.

The Involuntary Resettlement Policy was initially formulated in 1995, and was based on a similar involuntary resettlement policy by the World Bank.[94] With the growing complexity of ADB-financed projects, many projects had to handle impacts arising from the projects in relation to property, assets and more critically the loss of livelihoods of homes without physical relocation. Particular relevance lies in projects involving the development of urban areas, home to many informal settlers who might be unable to relocate.

Through implementation and experience, the ADB identified areas of improvements,[95] including the treatment of people without clear land titles, the scope of resettlement compensation and the ambiguous definition of 'affected' versus 'displaced' persons, as well as the capacity development of DMCs in planning, assessing and implementing involuntary resettlement.

ADB's Current Involuntary Resettlement Safeguards: The 2018 SPS

Following a review in 2006, the ADB's involuntary resettlement safeguard policy evolved to first avoid involuntary resettlement wherever possible.[96] If unable to avoid involuntary resettlement, the ADB would encourage the borrower to minimise the need for involuntary resettlement by exploring plausible alternatives through project design. If involuntary resettlement is required nonetheless, the borrower is required to

[92] Ibid.
[93] ADB (22 March 2018). Involuntary resettlement. www.adb.org/site/safeguards/involuntary-resettlement.
[94] ADB, *Safeguard Policy Statement*, p. 7.
[95] Ibid, p. 7.
[96] ADB, Involuntary resettlement.

at least restore, if not enhance, the livelihoods of the entire displaced population to the pre-project levels, and to improve the living standards of displaced vulnerable groups. The SPS requires consultation with the affected population and compensation of loss and the provision of assistance, as well as special measures to support the poor and vulnerable displaced population. Preparation, implementation and post-project monitoring of time-bound resettlement plans are also necessary. Depending on the project's impact, certain assessment reports may be required.[97]

Indigenous Peoples

With nearly three-quarters of the world's Indigenous peoples living in the Asia Pacific region,[98] ensuring that all projects offer appropriate protections to safeguard the rights of Indigenous peoples is critical.

The ADB's Policy on Indigenous Peoples was first adopted in 1998,[99] yet at the outset faced difficulty in accurately determining the relevant cultural identity, ancestral property and resources of affected populations. Through a process of building meaningful consultation with Indigenous populations, gradually more culturally appropriate approaches and a fairer distribution of benefits could be developed.

Among its recommendations in 2007, the OED SES on Indigenous peoples safeguards recommended:[100] (1) clarifying ambiguous or misunderstood definitions and standards, including the definition of Indigenous peoples; (2) integrating policies regarding the protection of Indigenous peoples together with the issues of involuntary resettlement and environmental concerns; (3) clarifying consultation requirements in the pre-project preparation and implementation stages; (4) developing an approach for capacity building; and (5) developing a comprehensive plan regarding the implementation of the safeguard policy in the Indigenous community.

97 Ibid.
98 ADB (16 August 2017). Indigenous peoples. www.adb.org/site/safeguards/indigenous-peoples.
99 ADB, *Safeguard Policy Statement*, p. 7.
100 Ibid, p. 7.

ADB's Current Indigenous Peoples Safeguards: The 2018 SPS

At present, the safeguards regarding Indigenous peoples are targeted to ensure that ADB-financed projects encourage and foster respect for the rights of the Indigenous population, including through recognition and respect of their identity, dignity, human rights and livelihood as well as cultural traditions as defined by themselves.[101]

Where a project involves impacts on Indigenous peoples, the SPS requires a borrower to carry out meaningful consultation with the Indigenous population, and prepare relevant plans to assess potential risks and ensure that appropriate measures are taken to avoid and mitigate such risks.[102] In particular, BCS is required where an Indigenous population is deemed particularly vulnerable. Planning documents should include the Indigenous People's Planning Frameworks, which provide guidance on the screening, assessment, arrangements and procedures in preparation for board approval,[103] as well as Indigenous Peoples Plans, and reviewing the impacts and consequences of projects at the pre-project stage.

ADB's Post-Project Complaints Handling Mechanism

Following project implementation, two main channels for post-project complaints handling include interventions by the ADB itself or facilitated by the borrower client according to the ADB's policy.[104]

The ADB requires borrowers to establish a local grievance redress mechanism designed to receive and facilitate the redress of concerns and grievances from the affected population.[105] Such mechanism should be scaled according to the risks and impacts of the project; the higher the risk and impact level, the more extensive the project complaints handling mechanism. It should be designed to address the complaints promptly, by way of an accessible, transparent and understandable processes. It should also be gender-responsive and culturally appropriate.

[101] ADB, Indigenous peoples.
[102] Ibid.
[103] Ibid.
[104] ADB, *Safeguard Policy Statement*, p. 22.
[105] Ibid, p. 22.

Post-project complaints can also be handled by the ADB's AM,[106] which provides a channel for project-affected populations to submit complaints and seek resolution of their concerns. It also serves as a channel for reviewing alleged violations of the ADB's operational policies.

The AM is comprised of two different phases.[107] Firstly, the consultation phase is led by ADB's special project facilitator (SPF), who directly reports to the ADB President. The role of the facilitator is to assist in ascertaining the related facts surrounding the complaint. The second phase is the compliance review phase, led by a panel of three individuals who report to the ADB's Board of Directors. The panel is in charge of investigating any alleged violations of the ADB's operational policies and propose recommendations to ensure project compliance.

AIIB's Accountability Mechanism

The AIIB's[108] mission is to improve the economic and social conditions within Asian countries, and has been in operation since January 2016.[109] The AIIB enables its clients to build Infrastructure for Tomorrow (i4t), encouraging green infrastructure that upholds the values of sustainability, innovation and connectivity. It cooperates closely with other MDBs and bilateral development organisations to seek opportunities in maximising their efforts.[110]

Initially at the founding of the AIIB in 2016, it had fifty-seven founding members – thirty-seven of which were regional members and twenty of which were non-regional, with China as the largest shareholder. As of 2020, the AIIB has 103 approved members, which represent approximately 79% of the global population and 65% of the global GDP.

AIIB Pre-project Environmental/Social Approval Mechanism

As part of its Operational Policy on Financing, environmental and social due diligence is required prior to project approval.[111] The AIIB's ESF (the

106 Ibid, p. 22.
107 Ibid, p. 22.
108 AIIB (2016 – amended 2019). *Environmental and Social Framework* (pp. 1–57, policy paper), p. 1.
109 AIIB (n.d.). About AIIB. www.aiib.org/en/about-aiib/index.html.
110 AIIB, *Environmental and Social Framework*, p. 1.
111 AIIB (2016 – updated 2020). *Operational Policy on Financing* (pp. 1–25, policy paper), p. 5.

'Framework') was approved in February 2016 and subsequently amended in February 2019. The ESP[112] is supplemented by environmental and social standards (ESSs) that set out internal policy in relation to environmental and social assessment and management, involuntary resettlement and Indigenous peoples.[113]

The policy and standards aim to minimise operational and reputational risks in relation to adverse social and environmental consequences arising from the projects it finances, and to avoid and/or mitigate unwanted negative impacts of projects in the wider society, community and environment. The Environmental and Social Exclusion List, on the contrary, expressly articulates excluded activities that the AIIB will not knowingly finance.[114]

The ESP

Similar to the IFC/World Bank and ADB, under the AIIB's ESP, a proposed project is categorised by assessing its nature and impact, before determining its level of environmental and social risk and relevant requirements.[115] In its categorisation, the AIIB takes into account the nature, location, sensitivity and scale of the project.

Projects are assigned a category – Category A, B, C or FI. Category A projects are likely to have significant adverse environmental and/or social impacts that are irreversible, diverse, cumulative or unprecedented. Category B projects have limited potentially adverse impacts that are not unprecedented, and very few of which are irreversible or cumulative; the impacts are also often limited to the project area and can be properly managed if adequately regulated. Category C projects are projects that are likely to have no or minimal adverse environmental and/or social impacts. Category FI are projects that involve a financial intermediary or funds in the financing structure, where the AIIB delegates most of the decision-making process to the financial intermediary, including decisions relating to the use of AIIB's funds, and the selection, appraisal, approval and monitoring of the subprojects financed by the AIIB. If a project is a Category FI project,

112 AIIB, *Environmental and Social Framework*, p. 1.
113 Ibid, p. 1.
114 Ibid, p. 1.
115 Ibid, pp. 9–11.

the AIIB requires the financial intermediary client to screen and categorise each of the sub-projects into either Category A, B or C, and observe the standards accordingly.[116]

Environmental and social due diligence is conducted by the AIIB under the ESP as an integral element of its appraisal of proposed projects. During the review process, the AIIB reviews the potential borrower's environmental and social assessment documentation to identify key risks and impacts, measures incorporated into the project design to avoid, minimise or mitigate such impacts, the client's understanding of the ESP and ESS requirements, and the role of third parties, and ensures that all relevant consultations have been conducted with the affected population.[117]

The Environmental and Social Assessment and ESSs[118]

The AIIB generally requires that clients adopt an integrated approach to assessment both in public- and private-sector projects. However, where the country's legislation requires that a separate set of documents be prepared, the AIIB allows client documents to be prepared according to standards of their national jurisdictions, and ensures that the standards adopted are in line with the AIIB's policies and standards.[119]

If the AIIB finds that a project potentially poses adverse environmental or social risks, the clients must work to mitigate such impacts through observing relevant ESSs. Under ESS 1, the borrower client has to conduct all relevant assessments and design the appropriate measures to avoid, minimise, mitigate, offset or compensate for related risks and impacts. If the impact includes the involuntary resettlement of people, a more detailed report needs to be completed together with a resettlement plan or a resettlement planning framework as required under ESS 2. Similarly, if the project involves actual or projected risks to Indigenous peoples, a comprehensive section is required alongside an Indigenous peoples plan or planning framework under ESS 3.[120]

116 Ibid.
117 Ibid.
118 Ibid, pp. 13–14.
119 Ibid.
120 Ibid.

Project assessment may include the following elements, depending on the risk categorisation: (1) project description; (2) policy, legal and administrative framework; (3) scope, including relevant stakeholders and consultation plans; (4) analysis of alternatives; (5) baseline environmental and social data; (6) evaluation of risks and impacts; (7) information disclosure and public consultation; and (8) measures designed to mitigate, monitor and manage said risks and impacts.

Standards Regarding Community Consultation

Community consultation before obtaining financing approval is required by the AIIB under the Framework.[121] The consultation process aims to address the scope of project design, mitigation measures, monitoring, sharing of development benefits and opportunities, and project implementation. Clients are required to engage in meaningful consultation with stakeholders to ascertain the opinion and views of the parties during the process of project preparation and implementation, with reference to the level of risks and impact. Depending on the category of the project, the level and standards of consultation may differ.

If a proposed project involves significant adverse environment and/ social impacts, involuntary resettlement or impacts on Indigenous communities, the AIIB may require the borrower client to include the Bank itself as part of the consultation process to better understand the impact and concerns of the affected population. This also increases accountability as the AIIB may take part in ensuring that the borrower client properly address concerns in the proposed project's design, plans and frameworks. The borrower client is also required to keep a record of the consultations and proper documentation regarding the list of participants.

Standards of Community Consultation for Projects Involving Indigenous Peoples

Special community consultation standards are applicable when a proposed project involves Indigenous peoples.[122] In such cases, the AIIB requires the borrower to engage in FPIC processes with affected Indigenous populations;

[121] Ibid, p. 21.
[122] Ibid, pp. 21–22.

however, unlike the ADB or IFC/World Bank, neither BCS nor prior informed consent is required. Such engagement is required where the project affects land or natural resources that are subject to traditional ownership by the Indigenous population or under customary occupation or use, or where the project requires the relocation of Indigenous peoples from the land or natural resources, or finally where the project significantly affects the cultural heritage of the Indigenous peoples. The borrower is required to engage suitable experts – qualified, experienced and independent – to assist in identifying the risks and impacts on the Indigenous population.[123]

General Standards on Information Disclosure

Under the Articles of Agreement of the AIIB, the AIIB aims to promote operational transparency through information disclosure.[124] The Public Information Interim Policy was initially adopted in January 2016 by the AIIB's board. In October 2017, the AIIB conducted a benchmarking exercise with six other MDBs to learn and benefit from their past experiences. The draft Policy on Public Information (PPI) was made public in January 2018 following public consultations and later finalised and approved in September 2018.

The PPI governs the type of information that the bank is required to disclose and the timing of such disclosure. The overarching principles in determining the practice of information disclosure includes: (1) the presumption in favour of disclosure – in order to uphold the fundamental values of openness and transparency; (2) the duty of proactive disclosure – requiring the bank to initiate the release information voluntarily – and (3) the equal treatment and non-discriminatory nature of disclosure requests – which requires the bank to observe the principles of non-discrimination and fairness when assessing the different requests for information disclosure.

Post-Project Complaints Handling Mechanism

In the event of post-project complaints regarding AIIB-financed projects, the project-affected population may first raise their concerns through the project-level grievance redress mechanisms or the AIIB Management's

[123] Ibid, pp. 21–22.

[124] AIIB (n.d.). Introduction: policy on public information. www.aiib.org/en/policies-strategies/public-information/introduction/index.html.

processes.[125] The AIIB's policy requires the borrower to establish an appropriate GM to handle disputes raised by the project-affected population. Such GMs are scaled according to the potential risk of the project. This may include either formal or informal methods of dispute resolution. It should aim to address the affected population's concerns promptly and transparently, and the mechanism itself must be designed to be easily understandable, culturally appropriate and readily accessible. The anonymity option, if so requested, should be made available to protect complainants from possible retaliation.[126]

If the GM does not satisfactorily address stakeholders concerns, they may raise these concerns with the client and/or AIIB during the preparation process, and throughout its implementation through the Project-Affected People's Mechanism (PPM).[127]

Project-Affected People's Mechanism

The AIIB initiated the development of a complaint handling mechanism in early 2017. The PPM was introduced as a channel to independently and impartially assess complaint submissions from a project-affected population in contravention of the AIIB's ESP.[128] The PPM took effect on 31 March 2019 and is guided by the Policy on the PPM (PPM Policy) and Rules of Procedure of the PPM (PPM Rules of Procedure).

The PPM is operated by the Complaints-resolution, Evaluation and Integrity Unit (CEIU), established in 2016 as an independent unit within the AIIB. The CEIU forms part of AIIB's Oversight Mechanism under Article 26(iv) of the AIIB's Articles of Agreement, which empowers the Board to set up such an oversight mechanism to supervise the management and operation of the AIIB.[129] The CEIU assesses the quality and results of the Bank's investment portfolio, processes external complaints relating to the AIIB's ESP under the PPM, and investigates any allegations of fraud or corruption (F&C) in relation to AIIB-financed projects.[130]

125 AIIB (n.d.). How we assist you. www.aiib.org/en/about-aiib/who-we-are/project-affected-peoples-mechanism/how-we-assist-you/index.html.
126 AIIB, *Environmental and Social Framework*, pp. 23–24.
127 AIIB, How we assist you.
128 Ibid.
129 AIIB (n.d.). Introduction to CEIU. www.aiib.org/en/about-aiib/who-we-are/complaints-resolution-evaluation-integrity-unit/introduction/index.html.
130 AIIB, How we assist you.

The PPM operates on the basis of a three-tiered complaints handling process. First, the Project Processing Queries (PPQs) system enables project-affected people to seek a relatively quick resolution to their concerns on simple matters arising from the screening, categorisation and assessment of social and/or environmental impacts. The mechanism is designed for queries that do not require any dispute resolution. For instance, queries in relation to the proposed project's consultation process, or requests by project-affected people to address environmental nuisances such as dust or noise pollution, or mobility restrictions during project preparation, are items that fall under the PPQ.[131]

Second, the Requests for Dispute Resolution (RDR) is designed to enable the PPM to address disputes arising during the process of project implementation. Dispute resolution may include multiple parties, including the client borrower and the requestors, and at times the management, contractors or any other parties involved in the process or implementation of the project. The RDR aims to monitor the discussion of potential actions that can be taken to mitigate adverse impacts and reach a time-bound agreement. In the process of the RDR, the PPM actively encourages the parties concerned to explore dispute resolution mechanisms through a consultative dialogue, information sharing, joint-fact finding, mediation or other acceptable methods.[132]

And finally, the Requests for Compliance Review (RCR) is a process by which the PPM investigates allegations raised by project-affected populations relating to the AIIB's failure to comply with its obligations under the ESP. The findings together with PPM's review of monitoring reports regarding the implementation of the Management Action Plan are also submitted to the board for review.[133]

Thus far, unlike the IFC/World Bank or ADB, summaries and outcomes of prior complaints are not yet available on the AIIB website.

Why Might Expanded Grievance Channels Reduce Grievances?

Procedural justice and dispute prevention research[134] has found that when given the choice between satisfaction with the process (procedural justice)

[131] Details on the process and procedures of a PPQ can be found in Sections 3–6 (especially 6.5) of the PPM Rules of Procedure.

[132] Ibid.

[133] Ibid.

[134] Tyler, T. R. (2003). Procedural justice, legitimacy, and the effective rule of law. *Crime and Justice*, *30*, 283–357, 283.

or satisfaction with the outcome (distributive justice),[135] parties tend to show preference for process satisfaction in shaping willingness to defer to decisions made by authorities. While this does not mean that distributive justice concerns are irrelevant, procedural justice has been shown to contribute to legitimacy of outcomes.[136] Whether this dynamic applies in the context of community relations with MDBs is an open question.

According to Tom Tyler's research, people's subjective judgments about the fairness of the procedures deployed[137] determine the extent to which they abide by such judgments. How is fairness perceived? One key element is the quality of decision making; individuals think that decisions are fairly made when authorities are neutral and unbiased and make their decisions using objective indicators, and not personal views.[138] People also value the quality of their interpersonal treatment, whether they feel they are being treated with dignity and respect by the authorities with whom they deal.[139]

Procedural justice perceptions are especially important in shaping behaviour over time. Individuals are more willing to accept a decision and adhere to it if they feel that it was fairly made.[140] Follow-up studies[141] have found that fair procedures support feelings of inclusion within a community.[142] Findings indicate that voice, neutrality, respect and trust are primary drivers in the achievement of legitimacy.[143] While the determination of truth and achievement of substantive justice shape legitimacy, neither is primary.[144] People react both to whether they believe decisions are fairly made and whether they think that parties are fairly treated.[145] Apart from the notion that adjudicators establish the truth, the other important element is relational.[146]

The importance of effective communication channels in preventing disputes has been highlighted by William Felstiner, Richard Abel and

[135] Ibid, p. 292.
[136] Ibid, pp. 292–294.
[137] Ibid.
[138] Ibid, p. 298.
[139] Ibid.
[140] Ibid, p. 296.
[141] Tyler, T. R., & Sevier, J. (2013/2014). How do the courts create popular legitimacy?: The role of establishing the truth, punishing justly, and/or acting through just procedures. *Albany Law Review*, *77*, 102–143, 102.
[142] Ibid, p. 103.
[143] Ibid.
[144] Ibid.
[145] Ibid.
[146] Ibid, p. 134.

Austin Sarat's work examining the dynamics of dispute transformation.[147] Not all disputes transform from conflicts into legal disputes. The extent to which communication channels effectively address early stages of 'naming' and 'blaming' can prevent a dispute from reaching the final stage of 'claiming'.[148] Further, institutional frameworks supporting relational and cultural understanding are important factors in mitigating disputes.[149]

With respect to citizen participation in resource-use decisions,[150] studies have found that although communities might prefer greater autonomy over private land dealings, the public generally views regulation of public land as desirable.[151] In this context, individuals expressed a willingness to accept decisions made using court hearings (75%); referenda (61%); administrative litigation (60%); negotiated solutions (49%) and public hearings (46%).[152] Results also indicate that the justice of procedures is always a significant independent influence on their acceptability.[153]

A further study examined the role of citizen participation in environmental compliance and enforcement measures.[154] Apart from outcome-driven considerations, including prosecuting environmental non-compliance, respondents placed significant weight on the importance of neutral procedures.[155] This included procedures contributing to factually based decisions; legally appropriate outcomes; a right of appeal; and consistent application of the law.[156] Participants also valued evidence that decision-makers could be regarded as trustworthy.[157]

147 Felstiner, W. L. F., Abel, R. L., & Sarat, A. (1980). The emergence and transformation of disputes: Naming, blaming, claiming . . . *Law & Society Review, 15*(3–4), 631–654.
148 Ibid.
149 Gulliver, P. H., & Greenhouse, C. (1978). *The Disputing Process: Law in Ten Societies*. New York: Columbia University Press.
150 Tyler, T., & Markell, D. L. (2010). The public regulation of land use decisions: Criteria for evaluating alternative procedures. *Journal of Empirical Legal Studies, 7*, 538. https://ssrn.com/abstract=1475378.
151 Ibid, pp. 7–8.
152 Ibid.
153 Ibid, p. 24.
154 Markell, D. L., & Tyler, T. R. (2008). Using empirical research to design government citizen participation processes: A case study of citizens' roles in environmental compliance and enforcement. *Kansas Law Review 57*, 1–38.; Ali, S. (2016). *Governing Disasters: Engaging Local Populations in Humanitarian Relief*. Cambridge: Cambridge University Press.
155 Ibid.
156 Ibid.
157 Ibid.

These findings imply that for complex, long-term, multi-year infrastructure development initiatives, attention to process fairness in addition to substantive outcome fairness is vital.

MDBs' Adoption of FPIC and GMs

Playing an important role in risk management and project outcome optimisation, MDBs' ESFs have increasingly been designed to avoid and mitigate the negative social and environmental impacts of project investments. Key MDBs in this domain are the World Bank, Inter-American Development Bank (IDB), ADB, European Bank for Reconstruction and Development (EBRD), European Investment Bank (EIB) and AIIB. In recent policy updates, there has been an increased focus on prevention and mitigation. The IFC Sustainability Framework ('IFC Framework') approved in 2009 stems from the World Bank's ESF, with specific modifications catered towards the IFC's focus on the private sector. The Framework comprises IFC Performance Standards for Environmental and Social Sustainability and IFC Performance Standards.[158]

During the period between 2010 and 2019, alongside the IFC/World Bank, ADB and AIIB, the majority of the world's MDBs amended or introduced ESP frameworks, requiring (1) pre-project due diligence, consultation and FPIC in appropriate cases; (2) information disclosure on potential impacts; and (3) GMs into internal bank policies (Table 1). Such policies have evolved during this period, from an understanding of consultation as a top-down 'notification' process to one that may require 'free, prior and informed consent' for higher-risk undertakings that significantly impact the environment, require population relocation or impact Indigenous populations. This includes the necessity of information disclosure, meaningful consultation with relevant stakeholders and establishing relevant GMs.

Multilateral development banks' ESFs cover ten main ESSs; ESSs 5, 7 and 10 cover specific areas that relate to community involvement. ESS 5 (land use and resettlement) concerns the impacts on the local community due to construction and includes community engagement as a parameter. ESS 7 (Indigenous communities) are narrower in the sense that it assesses engagement with the Indigenous people affected, recognises the importance of obtaining FPIC from them, and evaluates GMs in place. ESS 10

[158] IFC (n.d.). *E&S Performance Standards.* www.ifc.org/wps/wcm/connect/Topics_Ext_Content/IFC_External_Corporate_Site/Sustainability-At-IFC/Policies-Standards/Performance-Standards/.

(stakeholder engagement) emphasises information disclosure and meaningful consultation with stakeholders involved in the project, which is relevant to not only the project financers and contractors but also local communities. There is a high degree of consensus among MDBs as to appropriate coverage of environmental and social impacts, pollution prevention and Indigenous communities ESSs.[159]

A number of NDBs have adopted their own sets of safeguards in parallel with MDB standards towards sustainable investment and financing. Generally, NDBs' ESFs are a step behind MDBs', with critical gaps existing in relation to certain ESSs among the NDBs.[160]

Evolution of Engagement, Monitoring and Evaluation Mechanisms in MDBs

In an effort to advance monitoring and evaluation of sustainability objectives, MDBs have established a variety of mechanisms to assess the performance of projects that are outlined here.[161] From reviewing these mechanisms, it is clear that there has been significant harmonisation in standards by multilateral development finance institutions as a whole, while NDBs continue to improve in the development of ESSs, GMs, independent monitoring and impact assessments. While most MDBs include public consultations with affected local communities in EAs, historically only a smaller proportion provided project-level GMs for environmental disputes.[162]

In reviewing the stakeholder engagement policies and GMs of twelve major MDBs, growing convergence can be found in the aspirations and structure of internal ESP Frameworks and the existence of project-level GMs among ten MDBs. At the same time, variation exists between banks, including the degree of transparency relating to the publication of grievance processes and whether higher FPIC norms are referenced in projects impacting on Indigenous communities and requiring relocation or whether reference is made to generally lower national standards.

[159] UN Development Programme (6 November 2019). *Harmonizing Investment and Financing Standards towards Sustainable Development along the Belt and Road.* www.cn.undp.org/content/china/en/home/library/south-south-cooperation/harmonizing-investment-and-financing-standards-.html.

[160] Ibid.

[161] Ibid.

[162] Gallagher, K. P., & Yuan, F. (2017). Standardizing sustainable development: A comparison of development banks in Latin America. *Journal of Environment and Development*, *26*(3), 243–271.

Table 1 *Selected MDB policies.*

Bank policy	FPIC?	Pre-project consultation/stakeholder engagement	GMs	Grievance cases published? Transparent?
World Bank/International Bank for Reconstruction and Development (IBRD)/ International Development Association/IFC Environmental and Social Framework 2016 Effective: 1 October 2018	Yes	Yes. ESS 10 – requires that borrowers will engage with stakeholders throughout the project life cycle, commencing such engagement as early as possible in the project development process and in a time frame that enables meaningful consultations with stakeholders on project design. The process of stakeholder engagement will involve the following: (1) stakeholder identification and analysis; (2) planning how the engagement with stakeholders will take place; (3) disclosure of information; (4) consultation with stakeholders; (5) addressing and responding to grievances; and (6) reporting to stakeholders.[163]	Yes	Bank policy
IDB Environmental and Social Policy Framework (ESPS)	Yes	Yes. Under ESPS 10, the borrower shall engage with stakeholders throughout the project life cycle. It will commence such engagement as early as possible in the project development process and in a time frame that	Yes	Yes, the outcomes of grievance cases are available for review at www.iadb.org/en/who-we-are/transparency/administra

[163] World Bank (2017). *World Bank Environmental and Social Framework.* Washington, DC, pp. 97–100. The borrower will undertake a process of meaningful consultation in a manner that provides stakeholders with opportunities to express their views on project risks, impacts and mitigation measures, and allows the borrower to consider and respond to them. Meaningful consultation will be carried out on an ongoing basis as the nature of issues, impacts and opportunities evolves. Meaningful consultation is a two-way process, which: (a) begins early in the project planning process to gather initial views on the project proposal and inform project design.

September 2020		enables meaningful consultations with stakeholders on project design and development. The nature, scope and frequency of stakeholder engagement will be proportionate to the nature and scale of the project, its development and implementation timeline, and its potential risks and impacts.[164]		tive-tribunal/administrative-tribunal-decisions.
EIB Environmental and Social Sustainability Framework/ Climate Roadmap 2020[165]	Yes	Yes. The borrower is required to identify stakeholders and comply with additional mandates for projects within the European Union (EU) and the European Free Trade Association (EUFTA). Meaningful consultation is a two-way process that: is initiated as early as possible to allow for effective stakeholder participation in the design of project activities or mitigation measures that could potentially affect them either positively or negatively.[166]	Yes	Yes, the outcomes of grievance cases are available for full review.[167]

164 IDB (2020). *Environmental and Social Policy Framework of Inter-American Development Bank*, p. 104–110. The language parallels that of the World Bank ESF.
165 EIB (2020). Climate roadmap. www.eib.org/attachments/thematic/eib_group_climate_bank_roadmap_en.pdf.
166 EIB (2022). *European Investment Bank's Environmental and Social Standards*. Luxembourg: EIB, pp. 17–18, [36]–[37].

> The promoter shall undertake a meaningful consultation process that provides opportunities to stakeholders to express their views on the project on an ongoing basis, as well as the identified environmental, climate and/or social impacts and risks and the proposed measures and actions to address them. The promoter shall engage with the identified stakeholders in a collaborative process to respond to and address their opinions and concerns as they arise, and document and disclose information about this process.

167 EIB (2025). Complaints. www.eib.org/en/about/accountability/complaints/cases/index.htm?q=&sortColumn=_complaintMetadata_receivedDate&sortDir=desc&pageNumber=0&itemPerPage=25&pageable=true&language=EN&defaultLanguage=EN&yearFrom=&yearTo=&orCountries=true&orContents.EN.content.type=true.

Table 1 (*cont.*)

Bank policy	FPIC?	Pre-project consultation/stakeholder engagement	GMs	Grievance cases published? Transparent?
EBRD Environmental and Social Policy 2019	Yes	Yes. Apart from a management plan, Category A projects with significant environmental and social impacts require impact assessment. If the client has already engaged in such a process, they will provide adequate documented evidence of such an engagement.[168]	Yes	Yes, the outcome of grievance cases are available for review at www.ebrd.com/work-with-us/project-finance/project-complaint-mechanism/pcm-register.html.
African Development Bank (AfDB) Integrated Safeguard System 2013	Yes	Yes. Stakeholder consultation is part of the Bank's Integrated Safeguards System, a portal that provides access to the impact assessment documents throughout the life cycle of the project. When the borrower/client has identified vulnerable communities that would potentially be affected by the project, the borrower/client engages in meaningful ICP with the vulnerable communities, beginning as early as possible in the project cycle before Board consideration and continuing throughout. The borrower/client demonstrates that consulted individuals or groups can effectively represent the affected groups and should involve representative bodies.[169]	Yes	Yes, the outcome of grievance cases are available for review at https://irm.afdb.org/en/page/registered-complaints. An Independent Review Mechanism (IRM) is in place for project-affected persons in matters concerns violation of the Bank's policies and procedures.
Islamic Development Bank (IsDB)	No	Discretionary. Environmental and social impact assessment is at the discretion of the Bank. Reference is made to national law. The IsDB requires the client to	Yes – scaled	No, the outcomes of grievance cases are not available for

168 EBRD (2019). *European Bank for Reconstruction and Development's Environmental and Social Policy*, p. 48, [19]–[20].
169 AfDB (2013). *African Development Bank Group's Integrated Safeguards System*, vol. 1, p. 27.

Environmental and Social Safeguards Policy 2020		engage in meaningful consultation with stakeholders during the project's preparation and implementation, in a manner commensurate with the risks to, and impacts on, the project-affected people. This consultation covers project design, mitigation and sharing of development benefits.[170]		review and no public statistics are available.
New Development Bank (NDB) Environment and Social Framework 2016	No	Discretionary. The NDB requires the client to conduct a meaningful consultation process, which is compliant with national laws and regulations and this policy, and (1) engages with communities, groups or people affected by proposed projects; (2) begins early and is carried out on an ongoing basis; (3) provides timely disclosure of relevant and adequate information that is understandable and readily accessible, is undertaken in an atmosphere free of intimidation or coercion; (4) is gender-inclusive and responsive, tailored to the needs of vulnerable groups; and (5) enables the incorporation of all relevant views.[171]	Yes – scaled	No, the outcomes of grievance cases are not available for review.
AIIB Environmental and Social Framework 2016 (amended in 2019)	Partial	Yes, as early as possible during assessment of the project, the Bank independently discloses to the public draft environmental and social assessment reports, resettlement plans, request for proposals and Indigenous peoples plans.	Yes	Partial, a summary, not full reports, are available for review at www.aiib.org/en/about-aiib/who-we-are/project-affected-peoples-

[170] IsDB (2020). *Environmental and Social Safeguards Policy*, p. 8.
[171] NDB (2016). *New Development Bank Environment and Social Framework*, p. 10.

Table 1 (*cont.*)

Bank policy	FPIC?	Pre-project consultation/stakeholder engagement	GMs	Grievance cases published? Transparent?
		Yes, community consultation before obtaining finance approval is required by the AIIB under the Framework.[172]		mechanism/submission/track-all-submission.html.
ADB SPS/Climate Risk Screening[173] 2010/2013/2016 (SPS update)	Yes	Yes, a robust pre-project community consultation requirement exists. For projects that pose significant environmental, involuntary resettlement or impacts Indigenous peoples, the Bank participates in consultation activities to understand the concerns of affected people and ensure that such concerns are addressed in project design and safeguard plans. In addition to ensuring appropriate information disclosure, public consultation and community participation is a key requirement.[174]	Yes	Yes, the outcome of grievance cases are available for review at http://compliance.adb.org/dir0035p.nsf/alldocs/BDAO-7XGAWN?OpenDocument.

172 AIIB, *Environmental and Social Framework*, p. 21. The consultation process aims to address the scope of project design, mitigation measures, monitoring, sharing of development benefits and opportunities, and project implementation. Under the Framework, the client is required to engage in meaningful consultation with stakeholders to ascertain the opinion and views of the parties during the process of project preparation and implementation, with reference to the level of risks and impact. Depending on the category of the project, the level and standards of consultation expected may differ.

173 www.adb.org/sites/default/files/institutional-document/736256/sps-review-update-policy-architecture-study-draft_0.pdf. Further updates to the SPS were made in 2016.

174 ADB, *Safeguard Policy Statement*, pp. 20–21. The ADB aims to work with borrowers to facilitate meaningful consultation early on in the preparatory stages of the project and invite ongoing participation in the consultation process throughout the project cycle. Meaningful consultation includes the provision and timely disclosure of information that is readily accessible and easily understood by the affected population. Project consultation should be undertaken freely and voluntarily, without intimidation or coercion. The consultation should be gender-inclusive, responsive and should be tailored to the needs of vulnerable groups. Invitations to participate should be extended to the affected population, and the ADB is required to incorporate all relevant views into its decision-making process. This means taking into account the management of the project's design, mitigation measures and development benefits and opportunities.

Stakeholder Engagement

Common Standards

Stakeholder engagement through a consultative process has featured in most all the multilateral banks' policies regarding project funding and is generally a pre-requisite to project approval. There appears to be a consensus that borrowers should identify the relevant stakeholders affected by the project and conduct meaningful consultation with them as soon as the planning or preparatory stage of the project commences, and should remain ongoing throughout the various cycles in a project. However, the degree of stakeholder engagement varies, with two banks making reference to potentially lax and discretionary national rules and policies.

The policies of the World Bank, the IDB, the EIB, the EBRD, the AfDB, the ADB and the AIIB are generally consistent in stakeholder engagement requirements. Under its 2016 ESF,[175] the World Bank requires borrowers to identify stakeholders, develop a Stakeholder Engagement Plan in consultation with the Bank and disclose project information in a time frame that enables meaningful consultation on project design. The Framework requires borrowers to engage with and provide information, including changes to a project resulting in additional risks and impacts, to stakeholders throughout the life cycle of the project. Specific personnel are to be designated to implement and monitor the stakeholder engagement activities.

Similarly, the 2021 ESP Framework[176] of the IDB adopts the World Bank model. It mandates identification of stakeholders and development of a Stakeholder Engagement Plan. The information disclosure and meaningful consultation aspects are identical to the World Bank's Framework, including the requirement to engage throughout the life cycle of the project.

Likewise, the EIB's 2022 ESSs[177] largely adopt the World Bank's structure with the inclusion of certain additional compliance components and special requirements for projects located in the EU, EUFTA, EU candidate and potential candidate countries. The requirements unique to the Bank are that the project should also comply with applicable national standards, an explicit requirement that the stakeholder

[175] World Bank, *Environmental and Social Framework.*
[176] IDB, *Environmental and Social Policy Framework.*
[177] EIB, *Environmental and Social Standards.*

engagement process be respectful of human rights and data and privacy protection rights.

The EBRD updated its ESP in 2019,[178] largely mirroring the World Bank's framework. A major addition in the EBRD's policy is the demarcation of certain projects as 'Category A' – projects that may result in potentially significant environmental and/or social impacts requiring environmental and social impact assessment. Borrowers in such projects are additionally required to engage with stakeholders in a formalised way, including participatory disclosure and consultation process built into each stage of an impact assessment.

Although the AfDB's 2013 Integrated Safeguards System[179] has not been updated after the World Bank's policy update in 2016, the key elements of stakeholder consultation are present in the Bank's Integrated Safeguards System. A distinctive feature of the 2013 policy is the Integrated Safeguard Tracking System – a portal for the public to access environmental and social impact assessment documents throughout the project's life cycle. Different timelines for publication of documents apply to projects based on their categorisation.

The ADB's 2009 SPS is considerably ahead of its time, compared to pre-2010 policies that other major banks had in place.[180] The Bank requires borrowers/clients to engage with project-affected persons of proposed projects, and with civil society through information disclosure, consultation and informed participation in a manner commensurate with the risks to and impacts on affected communities. For projects with significant adverse environmental, involuntary resettlement or impacts Indigenous peoples, ADB project teams participate in consultation activities to understand the concerns of affected people and ensure that such concerns are addressed in project design and safeguard plans. The Bank also categorises projects based on their potential environment impacts but employs some form of impact assessment/review for all categories.

The Asian Infrastructure Investment Plan amended its 2016 Environment and Social Framework in 2019.[181] The Bank aims to ensure effective information disclosure and consultation by the borrower by also independently disclosing draft environmental and social assessment reports, resettlement plans, request for proposals, Indigenous peoples

178 EBRD (2019). Environmental and Social Policy.
179 AfDB, *Integrated Safeguard System.*
180 ADB, *Safeguard Policy Statement.*
181 AIIB, *Environmental and Social Framework.*

plans or other approved forms of documentation as early as possible during the Bank's assessment of a project. The Bank also categorises projects on the basis of impact but conducts its own review of environmental and social risks and impacts associated with the project regardless of the categorisation.

Divergence

While general consultation requirements feature in all bank safeguard policies, the IsDB and NDB generally feature discretionary policies that reference national requirements, resulting in varied compliance requirements for pre-project consultation.

By its 2020 Environmental and Social Safeguards Policy,[182] the IsDB also follows the categorisation of projects commensurate with a risk and impact model. While elements of information availability for project-affected persons and meaningful consultation feature in the policy, the requirement for environmental and social impact assessment appears to be at the discretion of the Bank and not universally applicable to all projects.

The NDB published its Environment and Social Framework in 2016.[183] The Framework adopts the categorisation model and is based on potential environment impacts. The screening criteria cover three types of concerns – environment, involuntary resettlement and Indigenous peoples. The information disclosure and public consultation provisions of the Framework are of a similar nature as the those of other major development banks. However, the requirement to conduct environmental and social impact assessment is limited to Category A and B projects.

Free, Prior and Informed Consent

Standards defining the requirements for consultation and consent in advance of infrastructure development projects have evolved over time, particularly as they relate to the rights of Indigenous peoples and project-affected communities who may be required to relocate. Free, prior and informed consent is an international legal standard articulated in the UN Declaration on the Rights of Indigenous Peoples (UNDRIP)[184] that

[182] IsDB, *Environmental and Social Safeguards Policy.*
[183] NDB, *Environment and Social Framework.*
[184] UNDRIP, General Assembly Res. 61/295 (adopted on 13 September 2007).

applies to the process by which Indigenous communities are given the opportunity to approve or reject projects affecting them or their territories prior to the commencement of operations.

Besides being an established international legal norm, FPIC also aims to serve the interests of all stakeholders, as projects lacking community consent are often fraught with financial and reputational risks.[185]

In 2012, the IFC included FPIC as a requirement in its Environmental and Social Performance Standards.[186] Prior to this, a 1998 'Good Practice Manual' for doing better business through effective public consultation and disclosure[187] laid the foundation for the legal norm that has come to now be widely recognised. Corporations were urged to consider engaging with local communities, and management principles recommended pre-project disclosure as follows:

> public consultation may provide project sponsors with significant opportunities to benefit people living in the proposed project area(s). Consultation can help make corporate investments more effective by identifying communities' priority needs and designing locally appropriate responses. Greater interaction with their communities may increase local employees' commitment and morale. The goodwill generated by the project may help build local support, which can be valuable to the project sponsor if unanticipated problems occur.[188]

Free, prior and informed consent builds on and expands the process of ICP and is required to be established through good faith negotiation between a project proponent and affected communities of Indigenous peoples.

The borrower is required to document mutually accepted process between the borrower and affected communities of Indigenous peoples, and provide evidence of agreement between the parties as the outcome of the negotiations. Free, prior and informed consent does not necessarily require unanimity and may be achieved even when individuals or groups within the community explicitly disagree.

185 Nagar, A. (2021). The Juukan Gorge incident: Key lessons on free, prior and informed consent. *Business and Human Rights Journal*, 6, 377–383.

186 IFC (1 January 2012). Performance Standard 7: Indigenous Peoples. www.ifc.org/wps/wcm/connect/3274df05-7597-4cd3-83d9 2aca293e69ab/PS7_English_2012.pdf?MOD=AJPERES&CVID=jiVQI.D.

187 www.ifc.org/wps/wcm/connect/6dff50aa-212e-4bfc-8b97 6cecd734e6f1/PublicConsultation.pdf?MOD=AJPERES&CVID=nXvb496.

188 Ibid.

The key elements of FPIC have evolved over time.[189] 'Free' refers to consent given voluntarily and without coercion, intimidation or manipulation. It also refers to a process that is self-directed by the community from whom consent is being sought, unencumbered by coercion, expectations or timelines that are externally imposed. 'Prior' means that consent is sought sufficiently in advance of any authorisation or commencement of activities, at the early stages of a development or investment plan, and not only when the need arises to obtain approval from the community. 'Informed' refers mainly to the type of information that should be provided prior to seeking consent, and also as part of the ongoing consent process. 'Consent' refers to the collective decision made by the rights-holders and reached through the customary decision-making processes of the affected Indigenous peoples or communities. Consent must be sought and granted or withheld according to the unique formal or informal political-administrative dynamic of each community. Indigenous peoples and local communities must be able to participate through their own freely chosen representatives, while ensuring the participation of youth, women, the elderly and persons with disabilities as much as possible.[190]

The rationale behind the development of the FPIC requirement arose in the post-World War II era based on a recognition[191] that Indigenous communities, peoples and nations have a historical continuity with pre-invasion and pre-colonial societies that developed on their territories and considered themselves distinct from other sectors of the societies now prevailing in those territories. They have a special role to play in preserving, developing and transmitting to future generations their ancestral territories and ethnic identity, as the basis of continued existence as peoples, in accordance with their own cultural patterns, language, social institutions and legal systems.

Perhaps the most significant recognition of Indigenous peoples at the international level was the UN General Assembly's affirmation of their unqualified right to self-determination, which constitutes the foundation for their collective rights. This followed over twenty years of negotiations,

[189] UN Food and Agriculture Organization (2016). Free prior and informed consent an Indigenous peoples' right and a good practice for local communities. www.fao.org/3/i6190e/i6190e.pdf.

[190] Ibid.

[191] www.un.org/development/desa/indigenouspeoples/publications/martinez-cobo-study.html.

culminating in the adoption of the UNDRIP in 2007.[192] The Convention followed the International Labour Organisation's Convention on Indigenous and Tribal Peoples Convention 1989, the first major international binding convention on the subject, which came to be ratified by twenty-four countries.[193]

A report of the UN Human Rights Council submitted that when activities may affect Indigenous peoples, the business enterprise must take adequate steps to ensure meaningful and effective engagement. As part of implementing their responsibility, business enterprises engaged in extractive activities must ensure that employees have an understanding of the content of Indigenous peoples' rights, including their right to participate in decision making.[194]

Immediately following the UNDRIP, the EBRD in its 2008 ESP[195] introduced FPIC as a special requirement where Indigenous people were affected by a project.

Common Standards

Of the MDBs' policies surveyed, a majority adopt explicit requirements for FPIC with regards to Indigenous or other vulnerable groups; although, the banks adopt different definitions when it comes to these groups, perhaps resulting from the different geographical regions these banks serve. Two banks, the IDB and NDB, do not explicitly specify a requirement for FPIC.[196]

In the World Bank's Environment and Social Framework of 2016, a separate set of environment and social standard requirements have been identified for Indigenous peoples/Sub-Saharan African Historically Underserved Traditional Local Communities.[197] In recognition that they may be particularly vulnerable to the loss of, alienation from or

192 Doyle, C. (2022). Free prior and informed consent and Indigenous rights: A bulwark against discrimination and platform for self-determination. In D. Newman (Ed.). *Research Handbook on the International Law of Indigenous Rights* (pp. 96–128). Cheltenham: Edward Elgar.

193 As on 14 January 2023.

194 Advice No. 4 (2012): Indigenous peoples and the right to participate in decision making, with a focus on extractive industries. UN Human Rights Council, Expert Mechanism on the Rights of Indigenous Peoples, 2012.

195 EBRD (2008). *Environmental and Social Policy.* www.ebrd.com/downloads/research/policies/2008policy.pdf.

196 IsDB, *Environmental and Social Safeguards Policy.*

197 World Bank, *Environmental and Social Framework*, p. 79.

exploitation of their land and access to natural and cultural resources, the borrower is required to obtain the FPIC of such persons in projects that are likely to have adverse impacts on land, natural resources subject to traditional ownership or under customary use or occupation; cause relocation of such persons from land and natural resources subject to traditional ownership or under customary use or occupation; or have significant impacts on their cultural heritage that is material to the identity and/or cultural, ceremonial or spiritual aspects of their lives.[198]

The IDB requires FPIC[199] but defines Indigenous people differently. Indigenous people are defined as a distinct social and cultural grouping possessing characteristics in varying degrees of: (1) self-identification as members of a distinct Indigenous cultural group and recognition of this identity by others; (2) collective attachment to geographically distinct habitats or ancestral territories in the project area and to the natural resources in these habitats and territories; (3) customary cultural, economic, social or political laws and institutions that are distinct from those of mainstream society or culture; or (4) a distinct language or dialect, often different from the official language or languages of the country or region in which they reside.[200]

The EIB recognises the need for additional safeguards for vulnerable or marginalised persons and groups,[201] and identifies them as those that are usually exposed to risks and adverse impacts, and more sensitive to those risks and impacts, often having been subject to pre-existing discrimination and due to limited access or rights to required assets and/or resources. In so far as the components of FPIC are concerned, the Bank adopts the World Bank's model. Free, prior and informed consent itself is identified as an iterative process whereby the affected community of Indigenous peoples arrives at an agreement reached within sufficient time and in accordance with their cultural traditions and practices.[202]

The EBRD, apart from recognising the need to protect the rights of Indigenous people by requiring the borrower to obtain FPIC, acknowledges that borrowers can benefit from Indigenous knowledge.[203] The Bank recognises that Indigenous peoples have rich and distinct identities and livelihoods, while at the same time, they may be amongst the most

198 IsDB, *Environmental and Social Safeguards Policy.*
199 IDB, *Environmental and Social Policy Framework*, p. 88.
200 Ibid, p. 24.
201 EIB, *Environmental and Social Standards*, p. 49.
202 Ibid, p. 56.
203 EBRD (2019), *Environmental and Social Policy*, p. 39.

marginalised and vulnerable segments of the population. Their economic, social and legal status may limit their capacity to defend their rights to and interest in lands and resources (both natural and cultural). This, combined with their economic and spiritual connection with these lands and resources, may make them particularly susceptible to adverse impacts of projects. Indigenous peoples have unique knowledge and abilities and can be seen as potential partners in sustainable development, both contributing to and benefiting from the planning and implementation of project-related activities.[204]

Although the AfDB, which adopts FPIC, has not published a policy document on the detailed elements of FPIC, its Integrated Safeguard System stipulates that public consultation must meet the requirements of being 'free, prior and informed' and of achieving BCS, especially in high-risk projects or projects affecting vulnerable groups. Vulnerable groups are identified as groups whose lives are likely to be adversely affected by a bank-financed project. Depending on the specific context of the project, vulnerable groups might include landless people; people without legal title to assets; ethnic, religious or linguistic minorities; some categories of children (orphans, homeless); marginalised social groups; and Indigenous peoples.[205]

Since the ADB's SPS was released in 2009,[206] the term 'FPIC' has not been used; however, consent of Indigenous people is ascertained for projects where there is likely commercial development of the cultural resources and knowledge of Indigenous peoples; physical relocation from traditional or customary lands; and commercial development of natural resources within customary lands under use that would impact the livelihoods or cultural, ceremonial or spiritual uses that define the identity and community of Indigenous peoples. 'Consent of affected Indigenous peoples' communities' in the statement refers to a collective expression by the affected Indigenous peoples' communities, through individuals and/or their recognised representatives, of BCS for the project activities. Such BCS may exist even if some individuals or groups object to the project activities.[207]

[204] Ibid, p. 39.

[205] Ibid, p. 16.

[206] ADB, *Safeguard Policy Statement*, p. 56.

[207] Ibid, glossary; 'Indigenous people' is used in a generic sense to refer to a distinct, vulnerable, social and cultural group self-identifying as members of a distinct Indigenous cultural group and recognition of this identity by others, collectively attached to geographically distinct habitats or ancestral territories in the project area

Divergences

Some MDBs do not require FPIC. The IsDB in its Environment and Safeguards Policy[208] does not include any provisions related to FPIC. Similarly, the NDB does not impose any FPIC requirements on borrowers. However, the public consultation requirement applicable to all projects remains in place.[209] The NDB requires the development of an Indigenous People's Plan based on a social impact assessment with the assistance of qualified experts and is required to draw on Indigenous peoples' knowledge and participation.[210]

The AIIB in its Environment and Social Framework[211] adopts the definition of Free Prior and Informed Consultation, which does not require the explicit consent of Indigenous peoples in projects that affect them.

Grievance Mechanisms

All MDBs share a common requirement that mechanisms be established during a project's life cycle to address stakeholder grievances. They differ in the stringency of obligations placed on the borrower to provide specific protections to affected communities and whether such grievances are made publicly available.

Common Standards

Several banks including the World Bank, IDB, EIB, EBRD and AfDB maintain their own independent mechanisms that afford a platform for affected stakeholders to channel their complaints about projects' non-

and to the natural resources in these habitats and territories, possessing customary cultural, economic, social or political institutions that are separate from those of the dominant society and culture; and a distinct language, often different from the official language of the country or region. The Indigenous peoples' safeguards are triggered if a project directly or indirectly affects the dignity, human rights, livelihood systems or culture of Indigenous peoples, or affects the territories or natural or cultural resources that Indigenous peoples own, use, occupy or claim as their ancestral domain. In addition to what are now standard safeguards in instances of likely impact on Indigenous people, the statement provides for an 'Indigenous Peoples Plan' that the borrower is required to prepare in conjunction with qualified and experienced experts.

208 IsDB, *Environmental and Social Safeguards Policy.*

209 NDB, *Environment and Social Framework*, p. 10.

210 Ibid, p. 24.

211 AIIB, *Environmental and Social Framework.*

compliance with the banks' policies. These same banks similarly mandate that the borrower establish a mechanism for redressal of project-related environmental and social grievances. The mechanism is required to be available throughout the life cycle of a project, proportionate to the scale of the project, culturally appropriate, understandable and transparent, at no cost and without retribution to the complainant, accessible and should not impede access to other judicial or administrative remedies or substitute collective agreements.

Additional onus is placed on borrowers by the EBRD in requiring that it collaborate with respective government agencies in managing the risks and impacts on Indigenous people if the government has a defined role in their management. The Bank also requires the borrower to bring to the Bank's immediate attention any conflicts between Indigenous people and the borrower that remain unresolved after having gone through the GMs.

The World Bank, IDB, EIB and ADB maintain an independent complaint/investigation mechanism to serve as a forum for redress for stakeholders in matters of non-compliance with the bank's policies and publish full case reports of grievances and follow-up actions. The AfDB has in place an IRM for project-affected persons in matters concerning violation of the bank's policies and procedures.

The AIIB also incorporates provisions similar to the Work Bank's Framework but does not specifically include recourse to any internal redressal mechanism for grievances pertaining to non-compliance with the Bank's policies. The AIIB additionally requires borrowers to maintain a publicly accessible case register with reports on action taken/outcomes of complaints raised, although to date, the register only provides a brief summary of case complaints with limited information on follow-up actions.

Divergences

The GM policies of the IsDB and NDB, while not as comprehensive, provide for some safeguards, generally making reference to national requirements that vary in rigour. The banks require the borrower to establish a suitable grievance redressal mechanism scaled to the project's environmental and social risks and impact. However, these banks do not make grievance case information available to the public, even in summary fashion.

A Closer Look at MDB GMs

Understanding the unique structure of MDB GMs is important in identifying areas of commonality and distinction.

World Bank

The GM established by the World Bank, amongst the first to be developed by the worlds MDBs, is known as the Grievance Redress Service (GRS), which provides affected groups with a direct avenue to submit complaints related to World Bank-supported projects, and serves as a supplementary tool for pre-existing project-level grievance redress mechanisms.[212]

The GRS offers various services to support World Bank teams and complainants in addressing grievances, including reviewing project documents, identifying compliance issues with Bank policies, facilitating dialogue between project teams and communities, advising on possible solutions and sharing best practices.[213]

Complaints through the GRS may be submitted online, by mail or delivery, or through email, and are admissible when the complaint is about a project that was either finished within the last fifteen months, is presently being worked on or is being supported by the World Bank; the complaint is submitted by people or communities affected by a project sponsored by the World Bank; or by a designated representative on their behalf, or the complainant(s) allege that the project sponsored by the World Bank has negatively impacted them or will continue to do so.[214]

Complaints should also include information such as the specifics of the project being complained about, the detrimental effects experienced and name the person(s) submitting the complaint and if they are speaking on behalf of a community of affected individuals. Anonymous complaints are deemed inadmissible. Nevertheless, complaints are treated confidentially, and the GRS does not divulge personal identifying information without the complainants' permission.[215]

If approved by the complainant(s), the GRS implements the response plan in accordance with the procedure and timeline. After the original proposal is made, an agreement on the plan should be obtained within

212 World Bank (n.d.). Grievance redress service. www.worldbank.org/en/projects-operations/products-and-services/grievance-redress-service.
213 Ibid.
214 Ibid.
215 Ibid.

thirty business days. The time frame for implementation will vary depending on the nature of the actions required. The GRS should provide the complainant(s) with an explanation of the action plan's scope and the designated time frame.[216]

If the complaint cannot be resolved using the specified methods, the GRS then notifies the parties that no resolution can be reached. When this occurs, the GRS instructs the complainant(s) to consider alternative avenues for remedy.[217]

Asian Development Bank

The ADB's AM, implemented in 2012 to replace the previous 2003 AM policy, addresses grievances raised by individuals or communities adversely affected by ADB-funded projects. It consists of two offices: (1) the Office of the SPF; and (2) the Office of the Compliance Review Panel (CRP). The former operates to resolve complaints – facilitating a flexible and dialogue-oriented process where relevant parties collaborate to find solutions without assigning blame, while the latter functions as compliance review.[218]

The CRP consists of a full-time panel chair and two part-time panel members who report to the ADB's Board of Directors. It utilises multiple layers of checks and balances to ensure accountability. Through collaboration with the ADB's Board and President, it serves as an important stage of compliance review when complaints are raised through assessing whether non-compliance with these policies has resulted in 'direct adverse and material harm' to project-affected people. If non-compliance is found, the CRP reviews action plans proposed by the ADB management to address the issues raised. Both the SPF and CRP share a Complaint Receiving Officer (CRO) who acts as the initial point of contact for the AM. The CRO's role involves receiving, acknowledging and forwarding complaints to the relevant AM offices.[219]

[216] Ibid.

[217] World Bank Consultations (n.d.). Operational procedures for the World Bank's grievance redress service (GRS). https://consultations.worldbank.org/en/consultations/detail/operational-procedures-world-banks-grievance-redress-service-grs.

[218] SOMO (July 2018). The Asian Development Bank's accountability mechanism. www.somo.nl/wp-content/uploads/2018/07/The-Asian-Development-Banks-Accountability-Mechanism.pdf.

[219] ADB (2025). Accountability mechanism: A 25 year story. www.adb.org/multimedia/accountability-mechanism-25-years/index.php.

Complainants have the option of choosing which function they wish to engage with or may request the involvement of both the problem-solving and compliance review functions. While the ADB's AM does not require complainants to engage in problem-solving before their complaint may be considered for compliance review, once a compliance review has started or if the issues have already been addressed in a review, complainants are not allowed to request problem-solving. However, if a problem-solving attempt fails to reach a resolution or if it is successful, complainants have the right to ask for a compliance review.[220]

Together, these measures ensure that the ADB complies with its policies and procedures. The AM serves as an internal entity within the ADB while maintaining independence, providing an opportunity for affected groups to express their concerns and assist the ADB in working towards finding solutions to better its practices.[221]

International Bank for Reconstruction and Development, World Bank Group

The World Bank Group supports dialogue with a wide variety of stakeholders, including government, civil society, media, academia and the private sector.[222] Individuals and communities can access the GRS to submit complaints directly to the World Bank if they believe that a World Bank-supported project has or is likely to have adverse effects on them, their community or their environment. There are an average of 125 complaints a year, covering a wide spectrum of project-related issues.[223] A complaint is admissible if the complaint relates to a World Bank-supported project that is under preparation, active or has been closed for less than fifteen months and is submitted by individuals or communities affected by a World Bank-supported project, or by their authorised representative. The complainant(s) must also allege that they have been or will be affected by the World Bank-supported project.[224]

In lodging a complaint, individuals should identify the subject of the complaint, clearly state the project's adverse impact(s), identify the individual(s) submitting the complaint, specify if the complaint is

220 Ibid.
221 Ibid.
222 World Bank (n.d.). Consultations. https://consultations.worldbank.org/?map=1.
223 World Bank (n.d.). Grievance redress service. www.worldbank.org/en/projects-operations/products-and-services/grievance-redress-service.
224 Ibid.

submitted by a representative of the person(s) or community affected by the project, and include the name, signature, contact details and written proof of authority of the representative if the complaint is submitted by one. All complaints are treated as confidential.

At the conclusion of the review process, solutions and timelines will be proposed to the complainants. If agreed, the project team and project implementing agency will implement the proposals, which are monitored by GRS. The complaint will be closed when the solution is fully implemented.[225]

Inter-American Development Bank

The Independent Consultation and Investigation Mechanism (MICI) is an office of the IDB Group. It is independent of the Bank's management and project teams, and addresses the environmental and social grievances of communities potentially affected by the Group's operations. It works impartially and objectively to look for solutions with all parties concerned, including the communities alleging harm; the IDB Group, as the financier of the operation; and the borrower (company or government) executing the project.[226]

There are two courses of action for complainants who fear harm from projects financed by the Bank. First, there is a dispute resolution (Consultation Phase) whereby MICI will mediate to help the parties involved reach an agreement that resolves the problem, and monitor the implementation of a satisfactory solution. This is a free and voluntary dispute resolution process in which MICI acts as an independent facilitator between the parties including: the complainants, the borrower executing the project and the IDB Group. Second, there is an investigation (Compliance Review Phase) whereby MICI will conduct an independent investigation to verify whether the IDB Group complied with its environmental, social and access to information standards, recommend corrective actions and monitor their implementation. This phrase is a fact-finding process, similar to an internal audit, in which MICI acts as an independent investigator.[227]

Both phases provide a final opportunity to address environmental and social concerns.[228] Besides addressing the specific concerns of

[225] Ibid.
[226] IDB (n.d.). What is Mici? www.iadb.org/en/mici/what-mici.
[227] Ibid.
[228] Ibid.

complainants, MICI helps to generate lessons on environmental and social sustainability issues based on the analysis of the cases managed and the findings of its investigations. These lessons enable the Bank to take corrective actions, prevent the problems identified from recurring and make institutional changes.

Apart from MICI, there is a Public Consultation Process portal[229] that allows stakeholders to participate in the public consultation process. Participants can share their comments, suggestions and perspectives on relevant topics. By registering for public consultations, one can access relevant information about public consultations and include comments, suggestions and perspectives via a computer and mobile device.

European Investment Bank

At the project level, designated 'promoters' are required to implement open and transparent engagement with all relevant stakeholders in operations financed by the EIB. The EIB has a Complaints Mechanism – a citizen-driven accountability tool that collects people's concerns about an EIB Group project or activity. It also coordinates the EIB Group's response to complaints received by the European Ombudsman concerning the Group's actions, decisions or omissions, and engages periodically in communication and outreach activities with the public and with CSOs.[230]

The Complaints Mechanism is one of the three independent control and accountability functions under the EIB Inspectorate General, together with its evaluation and investigation functions. It operates as a non-judicial, solution-driven mechanism based on the principles of independence and transparency. Its role is to investigate complaints to ensure the EIB Group complies with its policies and procedures, and to propose corrective actions if appropriate. Its team handles complaints about various topics concerning EIB Group-financed operations. This may include a potential lack of consultation with stakeholders, environmental degradation, involuntary resettlement and related compensation matters, and threats to community health and safety. The mechanism also supports complainants who encounter other issues concerning EIB Group activities, such as difficulties in accessing information.[231]

229 https://iadb.force.com/IDBPublicConsultation/s/?language=en_US.

230 EIB (2021). *European Investment Bank Group Complaints Mechanism Report 2021*. Luxembourg: EIB, p. 11.

231 Ibid, p. 3.

If a complaint is found to be admissible, the Complaints Mechanism will carry out a preliminary review of the allegations. This process includes desk reviews and meetings with EIB Group departments and with external stakeholders on-site, as necessary. After gathering information, it decides whether further investigation is needed. During a compliance review, the Complaints Mechanism investigates whether the EIB Group has followed the standards, rules and procedures that govern its operations. It then presents the findings, conclusions and any recommendations in a conclusions report.[232]

The Complaints Mechanism also offers complainants the possibility of resolving the issues underlying their complaint through a dispute resolution process. The Complaints Mechanism may propose and facilitate this approach if it determines that the issues can be resolved through the involved parties' participation. If the parties agree to certain commitments during the resolution process, these will generally be documented together with the agreed timetable in a written mediation agreement.[233]

European Bank for Reconstruction and Development

The ERBD's GM is designed to be proportionate to the risks and potential adverse impacts of a project. In particular, the principles that outline its approach include addressing concerns 'promptly and effectively, in a transparent manner that is culturally appropriate, free from manipulation, interference, coercion, intimidation and retribution, and readily accessible to all affected parties, at no cost'.[234] The mechanism does not prevent access to judicial or administrative remedies. It reports regularly to the public on its implementation, protecting the privacy of affected individuals. For projects where there are significant community concerns, the client is encouraged to provide the option of mediation. The ERBD monitors the implementation of the GM and analyses trends.

The Independent Project AM reviews environmental, social and transparency-related concerns raised by project-affected people and CSOs about bank-financed projects through two non-judicial and non-adversarial mechanisms:[235] The first approach is through problem solving and mediation. Mediation may be facilitated between project-affected

[232] Ibid, p. 12.
[233] Ibid, p. 12.
[234] EBRD (n.d.). *About the Independent Project Accountability Mechanism*. www.ebrd.com/project-finance/independent-project-accountability-mechanism/about.html.
[235] Ibid.

people, clients and other stakeholders to help find mutually satisfactory solutions. In addition to facilitated dialogue and mediation, solutions can be reached through conciliation, information sharing, joint fact finding or supported negotiation.[236]

The second non-judicial approach is compliance review: Independent Project Accountability Mechanism (IPAM) reviews the environmental and social performance of the bank project to determine whether the EBRD has complied with its commitments under the bank's ESP and Access to Information Policy. If the EBRD is found to be non-compliant, IPAM will propose changes to the Project and to the Bank's procedures to address the non-compliance, prevent future non-compliance, and promote institutional learning.

African Development Bank

Over the past decade, the AfDB has focused on increasing its transparency and accountability in relation to the broader public. The CSO Engagement Framework 2008–2012 is designed to strengthen and sustain the bank's engagement with CSOs.[237]

The IRM (administered by Compliance Review and Mediation Unit (BCRM)) provides individuals adversely affected by a project financed by the AfDB Group with an independent mechanism through which they can request the AfDB to comply with its own policies and procedures. The IRM intervenes when affected people or communities submit a complaint. In this way, the IRM is a recourse instrument for project-affected people who have previously been unable to resolve their problems with AfDB's management.[238]

In a request for problem solving, BCRM will open dialogue between the requestors and any interested persons with the aim of resolving underlying issues without seeking to attribute blame or fault to any party. The compliance review function is handled by the IRM Roster of Experts comprising of three external professionals, appointed by the Board of Directors for a five-year non-renewable term.[239]

236 Ibid.

237 AfDB (2019). *AfDB's Civil Society Engagement Framework*. www.afdb.org/en/consultations/closed-consultations/afdbs-civil-society-engagement-framework.

238 AfDB (17 May 2022). *Independent Review Mechanism (IRM)*. www.afdb.org/en/independent-review-mechanism-irm.

239 AfDB (16 July 2019). *Independent Review Mechanism – What we do?* www.afdb.org/en/independent-review-mechanism/about-irm/what-we-do.

Islamic Development Bank

While the IsDB does not have a project-affected community complaints handling mechanism similar to those already outlined, it does address procurement-related complaints,[240] including allegations of F&C, or any prohibited practice under IsDB Group Anticorruption Guidelines (January 2012), IsDB Group Integrity Policy (August 2010) and IsDB Group Integrity Principles and Guidelines (June 2012). Procurement-related complaints can only be brought to the beneficiary or IsDB by an 'Interested Party' including bidders, firms and suppliers.[241]

In addressing a procurement-related complaint, the beneficiary should ensure the timely and meaningful review of the complaint, including providing all relevant documentation and facts related to the complaint, while maintaining the confidentiality of information provided by the bidders.[242]

Central American Bank for Economic Integration

The Central American Bank for Economic Integration (CABEI) has a reporting channel designed to receive reports and allegations of irregularities, prohibited practices or regulatory breaches in the use of its funds or resources. Reports about environmental and/or social issues or damages related to CABEI's projects can be reported as well.[243]

Individuals including CABEI's staff or related third parties can submit a report/complaint. Anonymous reports are also admitted and the identity of reporting individuals as well as the results of the investigation are kept confidential.[244]

New Development Bank

While the NDB does not have a formalised GMs, its Information Disclosure Policy provides a channel for engagement with stakeholders.[245] This general engagement includes regular meetings between the Bank's management with representatives of CSOs during annual meetings, BRICS summits

[240] IsDB (2018). *IsDB's Guidance Note on Procurement Related Complaints Handling* (p. 1).
[241] Ibid, p. 5.
[242] Ibid, p. 9.
[243] CABEI (30 March 2020). *Reporting Channel*. www.bcie.org/en/about-cabei/reporting-channel/general-information.
[244] Ibid.
[245] NDB (6 August 2020). *Academia and Civil Society Organizations*. www.ndb.int/partnerships/civil-academic-societies/.

and other events, public lectures and discussions, and expert group meetings.[246] While the NDB has whistleblower procedures,[247] it seeks to deal with reported incidents of misconduct internally rather than though project-related dispute resolution mechanisms.

Asian Infrastructure Investment Bank

The PPM was established in 2019 by the AIIB to provide a channel to address grievances and concerns raised by people who have been adversely affected by the AIIB's failure to implement its ESP. It operates in accordance with the PPM Policy and Rules of Procedure,[248] including PPQ, RDR and RCR. Project Processing Queries are intended for the AIIB to address straightforward issues that come up during a project's environmental and social due diligence. These issues can be settled quickly through consultation and discussion, negating the need for dispute resolution. Requests for Dispute Resolutions are initiated where disputes arise over measures to lessen a project's negative social and environmental impacts. The PPM helps the parties resolve disagreements, with the goal of prioritising a time-bound, monitorable agreement on steps to mitigate the effects. Requests for Compliance Reviews involve investigations by the PPM into allegations of AIIB's non-compliance with its ESP during project preparation or implementation. If non-compliance is identified, the AIIB management prepares an action plan to address the issues raised, subject to approval by AIIB's Board.

As confidentiality is a key consideration in the PPM process, complainants may request that their personal particulars be kept confidential, and the PPM must make reasonable efforts to grant it. The PPM should also assess the risk of retaliation and take steps to protect the safety of the requesters and relevant individuals if there is a risk. Nevertheless, if requests for confidentiality impede the assessment or resolution of the submission, the PPM may advise the requestors and, if agreement cannot be reached, terminate the review process.[249]

[246] Ibid.
[247] www.ndb.int/about-us/whistleblowing/
[248] AIIB, How we assist you.
[249] AIIB (n.d.). Frequently asked questions – project-affected people's mechanism. www.aiib.org/en/about-aiib/who-we-are/project-affected-peoples-mechanism/faq/index.html.

Do Expanded Grievance Channels Lead to Fewer Disputes? Statistical Analysis

This section examines data from ten MDBs in relation to the total number of projects financed and number of project-related complaints per year between the years from 1995 to 2021 in order to assess changes, if any, in the percentage of grievances raised after the introduction of heightened engagement standards between 2010 and 2020. The aim is to understand the contribution, if any, of robust pre-project consultation and GMs on the subsequent occurrence of disputes. Grievance data were collected from the EIB,[250] IBRD (of the World Bank Group),[251] ADB,[252] International Development Association (of the World Bank Group),[253] IDB,[254] EBRD,[255] AfDB,[256] AIIB,[257] CABEI[258] and the IFC (of the World Bank Group).[259] Data from the IsDB[260] and NDB[261] were excluded since these banks do not publish grievance data.

Grievance data were gathered from official figures contained in the MDBs' publicly released reports, including their annual reports and yearly financial reports accessed from their websites or database archives. Such data were cross-referenced with the MDBs' own interactive

[250] EIB (n.d.). *Publications.* www.eib.org/en/publications/all/index.htm?q=&sortColumn=relevant&sortDir=desc&pageNumber=0&itemPerPage=10&pageable=true&language=EN&defaultLanguage=EN&=&or=true&yearFrom=&yearTo=&orSubjects=true&category=5c5173c2fa70a5c4ddd73ecd&orCategory=true&orCountries=true&orRegions=true&orSeries=true&orTags=true.

[251] World Bank Group Open Knowledge Repository (n.d.). *World Bank Annual Reports & Financial Statements.* https://openknowledge.worldbank.org/handle/10986/2127.

[252] ADB (n.d.). *ADB Accountability Mechanism Annual Reports.* www.adb.org/documents/series/adb-accountability-mechanism-annual-reports.

[253] World Bank Group Open Knowledge Repository, *World Bank Annual Reports & Financial Statements.*

[254] IDB (n.d.). *Publications.* https://publications.iadb.org/en/publications?keys=annual%20report&f%5B0%5D=type%3A4621

[255] EBRD (n.d.). *PCM Registry.* www.ebrd.com/work-with-us/project-finance/project-complaint-mechanism/pcm-register.html.

[256] AfDB (n.d.). *IRM Register of Registered Requests as of August 2022.* www.afdb.org/en/independent-review-mechanism/management-of-complaints/registered-requests.

[257] AIIB (n.d.). *AIIB Annual Reports and Financials.* www.aiib.org/en/news-events/annual-report/overview/index.html.

[258] CABEI (n.d.). *Publications.* www.bcie.org/en/news-and-media/publications/anual-reports.

[259] World Bank Group Open Knowledge Repository, *IFC Annual Reports & Financial Statements.*

[260] IsDB (n.d.). *Publications.* www.isdb.org/publications?pub_q=&pubcat=annual–annual-report&search=.

[261] NDB (n.d.). *Data and Documents.* www.ndb.int/data-and-documents/annual-reports/.

representations on their websites, where available, for accuracy. The numerical data collected were then tabulated, the percentages calculated and together presented in individual and collective graphical forms (Figure 1).

Despite the general disclosure of relevant grievance figures through official publications, there are a number of limitations pertaining to the available data. These include unavailability of official figures (for both projects financed and project-related complaints) in certain years for some MDBs, and a lack of differentiated data for complaints handled by associated institutions under the umbrella of the World Bank Group.

Conclusion

Prior to the early 2000s, few projects, if any, provided pre-project consultation or mandated GMs. Consultation was conducted on an ad hoc basis, usually after major grievances occurred. Since the mid-2010s, greater attention has been placed on early-stage consultation and mitigation measures in nearly all MDBs.[262] Attention has also focused on the quality and depth of the consultation process. Bank leadership has taken on greater responsibility and oversight of GMs and cancelling projects not in compliance with environmental, social and governance policy.

From an initial review of community engagement, information disclosure, grievance, dispute resolution and compliance standards within the ten multilateral banks examined, it is clear that over time such standards have converged towards requiring increasingly higher levels of accountability and responsiveness within project-affected communities. This has meant greater attention to accessibility and the transparent disclosure of prior complaints and outcome. In most cases, BCS is required, while in some cases, consent is necessary for projects in the highest-risk categories. Overall, knowledge sharing between banks has supported a robust process of shared norm development. This has emerged out of crises, decentralised knowledge generation[263] resulting in legal innovations.

Overall, the key findings of the data analysis indicate that the percentage of grievances per project peaked at 15.4% in 2019 then dropped significantly in 2021 to 7.1%. This drop in percentage of grievances corresponds with the implementation of heightened MDB community

262 Ali, Davis & Lee, Multi-stakeholder dispute resolution.

263 Shahla, A. (2021). *Forming Transnational Dispute Settlement Norms: Soft Law and the Role of UNCITRAL's Regional Centre for Asia and the Pacific*. Cheltenham: Edward Elgar.

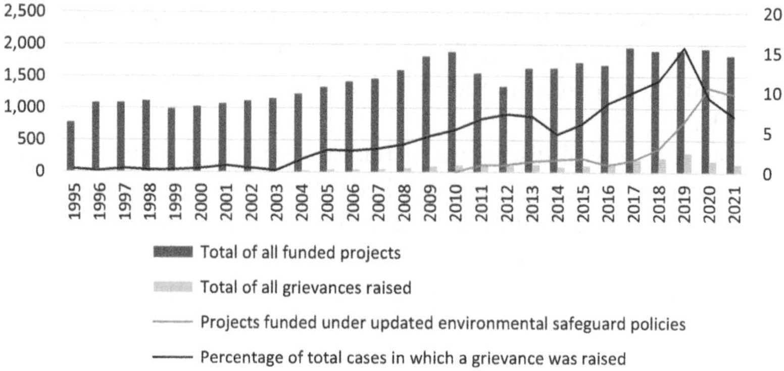

Figure 1 Total of all projects, total of all grievances raised.

engagement policies, including mandating pre-project consultation processes and GMs introduced between 2010 and 2020, taking into account an average three-year time lag between policy introduction and project implementation.

While this overall decline in the percentage of grievance cases could be due to a number of factors including self-help, lock down measures, resort to formal legal mechanisms or alternatively the effective screening of inappropriate or environmentally harmful projects and incorporation of community concerns mitigating the need for grievance claims, overall, the findings provide measured evidence supporting the development of increasingly robust community engagement channels, particularly for multilateral and national banks who have not yet implemented such policies. These engagement channels, far from aggregating complaints, conversely are correlated with a reduction in the overall proportion of project disputes. While more recent data from 2022 has shown a slight uptick in filed complaints,[264] at the same time, total project funding has likewise increased by approximately 6%, suggesting a modest levelling of grievances per project in recent years.[265] These data seem to reflect a growing awareness of the availability of such mechanisms and a higher number of complaints passing the eligibility threshold amidst post-Covid revived activity.

[264] See Accountability Council Report, A new decade of complaints.

[265] Based on estimated total MDB infrastructure development funding comparison between 2021 and 2022.

Significantly, new grievance data since 2021 show that the increased attention on the part of MDB's to pre-project consultation, disclosure and due diligence has been positively recognised by affected communities. This is demonstrated by the fact that before 2021, the lack of consultation, disclosure or due diligence was the single most cited cause of grievances amongst affected communities. After 2021, it was no longer the single most cited cause, but rather became the second issue cited issue after concerns regarding displacement became the primary concern amongst complainants.[266]

[266] See Accountability Council Report, A new decade of complaints.

PART II

Towards Greater Community Oversight in Practice

4

Practitioners' Insights into the Efficacy of Mitigation Measures

Introduction

Building on an examination of existing conflict mitigation mechanisms in multilateral banking institutions and the impact of heightened consultation and accountability standards on the frequency of subsequent disputes, this chapter explores the attitudes and perceptions of fifty-five practitioners engaged in infrastructure-related dispute prevention and resolution in the Asia Pacific region. The aim of the survey and follow-up interview conversations is to provide insights into the dynamics, challenges and lessons learned in engaging with communities to prevent and resolve disputes in the context of infrastructure projects.

The principal finding of this chapter, based on survey data and follow-up questions, is that from the perspective of regional practitioners, prior community consultation is considered the most effective approach to preventing infrastructure disputes. This finding is consistent with the results of the data analysis in the prior chapter correlating heightened consultation standards with a reduction in the proportion of project disputes. A number of challenges continue to exist in mitigation efforts, with the most challenging being the 'lack of agreement on shared economic benefits' and 'limited communication'. Overall, practitioners advised that most disputes arise because 'there was no consultation or inadequate consultation with a marginalised part of the community'.[1]

Respondents offered suggestions on how community–investor dispute resolution systems might be improved, including the need for more public awareness[2] of community consultation and grievance

[1] Survey No. 11 (22 September 2022 11:32 a.m.).
[2] Survey No. 19 (15 June 2022 08:10 a.m.).

mechanisms, a clear consultation process to encourage better understanding of those engaged[3] and more efforts to educate the community so that they 'understand … the risk of investment'.[4] Follow-up conversations between 2021 and 2023 with practitioners working in dispute mitigation offered additional insights into themes such as the duty of consultation and social license to operate, the development of hybrid forms of resolution, dispute mitigation through early consultation and dispute boards, the exploration of appropriate due diligence standards in infrastructure financing programmes, the internalisation of environmental, social and governance (ESG) standards into contracting agreements, and an emphasis on long-term contracting models and multi-tiered approaches to resolution.

Given the small n size of the survey sample (n = 40), the findings cannot be considered generalisable. As prior studies have noted, self-reported perceptions are subject to bias and statements may not always reflect actual practice.[5] However, the findings of this chapter demonstrate the overall significance of prior community consultation and effective grievance mechanisms in preventing disputes in the infrastructure context.

Summary of Findings

The findings of this chapter can be grouped into three areas. The first reports on the primary mechanisms deployed in preventing community–investor disputes. The second explores their relative efficacy alongside challenges encountered. The last examines areas of learning and recommendations for advancing infrastructure dispute mitigation.

'Prior community engagement and consultation' was identified as the most frequently used mechanisms in dispute prevention, constituting 15% of the total. Next in frequency of use was developing a 'shared benefits system' with 12% of the total and next in frequency were 'compliance review', 'mediation' and 'consensus building with local community on shared values, standards and goals', each with 11% of the total.

[3] Survey No. 22 (14 June 2022 18:33 p.m.).

[4] Survey No. 23 (14 June 2022 18:03 p.m.).

[5] Wall, J. A., & Kressel, K. (2012). Research on mediator style: A summary and some research suggestions. *Negotiation and Conflict Management Research* 5(4): 403–421.

In relation to the efficacy of selected mechanisms of dispute prevention, respondents identified a number of approaches as being either 'very effective' or 'effective', including: prior community engagement and consultation (82.35%, weighted 4.16); developing a shared benefits system (73.53%, weighted 3.97); prior informed consent (71.43%, weighted 3.90); consensus building with local community on shared values, standards and goals (67.65%, weighted 3.83) followed by mediation (58.82%, weighted 3.74); and compliance review (60.61%, weighted 3.59). Additional mechanisms were identified as moderately or less effective as will be examined later in this chapter.

Respondents also shared the challenges they encountered when engaging in dispute mitigation efforts on a scale of 1–9, with 1 being the most challenging and 9 the least. Amongst the most significant challenges included a 'lack of agreement on shared economic benefits' with a weighted average score of 3.05. Next was 'limited communication' with a score of 3.24. This was followed by 'political risk' with an average score of 3.52. Next was 'limited cultural or religious awareness' with an average score of 3.87 and 'complex local regulations' with a score of 4.25.

The final part of this chapter reports on insights from fifteen practitioners regarding suggestions for advancing the practice of community engagement and dispute mitigation. This included the need for more public awareness[6] of community consultation and grievance mechanisms, a clear consultation process,[7] and more efforts to educate the community so that they 'understand … the risk of investment'.[8]

Survey Data Collection Method

Survey data were collected from forty practitioners largely from the Asia Pacific region in order to gain insights into the dynamics of dispute prevention and the effectiveness of early-stage dispute mitigation mechanisms. The survey examined how dispute resolution practitioners viewed existing strengths, challenges and lessons learned in conflict

[6] Survey No. 19 (15 June 2022 08:10 a.m.).
[7] Survey No. 22 (14 June 2022 18:33 p.m.).
[8] Survey No. 23 (14 June 2022 18:03 p.m.).

prevention in the infrastructure development context. Given the small sample size (n = 40), the purpose of the survey is not to provide generalisable findings. Rather, the survey aims to supplement case studies by offering insights into how practitioners are engaging with dispute mitigation in practice.

Public discussions at the ADGM conference on Investor State Mediation and the Challenges of Energy Transition, the Asia Global Dialogue, the World Arbitration Update on Community Consultations and Environmental Protection and the Asia African Legal Consultative Organisation (AALCO) Arbitration Forum between 2021 and 2023, offered additional insights on the duty of consultation and social license to operate, hybrid forms of resolution, disclosure and dispute boards, enhancing mediator skills to address complex infrastructure disputes and recent developments within China.

What Is Your Region of Practice?

The survey questionnaire contained a quantitative part asking for yes-no answers and numerical responses in the form of percentage estimates, rankings and evaluations according to a five-point scale, as well as a supplemental part containing qualitative, open-ended questions asking for personal observations, judgments and proposals.

The first part of the survey asked for participants background information on their region of practice[9] and the nature of their engagement with conflict mitigation. The second part of the survey examined the efficacy, if at all, of various approaches to conflict prevention in the infrastructure context. The final part explored respondent's suggestions for improving systems of conflict prevention through community engagement. These findings will be discussed in greater detail here.

Responses were received from different continents (Figure 2). The majority, thirty-four in number and 87% of the total, came from Asia Pacific. Americas and Middle East/Africa each contributed two respondents, respectively 5% of the total. The remaining respondent was from Europe (3%).

[9] Ali, S. F. (2010). *Resolving Disputes in the Asia-Pacific Region: International Arbitration and Mediation in East Asia and the West.* Abingdon: Routledge.

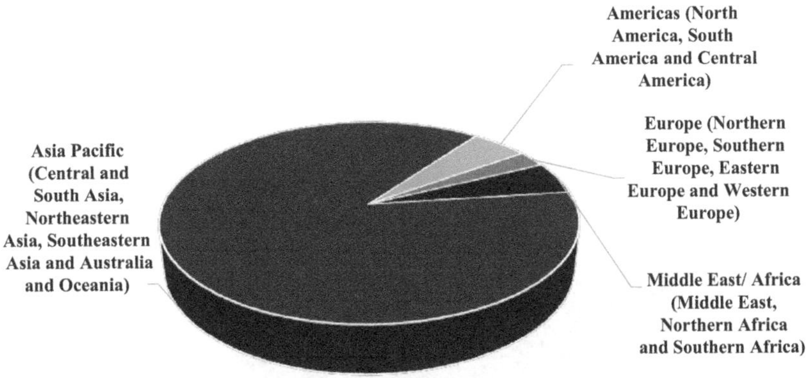

Figure 2 Region of practice.

How Would You Describe Your Institution of Practice?

The survey was conducted between May 2022 and December 2023. A total of eighty-five surveys were distributed in person at dispute resolution forums in the Asia Pacific and initiated via a web link portal and forty surveys were completed. Given the small sample size (n = 40), the survey aimed to provide insights into the dynamics of conflict prevention in the infrastructure context rather than provide generalisable findings. The sample pool consisted of a convenience sample of dispute resolution practitioners selected from contacts made with members of the Asian Development Bank (ADB), Asian Infrastructure Investment Bank (AIIB) and World Bank ombuds teams. In addition, the survey was distributed through contacts made at the Hong Kong Arbitration Week, and the ADGM conference on Investor State Mediation and the Challenges of Energy Transition. Of the respondents, 40% were either arbitrators, attorneys and/or members of a chamber of commerce, 13% were community dispute resolution service providers, 7% worked within a national or multilateral banking institution, and 33% of the total selected 'other', which included mediator, arbitrator, alternative dispute resolution expert, systems designer, claims and dispute resolver, mediation expert and a regional banking group member (Figure 3).

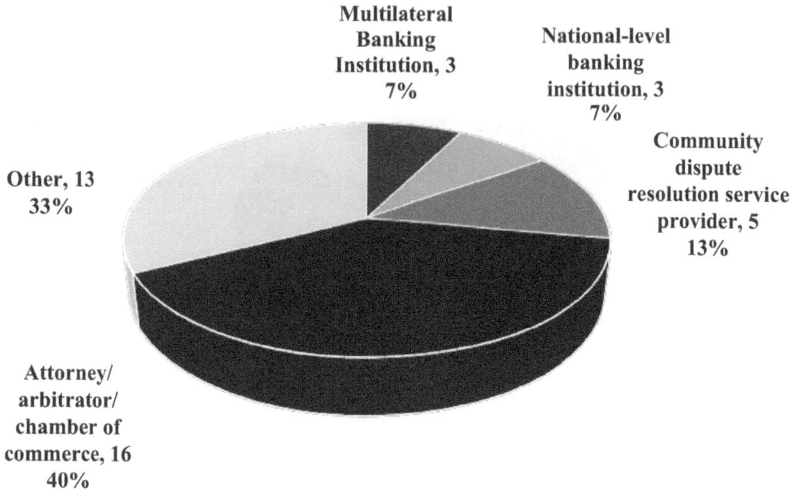

Figure 3 Institution type: how would you describe your institution?

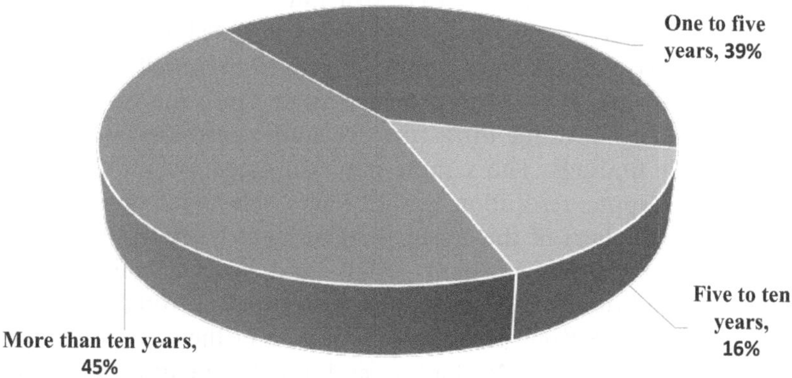

Figure 4 Years of experience in the field of dispute resolution.

How Long Have You Worked in the Field of Dispute Prevention?

Of those surveyed, approximately 45% respondents reported that they had over ten years of experience, while 39% were relatively new to the field, with one to five years of experience. The intermediate group, with five to 10 years of experience, made up 16% of the total (Figure 4).

What Are the Key Mechanisms Used in Preventing Community–Investor Disputes (Check All That Apply)

In relation to observations regarding the key mechanisms used in preventing community–investor disputes, the most frequently cited mechanism was 'prior community engagement and consultation', constituting 15% of the total. Not far behind was developing a 'shared benefits system' with 12% of the total. Next in frequency were 'compliance review', 'mediation' and 'consensus building with local community on shared values, standards and goals', each with 11% of the total. Next was 'prior informed consent', with 10% of the total. Finally, a number of mechanisms were less frequently cited, contributing less than 10% of the total, including 'administrative/regulatory dispute resolution' (8%), 'localised complaint handling/ grievance mechanism (ombudsperson) (8%), 'centralised complaint handling mechanism (ombudsperson)' (7%) and 'arbitration' with (4%). A few respondents noted 'other' mechanisms (3%), including: 'periodical claims and dispute management reviews with dedicated neutral', 'dispute boards/conflict avoidance boards', 'non-binding mechanisms such as OECD NCP (resolving disputes at an early stage) and company and industry grievance mechanisms', and 'state-sponsored community mediation and special mediation programme[s]' (Figure 5).

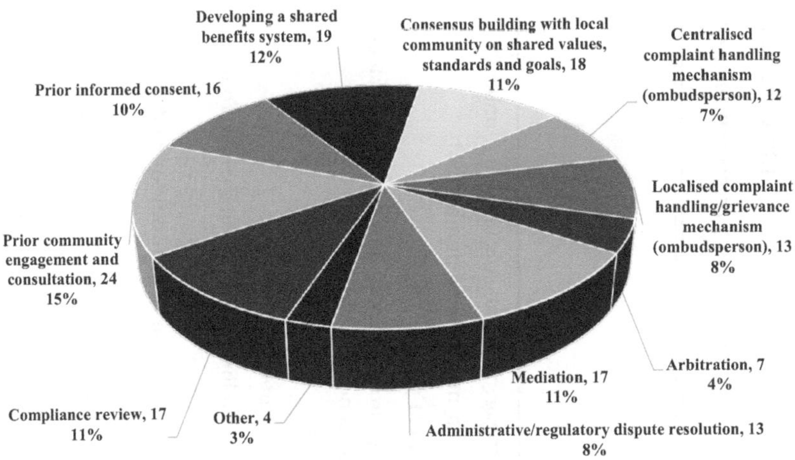

Figure 5 Key mechanisms used in preventing community–investor disputes.

Table 2 *Effectiveness of mechanisms in preventing disputes.*

	The degree of effectiveness of the following mechanisms in preventing disputes (in ranked order)					
	Very effective	Effective	Moderately effective	Not so effective	Very ineffective	Weighted
Prior community engagement and consultation number (%)	12 (35.29)	16 (47.06)	6 (17.65)	0 (0.00)	0 (0.00)	4.16 (1st)
Developing a shared benefits system number (%)	11 (32.35)	14 (41.18)	7 (20.59)	2 (5.88)	0 (0.00)	3.97 (2nd)
Prior informed consent number (%)	11 (31.43)	14 (40.00)	6 (17.14)	4 (11.43)	0 (0.00)	3.90 (3rd)
Consensus building with local community on shared values, standards and goals number (%)	8 (23.53)	15 (44.12)	9 (26.47)	2 (5.88)	0 (0.00)	3.83 (4th)
Mediation number (%)	11 (32.35)	9 (26.47)	9 (26.47)	5 (14.71)	0 (0.00)	3.74 (5th)
Compliance review number (%)	2 (6.06)	18 (54.55)	11 (33.33)	2 (6.06)	0 (0.00)	3.59 (6th)
Localised complaint handling/grievance mechanism (ombudsperson) number (%)	4 (11.43)	14 (40.00)	11 (31.43)	6 (17.14)	0 (0.00)	3.45 (7th)
Centralised complaint handling mechanism (ombudsperson) number (%)	5 (14.71)	12 (35.2)	9 (26.47)	8 (23.53)	0 (0.00)	3.39 (8th)
Administrative/regulatory dispute resolution number (%)	3 (9.38)	10 (31.25)	7 (21.88)	12 (37.5)	0 (0.00)	3.1 (9th)
Arbitration number (%)	1 (3.13)	10 (31.25)	11 (34.38)	6 (18.75)	4 (12.50)	2.92 (10th)

Table 3 *Most significant challenges in community dispute prevention.*

	The most significant challenges in community dispute prevention (1 most challenging to 9 least challenging) (in ranked order)										
	1	2	3	4	5	6	7	8	9	Total	Weighted score
Lack of agreement on shared economic benefits number (%)	6 (17.14)	3 (8.57)	9 (25.71)	7 (20.00)	5 (14.29)	1 (2.86)	2 (5.71)	1 (2.86)	1 (2.86)	35	3.05 (1st)
Limited communication number (%)	8 (21.62)	6 (16.22)	10 (27.03)	2 (5.41%)	5 (13.51)	5 (13.51)	1 (2.70)	0 (0.00)	0 (0.00)	37	3.24 (2nd)
Political risk and effective communication number (%)	3 (15.79)	6 (31.58)	3 (15.79)	1 (5.26)	2 (10.53)	0 (0.00)	3 (15.79)	1 (5.26)	0 (0.00)	19	3.52 (3rd)
Limited cultural, religious awareness number (%)	5 (13.89)	8 (22.22)	4 (11.11)	4 (11.11)	7 (19.44)	3 (8.33)	2 (5.56)	3 (8.33)	0 (0.00)	36	3.87 (4th)
Complex local regulations number (%)	5 (13.16)	6 (15.79)	4 (10.53)	6 (15.79)	8 (21.05)	1 (2.63)	3 (7.89)	3 (7.89)	2 (5.26)	38	4.25 (5th)
Environmental protection; sustainability number (%)	6 (17.14)	2 (5.71)	3 (8.57)	5 (14.29)	6 (17.14)	7 (20.00)	3 (8.57)	0 (0.00)	3 (8.57)	35	4.53 (6th)

Table 3 (*cont.*)

	The most significant challenges in community dispute prevention (1 most challenging to 9 least challenging) (in ranked order)										
	1	2	3	4	5	6	7	8	9	Total	Weighted score
The absence or instability of laws, regulations and policies number (%)	1 (5.00)	2 (10.00)	2 (10.00)	4 (20.00)	1 (5.00)	1 (5.00)	2 (10.00)	5 (25.00)	2 (10.00)	20	5.5 (7th)
Corruption; rent-seeking number (%)	2 (10.00)	3 (15.00)	2 (10.00)	2 (10.00)	2 (10.00)	2 (10.00)	1 (5.00)	4 (20.00)	2 (10.00)	20	5.05 (8th)
Gender number (%)	1 (2.63)	1 (2.63)	1 (2.63)	5 (13.16)	0 (0.00)	14 (36.84)	3 (7.89)	4 (10.53)	9 (23.68)	38	6.41 (9th)

Respondents were invited to rate the degree of effectiveness of several dispute prevention mechanisms, namely: compliance review; prior community engagement and consultation; prior informed consent; developing a shared benefits system; consensus building with the local community on shared values, standards and goals; centralised complaint-handling mechanism (ombudsperson); localised complaint-handling/ grievance mechanism (ombudsperson); arbitration; mediation; and administrative/regulatory dispute resolution (Table 2).

The following mechanisms were regarded as amongst the most effective (Table 3), with nearly 60% of the respondents recognising them as 'very effective' or 'effective': prior community engagement and consultation (82.35%, weighted 4.16); developing a shared benefits system (73.53%, weighted 3.97); prior informed consent (71.43%, weighted 3.90); consensus building with local community on shared values, standards and goals (67.65%, weighted 3.83); mediation (58.82%, weighted 3.74) and compliance review (60.61%, weighted 3.59).

The mid-range category of effectiveness included: localised complaint handling/ grievance mechanism (ombudsperson) and centralised complaint handling mechanism (ombudsperson). Concerning the former, 51.43% of the respondents opted for 'very effective' or 'effective', while around one-third chose 'moderately effective' (31.43%) with a weighted score of 3.45. Regarding the latter, 49.91% of the respondents regarded it as 'very effective' or 'effective'.

Survey respondents regarded the least effective dispute prevention mechanisms as arbitration and administrative/regulatory dispute resolution.

With respect to the key challenges faced in dispute prevention, respondents were asked to score the most significant challenges they faced in community dispute prevention on a scale from 1 (most challenging) to 9 (least challenging). Nine options were provided, namely: environmental protection sustainability; limited cultural, religious awareness; limited communication; lack of agreement on shared economic benefits; complex local regulations; gender; political risk and effective communication; corruption and rent-seeking; and absence or instability of [relevant] laws, regulations and policies.

The most significant challenge noted was 'lack of agreement on shared economic benefits' with a weighted average score of 3.05. Next was 'limited communication' with a score of 3.24. This was followed by 'political risk' with an average score of 3.52. Next was 'limited cultural or religious awareness' with an average score of 3.87 and 'complex local regulations' with 4.25. 'Environmental protection and sustainability' followed with an average score of 4.53, and 'corruption and rent seeking' with a score of 5.05. Finally, the least challenging issues included 'the absence or instability of [relevant] laws, regulations and policies' with a score of 5.05 and 'gender' with a score of 6.41.

Additional Challenges in Dispute Prevention

Elaborating on the previous question, respondents were asked 'what other challenges have you faced, if any, in the community–investor dispute prevention processes?' One respondent observed the challenge of individuals acting 'unreasonably in the face of conflict'.[10] Another respondent remarked on the 'lack of understanding of regulations',[11] while others noted challenges in ascertaining the 'benefit sharing system'[12] and 'commercial considerations'.[13]

Best Practice Experiences, Lessons Learned and Suggestions for Improvement

Survey respondents shared their best practice experiences in community engagement and consultation processes. One respondent observed that:

> informed consent is a higher standard and more powerful to prevent disputes, but requires (1) the opportunity for communities to design a consent protocol that reflects their traditional decision-making processes and values and (2) it requires respect for whatever outcome, including no project. 'Consultation' is weaker but can be effective if it is accompanied by: inaction (open invitations, meetings held on different days to accommodate different schedules, planned well in advance), prior information, information that is accessible (language, format), and information that is balanced (negative/risks as well as potential benefits).[14]

Another respondent stated: 'I think the most important thing is to properly identify the "community", which needs to be consulted. Most disputes I have seen arise because there was no consultation or inadequate consultation with a marginalised part of the community'.[15] A

[10] Survey No. 1 (15 June 2022 09:03 a.m.).
[11] Survey No. 4 (14 June 2022 18:33 p.m.).
[12] Survey No. 2 (15 June 2022 09:01 a.m.).
[13] Survey No. 3 (15 June 2022 08:10 a.m.).
[14] Survey No. 8 (05 October 2022 07:21 a.m.).
[15] Survey No. 11 (22 September 2022 11:32 a.m.).

practitioner in Nepal noted that 'road project [developers] are unaware of [the requirement of 'Free Prior and Informed Consent'] (FPIC) in Nepal'.[16] Finally, a lawyer noted that when a dispute enters the legal system, it is already 'in its late stage'.[17]

Respondents shared important lessons they have learned in administering effective community–investor dispute prevention mechanism. This included the importance of strict adherence to contracts,[18] and the perspective that 'communication beforehand is the key'.[19]

Finally, survey respondents offered suggestions on how the community–investor dispute resolution system might be improved including through information dissemination, simple programme design and community education. One respondent suggested the need for more public 'promotion'[20] of community consultation and grievance mechanisms, while another stressed that the consultation process be designed in a 'simple' way to encourage better understanding of those engaged.[21] Lastly, a practitioner called for more effort to educate the community so that they 'understand … the risk of investment'.[22]

Practitioners' Insights

Follow-up public discussions at the ADGM conference on Investor State Mediation and the Challenges of Energy Transition, the Asia Global Dialogue, the World Arbitration Update on Community Consultations and Environmental Protection, and with members of the Infrastructure Investment Banks in the Asia Pacific and the ALCO Arbitration Forum between 2021 and 2023 on dispute mitigation offered additional insights on themes such as shared learning between MDBs on the development of dispute mitigation mechanisms, the duty of consultation and social license to operate, the development of hybrid forms of resolution, mitigation through early consultation and dispute boards, and the importance of mediator training.

[16] Survey No. 12 (05 September 2022 12:03 p.m.).
[17] Survey No. 10 (22 September 2022 22:35 p.m.).
[18] Survey No. 15 (14 June 2022 19:51 p.m.).
[19] Survey No. 16 (14 June 2022 18:33 p.m.).
[20] Survey No. 19 (15 June 2022 08:10 a.m.).
[21] Survey No. 22 (14 June 2022 18:33 p.m.).
[22] Survey No. 23 (14 June 2022 18:03 p.m.).

Shared Learning between Multilateral Banks on Dispute Mitigation Mechanisms

Consultations with practitioners working in multilateral banking institutions in China highlighted shared learning process between multilateral development banks in advancing community engagement processes including drawing on experiences from peer banks such as the Inter-American Bank and ADB. A key area of development has been the adaptation and implementation of project-level grievance mechanisms with regular follow-up and support. Bank leadership likewise sets the 'tone in complaint handling' and providing 'resources to [conduct] due diligence well'. Complaints may increase, 'not because prevention is not working, but because people are more aware of their rights … leading to more complaints, accountability … [through] outreach'.[23]

Identifying the Community and Core Interests

Further discussions with dispute mitigation practitioners provided elaboration on best practices in stakeholder engagement including the composition of the constituents of a community. One practitioner noted that it is critical to identify who the relevant stakeholders are and the important interests that need to be considered. This could 'include investors, employees, customers, and suppliers – this can now also include communities, governments, and trade associations'.[24] It is important to think about 'primary stakeholders, secondary stakeholders, and key stakeholders – If we don't include all [relevant parties]– the durability and implementation can be affected.'[25] In terms of relevant issues, interests may include: 'economics, social change, time, environment, employment, health, safety, security'.

Levels of community engagement vary such that stakeholder engagement may be conceived of as 'concentric circles' according to one practitioner. For example, in consultations concerning the location of a mine in Australia, a practitioner noted that 'the local community may like this [project] for job creation and economic activity. However, there is a broader impact on fossil fuels in the wider environment. Who should be engaged? We need to work with parties to see what that looks like.'[26] She

[23] Background consultation, infrastructure bank in Asia.

[24] Dispute Resolution Practitioner 1, ADGM conference on Investor State Mediation and the Challenges of Energy Transition, 2021.

[25] Ibid.

[26] Ibid.

elaborated that 'what we have developed is preparing a high/low graph distinguishing individuals with whom we should collaborate, engage, and keep informed'.[27] This same practitioner noted that consideration must be given to 'what forms of dispute resolution are appropriate for impacts on climate change. This includes thinking about cultural impacts, values, communication styles, strategies for engagement and bridging cultural gaps.'[28] Finally, she noted the importance of a constructive orientation when engaging with the community – 'if we come to table with an adversarial mindset, this will impact parties'.[29]

Understanding the Duty of Consultation and Social License to Operate

The emergence of a 'duty of consultation' as outlined in the ICCPR and Article 23 of the American Convention on Human Rights has raised new questions as to how this duty is put into practice.[30] A growing number of cases surrounding this right are emerging including *Sarayaku* v. *Ecuador*, *Metalclad* v. *Mexico* and *Bear Creek Mining* v. *Peru.*

Emerging case law has made reference to the concept of a 'social license' to operate prior to the initiation of large-scale infrastructure projects. Related questions surrounding such a license include who has authority to grant such a license, and what are the parameters of the relevant community. One practitioner reflected, 'how close to the vicinity of the project must one be? What if the community is split and doesn't agree? For example, there is a case concerning proposed liquified natural gas that would impact tribal lands. The council supported it, but others [in the community] opposed. How to reconcile the split in the community?'[31] The issue of a split in community support likewise came up in the ICSID case of *Gabriel Resources Ltd* v. *Romania.* The local community supported 'the mine but environmental activities who are not local opposed [it]. The question then is how to reconcile the split?' Another question is the timing of support, 'if formal approval is given for a project, and then later it loses the

[27] Ibid.
[28] Ibid.
[29] Ibid.
[30] Practitioner 2, World Arbitration Update, 26 September 2022, Americas: Community Consultations and Environmental Protection in International Arbitration – providing that individuals have a right to participate in governance decision making.
[31] Practitioner 3, World Arbitration Update, 26 September 2022, Americas: Community Consultations and Environmental Protection in International Arbitration.

social license, what are the companies obligations to maintain the social license [over time if at all]?'[32] A related question is whether an investor 'has a legitimate expectation that it needs to maintain a social license' and to what extent does the lack of such a license 'highlight governance deficits in the host state' (i.e. Indigenous peoples not having representative voice in domestic decision making of the government that grants the license).[33] The obligations on investors need to be 'achievable'.[34] For example, conducting an environmental impact assessment is generally the responsibility of a state's regulatory body and not within the power of a private company.

Hybrid Forms of Resolution for Climate Disputes

Considering the need to address climate-related disputes through inclusion of a 'wider cross section of parties – including indigenous peoples and groups' in the context of 'polycentric disputes with multiple-parties',[35] new forms of resolution are developing including investor–state mediation and hybrid mechanisms. One practitioner noted the benefits of mediation in the investor–state context, given that it is 'unique and can be crafted on the basis of need, including the important advantage [of being able] to choose the neutral'.[36]

Flexible and creative forms of hybrid resolution are particularly relevant in the context of disputes arising from the 'early retirement of coal and nuclear, [and] early retirement of oil and gas'.[37] Attention to mitigating such disputes through early-stage due diligence and transparent and fair risk allocation prior to the initiation of a project is increasing. A dispute resolution practitioner noted that she is seeing more disputes arising in the context of renewable energy infrastructure projects since the 'technology is new and not tested, and [there are] competing objectives between stakeholders and states regulating energy transition'.[38] A

[32] Ibid.
[33] Ibid.
[34] Ibid.
[35] Dispute Resolution Practitioner 4, ADGM conference on Investor State Mediation and the Challenges of Energy Transition, 2021.
[36] Dispute Resolution Practitioner 5, ADGM conference on Investor State Mediation and the Challenges of Energy Transition, 2021.
[37] Dispute Resolution Practitioner 6, ADGM conference on Investor State Mediation and the Challenges of Energy Transition, 2021.
[38] Dispute Resolution Practitioner 7, ADGM conference on Investor State Mediation and the Challenges of Energy Transition, 2021.

risk 'balance must be found between investors and states … to allow transitions to new technologies'.[39] She observed that rather than late-stage mediation or arbitration, 'it's important to focus on dispute avoidance as much as possible … we will need to spend more time before signing an agreement than after a dispute arises … a stronger party can also be harmed by unbalanced risk allocation'.[40] Another practitioner noted that it is important to 'ensure that contracts are clear with where risk lies and who picks up the change in law … we need to think about how to manage disputes in an amicable way … [since] we will need to continue relationships'.[41]

Investing in Mitigation through Consultation, Disclosure and Dispute Boards

The emphasis on conflict avoidance through consultation, information disclosure and the establishment of dispute boards has advanced in recent years. An in-house lawyer for an energy company noted that 'avoiding conflicts from arising is where our focus should be'.[42] Within his company, he focused on 'understanding our risks, climate risks, physical, legal and policy' and 'reporting [through] carbon disclosures'. He observed that 'the more disclosure [and] transparency – the more we can avoid and mitigate risks'.[43] He added that because stakeholders 'are involved in our decisions', if a conflict arises, 'instead of going through litigation which would lead to breaking up relations and harming both parties', instead we seek 'more collaborative approaches – whether negotiation or mediation, to avoid the risk of conflict'.[44]

Project-based dispute boards represent a relatively new innovation in dispute mitigation for long-term projects. One practitioner noted the benefit of a standing group of advisors to 'hea[d] off conflicts [with] … the main emphasis on avoiding disputes'.[45] Another practitioner noted that given the growing 'complexity of the regulatory side, this makes the

[39] Ibid.
[40] Ibid.
[41] Dispute Resolution Practitioner 9, ADGM conference on Investor State Mediation and the Challenges of Energy Transition, 2021.
[42] Dispute Resolution Practitioner 8, ADGM conference on Investor State Mediation and the Challenges of Energy Transition, 2021.
[43] Ibid.
[44] Ibid.
[45] Dispute Resolution Practitioner 10, ADGM conference on Investor State Mediation and the Challenges of Energy Transition, 2021.

argument for the preventative side much stronger'.[46] Being involved from the start also helps Board Members understand the relevant background. In contrast, if one is appointed after a dispute arises, 'parties are entrenched, prospects for resolution are reduced … [initiating formal dispute resolution] sends a negative message … [it] seems like throwing a grenade – [it is] better to be there at start of project, [and] know the background'.[47] The language of the dispute board has an impact on the framing of the dispute. This same practitioner noted that it is 'better to avoid the word dispute – rather, let's get together and work this through'.[48]

Enhancing Mediator Skill to Address Complex Infrastructure Disputes

The need for experienced and well-trained neutrals capable of addressing infrastructure disputes was also highlighted by practitioners. An in-house counsel noted that 'there is a lot of effort by the government [to promote] mediation and settlement';[49] however, the 'skills to bring parties together is not there'.[50] He noted that he 'would prefer these cases to be handed over to better/higher quality mediation' and that legislation is needed to determine 'what mediation [is and] to make sure the safeguards of confidentiality/enforceability are available'.[51] This corresponds with findings of prior research on the need for enhanced mediator training both for voluntary and mandatory systems.[52]

Developments within China

In conversations with members of the multilateral development community in China, several trends can be observed, including exploration of appropriate diligence standards whether domestic or global in infrastructure financing programmes, the internalisation of ESG standards into

[46] Dispute Resolution Practitioner 11, ADGM conference on Investor State Mediation and the Challenges of Energy Transition, 2021.
[47] Dispute Resolution Practitioner 12, ADGM conference on Investor State Mediation and the Challenges of Energy Transition, 2021.
[48] Ibid.
[49] Dispute Resolution Practitioner 10, ADGM conference on Investor State Mediation and the Challenges of Energy Transition, 2021.
[50] Ibid.
[51] Ibid.
[52] Ali, S. (2018). *Court Mediation Reform: Efficiency, Confidence and Perceptions of Justice*. Cheltenham: Edward Elgar.

contracting agreements, an emphasis on long-term contracting models and multi-tiered approaches to resolution.

While China has been a major contributor to coal production and financing, efforts are advancing to reduce coal production and address intellectual property protection. In recent years, China and India have contributed significantly to global solar panel and wind energy production.[53] Deploying such technologies appropriately will result in economic dislocation in traditional energy sectors and require greater balance between state regulation and social innovation.[54]

Standard setting at the national level, similarly, has resulted in a wide range of standards when it comes to due diligence and sustainable infrastructure practice, with many national host government environmental policies containing significant gaps in community engagement, accountability and due diligence protections. Where economic development is prioritised over environmental protection, the result is significantly lower standards for community engagement on climate-related oversight. As noted by a senior official at the New Development Bank, 'we apply the country standards to our projects'.[55] Thus far, a similar approach has been taken by most national development banks in China in the context of overseas infrastructure investment. Recent experience has demonstrated that national standards, while diverse and evolving, have often not been sufficiently comprehensive in preventing environmental and social harm.

Increasingly, companies must adhere to relevant ESG standards in supply chains as a contractual obligation through due diligence and remedy clauses that may result in breach of warranty claims[56] and shareholder disputes[57] in the private law context. For example, the International Bar Association recently issued a report on the use of ESG contractual obligations and related disputes. This recent development has contributed to preventing some environmental harms and community level disputes by ensuring self-directed compliance at the company level.

Practitioners working in China's rail and port development shared their experiences in dispute prevention and resolution in the context of major infrastructure projects. One legal practitioner noted that the nature of recent contracting models in China have changed from

53 Asia Global Dialogue, 2023, Speaker 1.
54 Ibid.
55 Asia Global Dialogue, 2023, Speaker 2.
56 AALCO Conference 2023, Speaker 1.
57 AALCO Conference 2023, Speaker 2.

traditional contracts to 'Engineering, Procurement and Construction, and Build, Operate, Transfer, or Build, Transfer and financing over the past 10 years'[58] in mega construction projects 'with 80% of this business in Asian and African countries'.[59] This practitioner shared that China's contribution to global construction will remain 'an important part of international economic cooperation … for a long time in the future'.[60] The main areas of focus will be in 'energy and communications' with 'longer construction periods [and] decades of operation cycles'. China's legal standards are increasingly referenced in such projects in approximately 30% of such cases. For port operations, conflicts may arise in relation to 'contract disputes, port operations, leasing, warehousing, damages, clash of vessels, damage to cargo, rights of land use, environmental legislation and administrative disputes'.[61] The approach to resolving these disputes will largely 'depend on the dispute itself'.[62] Arbitration remains an attractive approach. This business executive mentioned that 'we used to be learners … [and] didn't have much choice [in the resolution method], but now we are the largest port operator in the world, so we have the power to choose the way to resolve disputes'.[63] Efficiency, neutrality, confidentiality, enforceability and cost are also important.[64]

An in-house counsel at a light rail company noted the utility of multi-tiered approaches to resolution. She observed that given the complexity of 'mega infrastructure projects', which 'are complex and technical in nature – involve[ing] multiple currencies, insurance, supply chain, complex legal documents, liquidated damages … over a long duration and involve[ing] a number of parties (government, consultants, contractors and sub-contractors)',[65] it is useful to resolve issues through use of 'multi-tiered dispute resolution processes, beginning with submitting the dispute to an engineer then to mediation, then arbitration'.[66] The company makes extensive use of 'non-contractual negotiation between senior parties, or through third party assessment … This allows you to use separate and distinct methods – leaving only the challenging disputes for more formal

58 AALCO Conference 2023, Speaker 3.
59 Ibid.
60 Ibid.
61 AALCO Conference 2023, Speaker 4.
62 Ibid.
63 Ibid.
64 Ibid.
65 AALCO Conference 2023, Speaker 5.
66 Ibid.

mechanisms – to save cost with minimal disruption to the project.'[67] In achieving resolution, neutrality and fairness are core concerns. Through this multi-tiered mechanism, a variety of disputes were resolved including a signalling issue and payment schedule through direct negotiation and a ground condition claim through third-party assessment. The counsel noted that there is 'no one size fits all when resolving mega infrastructure projects'[68] and 'different approaches will be appropriate, depending on the nature of the dispute and parties involvement. The key is the business relationship that allows the project to get delivered.'[69] She added that 'risk allocation has to be fair, you should want each party to benefit, otherwise one party will bring claim'.[70]

Conclusion

This chapter has examined the attitudes and perceptions of fifty-five practitioners engaged in infrastructure-related dispute prevention in the Asia Pacific region. The aim of the survey and follow-up conversations was to provide insights into the dynamics, challenges and lessons learned in engaging with communities to prevent and manage disputes in the context of infrastructure projects. The principal finding of this chapter, based on survey data and follow-up questions, is that from the perspective of regional practitioners, prior community consultation is considered the most effective approach to preventing infrastructure disputes. A number of challenges continue to exist in mitigation efforts, with the most challenging being the 'lack of agreement on shared economic benefits' and 'limited communication'. Overall, practitioners advised that most disputes arise because 'there was no consultation or inadequate consultation with a marginalised part of the community'.[71]

Respondents offered suggestions on how community–investor dispute resolution systems might be improved, including the need for more public 'promotion'[72] of community consultation and grievance mechanisms, and a clear consultation process to encourage better understanding of those engaged.[73] and more efforts to

[67] Ibid.
[68] Ibid.
[69] Ibid.
[70] Ibid.
[71] Survey No. 11 (22 September 2022 11:32 a.m.).
[72] Survey No. 19 (15 June 2022 08:10 a.m.).
[73] Survey No. 22 (14 June 2022 18:33 p.m.).

educate the community so that they 'understand ... the risk of investment'.[74] Follow-up conversations between 2021 and 2023 with practitioners working in dispute mitigation offered additional insights into themes such as shared learning between multilateral banks on the development of dispute mitigation mechanisms, the duty of consultation and social license to operate, the development of hybrid forms of resolution, mitigation through early consultation and dispute boards, the exploration of appropriate diligence standards whether domestic or global in infrastructure financing programmes, the internalisation of ESG standards into contracting agreements, an emphasis on long-term contracting models and multi-tiered approaches to resolution.

Given the small size of the survey sample, the findings cannot be considered generalisable. As prior studies have noted, self-reported perceptions are subject to bias and statements may not always reflect actual practice.[75] However, the findings of this chapter demonstrate the overall significance of prior community consultation and effective grievance mechanisms in the infrastructure dispute mitigation context, and provide insights into the dynamics of project data analysis findings in Chapter 3 and case study findings in the following chapters.

[74] Survey No. 23 (14 June 2022 18:03 p.m.).
[75] Wall & Kressel, Research on mediator style.

5

Discretionary Pre-project Community Engagement Cases in the Asia Pacific

Introduction

As discussed in Chapter 4, prior to 2013, the standards regarding pre-project community engagement and accountability on the part of infrastructure investment banks were less stringent than those in place following 2013. This chapter presents a series of six investor–community case studies in the Asia Pacific region during the pre-2013 period in order to understand the impact of relatively relaxed community engagement standards on subsequent grievance claims. This set of six cases will be compared with a set of six cases presented in Chapter 6 after heightened diligence standards were introduced after 2013.

The cases reviewed in this chapter were either sole-financed projects by the International Finance Corporation (IFC)/World Bank or collaborative projects with the Asian Development Bank (ADB) and European Investment Bank (EIB) in the Asia Pacific region. The sectors include investment in transport, the extractive industry and special economic zone (SEZ) development.

The key finding of this chapter is that during this pre-2013 discretionary community consultation phase (Table 4), the majority of cases resulted in either full or partial project cancellation, delay, suspension, compensation for harms or transfer to local courts for resolution. A small portion were dismissed due to insufficient information. In total, of the six cases examined, four were cancelled or stalled, one proceeded to court litigation and one was closed. The cases highlight the risks of insufficient attention to community consultation, the necessity of maintaining relationships with decision makers that emerge over the course of a project life cycle, the need for genuine multi-directional rather than 'uni-directional' consultation and the importance of thorough prior environmental and social (E&S) impact assessment (ESIA). Prior to 2013, standards for pre-project community engagement were relatively lax. The primary issues raised in

Table 4 *Phase 1: 'informing the community': pre-2013 multilateral development bank models of community engagement and resulting challenges.*

No.	Name	Country	Sector	Stakeholders	Issues	Year	Result
1	IFC/World Bank Cambodia Airport II project	Cambodia	Airport extension	Landowners, government	Societe Concessionaire de l'Aeroport (SCA) did not provide detailed information or consult the complainants; local residents were instructed to leave their homes without compensation and were unable to properly use their farmlands	2006	Grievances resolve, locals compensated; project in part cancelled: 10 m of 17 m loan undispersed

2	IFC/World Bank Mongolian Oyu Tolgoi community–investor dispute case	Mongolia	Copper and gold mine	Indigenous peoples/local community	Insufficient consultation, improper use of water in project threatened to disrupt livelihood of nomadic herders, dry up the local water systems, diminish yields and water supply to forests, posing a threat to local culture	2010	Resolved resettlement, compensation, herder services, and pastureland management plan issues; project faced complications for over seven years
3	World Bank Indonesia PT Weda Bay Nickel (WBN) project	Indonesia	Nickel and cobalt mine and a hydro-metallurgical processing plant	Indigenous peoples/local community	Forced relocation of Indigenous people from their community, lack of assessment or mapping to	2010	Case was transferred to Compliance Advisor Ombudsman (CAO) Compliance and

Table 4 (*cont.*)

No.	Name	Country	Sector	Stakeholders	Issues	Year	Result
					prevent damage to cultural heritage, inadequate information on impacts on biodiversity and pollution, lack of consultation with local community and of transparency, economic harm, likely grassroots resistance		was closed after being found to not merit an audit upon further review
4	ADB/IFC/EIB Bangladesh Lafarge Surma Cement (LSC) case	Bangladesh, India	Mining operation	Landowners, Indigenous peoples/local community	Use and transfer of land without consent of owners, disruption of livelihood, demographic	2005	Land issue referred to local courts for resolution; case closed; CAO reluctant to pursue investigation

					impact on Indigenous groups, unsustainable mining practices. Later concerns: insufficient local engagement, resettlement without prior full consent, inaccurate land documentation, limited external monitoring		without a broader group of individuals raising complaint
5	IFC Philippines Mindoro resources project	Philippines	Two-phased exploratory mining project	Local community and Indigenous population	Pollution of a nearby lake, threatening biodiversity and water supply, dis-turbances to Indigenous ways of life and tribal unity.	2000 (first), 2010 (second)	The project was ultimately suspended. The CAO found that any immediate risks were 'mitigated' by the suspension and

Table 4 (*cont.*)

No.	Name	Country	Sector	Stakeholders	Issues	Year	Result
					Dissatisfactory consultative process: consultation was uni-directional, consent given was not full prior consent, alleged issues of undue influence and illegitimate signatories		longer-term risks were reduced by agreement between the IFC and the company
6	IFC/World Bank Papua New Guinea (PNG) SEZ project	PNG	SEZ for fishery	Landowners, government	Lack of community consultation with landowners in the area, lack of environmental planning, impacts to fish populations, reefs and lagoons, and wider social, environmental impacts	2009	Introduced Madang Environmental Office project stalled for more than ten years

project complaints included insufficient community consultation, lack of environmental planning, inadequate compensation for relocation, damage to local resources including water and farmland, economic harm, forced land transfer, undue influence, lack of consent and limited external monitoring.

Phase 1 (Pre-2013) Case Overview

Overall, cases examined prior to 2013 highlight the risks of insufficient attention to community consultation, the necessity of maintaining relationships with new governmental decision makers that emerge over the course of a project life cycle, the need for genuine multi-directional rather than 'uni-directional' consultation and the importance of thorough prior ESIA. The IFC/World Bank Cambodia Airport II project demonstrates the importance of involving all key stakeholders at the outset of a project and providing full information disclosure. While compensation was ultimately provided for relocation, elements of the project had to be cancelled. The IFC/World Bank Mongolian Oyu Tolgoi community–investor dispute case demonstrates how insufficient pre-project consultation and water resource management planning resulted in seven years of project complications and delay. The World Bank Indonesia PT WBN project similarly demonstrated the dangers of a lack of consultation and transparency on subsequent project progression. The ADB/IFC/EIB Bangladesh LSC case, which implemented a lower standard of 'informed participation' rather than full consultation and consent, resulted in inaccurate land documentation, limited external monitoring and limited engagement, resulting in the subsequent transfer of the dispute to the local courts. The IFC Philippines Mindoro resources project demonstrated the importance of oversight of de-centralised consultative process involving local government authorities, company representatives and Indigenous populations. Risks arising from illegitimate consent, lack of transparency, ineffective social and economic audits and obfuscation of facts resulted in the dissolution of trust between parties and ultimate suspension of the project. Finally, the PNG SEZ project further demonstrated the link between the lack of sufficient prior consultation with community land owners and environmental impact assessment and the subsequent stalling of the project for ten years.

Overall, these cases highlight the significance of meaningful pre-project consultation for the prevention of delay, cancellation or litigation and achievement of the long-term success of the project. They also raise certain questions, including how large numbers of people might meaningfully engage in consultations regarding development initiatives that affect their community, how might these consultations be of a manageable size to facilitate meaningful and focused discussion, and the criteria that might be used to determine who participates in these consultations.

Overview of the Role of the CAO in Case Handling

The large majority of pre-2013 cases examined in this chapter were handled by the Office of the CAO. The CAO was amongst the first accountability and recourse mechanism established for investment projects undertaken or supported by the IFC and the Multilateral Investment Guarantee Agency (MIGA).[1] Both the IFC[2] and the MIGA[3] are member institutions of the World Bank Group, and have as their respective mandates the promoting economic growth in developing countries across the globe through the facilitation of foreign direct investment towards the private sectors of said countries.

The CAO serves three roles: dispute resolution, compliance and advisory.[4] Prior to the CAO's engagement of any of its three roles, the CAO undertakes a period of assessment of all relevant factors of the complaints by local communities claiming to be affected by the projects supported by either the IFC or the MIGA. The results of the assessment exercise determine whether the CAO will then proceed to dispute resolution or compliance.[5] The need for its advisory role will in turn be informed by whether the dispute resolution or compliance phases have revealed systemic issues in the IFC or the MIGA's approach towards assessing the E&S impacts of their supported projects that warrant a revision of its policies or guidelines.[6]

1 The Office of the CAO (n.d.). About the CAO: Who We Are. www.cao-ombudsman.org/about/whoweare/.

2 IFC (n.d.). About IFC. www.ifc.org/wps/wcm/connect/corp_ext_content/ifc_external_corporate_site/about+ifc_new.

3 Multilateral Investment Guarantee Agency, World Bank Group (n.d.). What We Do. www.miga.org/what-we-do.

4 The Office of the CAO (n.d.). About the CAO: Our Roles. www.cao-ombudsman.org/about/ourroles/index.html.

5 The Office of the CAO (2013). CAO Operational Guidelines 2013. www.cao-ombudsman.org/howwework/documents/CAOOperationalGuidelines2013_ENGLISH.pdf, p. 15.

6 Ibid, pp. 28–29.

CAO Dispute Resolution

The CAO dispute resolution process consists of a combination of joint fact finding, participant training, joint stakeholder consultations, shuttle diplomacy, mediation and facilitated resolution.

CAO Compliance Appraisal

If the CAO concludes that parties are not able to reach a facilitated solution after its assessment, the case is transferred to CAO Compliance for appraisal and potential compliance investigation.[7] The focus of the appraisal is on the IFC, not the client. The CAO assesses how the IFC assured itself of the performance of its business activity or advice, and whether the outcomes of its project are consistent with the intent of the relevant policy provisions. In assessing the performance of the project and IFC's implementation of measures to meet the relevant requirements, the CAO, in some cases, reviews the clients' actions and verifies outcomes in the field.[8]

The Compliance appraisal is conducted to determine whether a Compliance investigation is warranted. The Compliance appraisal is done to ensure that Compliance investigations are initiated 'only for those projects that raise substantial concerns regarding environmental and/or social outcomes, and/or issues of systemic importance to the IFC'.[9]

To guide the appraisal process, the CAO applies criteria to test the value of undertaking a compliance investigation. This is done as the CAO seeks to determine whether:

- There is evidence of potentially significant adverse environmental and/or social outcome(s) now, or in the future.
- There are indications that a policy or other appraisal criteria may not have been adhered to or properly applied by IFC/MIGA.
- There is evidence that indicates that IFC's/MIGA's provisions, whether or not complied with, have failed to provide an adequate level of protection.[10]

[7] CAO (2008). CAO Appraisal Report for Audit of IFC: Case of Wilmar Group (Report No. C-I-R6-Y08-F096). www.cao-ombudsman.org/sites/default/files/downloads/CAO_Appraisal_Report_C_I_R6_Y08_F096_ENGLISH.pdf, p. 3.

[8] Ibid, p. 3.

[9] Ibid, p. 3.

[10] Ibid, p. 3.

When conducting the appraisal, the CAO engages with the IFC team that worked on the project and other stakeholders to understand the criteria the IFC used to assure itself of the project's performance, how the IFC assured itself of the compliance with these criteria, how the IFC assured itself that these provisions provided an adequate level of protection, and whether a compliance investigation was the appropriate response. The CAO can close the case or initiate a compliance investigation after the Compliance appraisal has been completed.[11]

The CAO advises the IFC, the President of the World Bank Group, the Board, and the complainant of the conclusion of the Compliance appraisal in writing. The summary of the appraisal results will be made public. If the CAO decides to initiate a compliance investigation, the CAO will draw up terms of reference for the Compliance investigation in accordance with the CAO's Operational Guidelines.[12]

Case 1: IFC/World Bank Cambodia Airport II Project

Overview

The IFC/World Bank Cambodia Airport II Project case demonstrates the importance of involving all key stakeholders at the outset of a project, the need for flexibility and focus, awareness of external constraints and providing scope for parties to weigh various options for resolution.

Background

The SCA is a special purpose company that holds a forty-five-year concession (from 1995) from the Royal Government of Cambodia (RGC) to operate the Phnom Penh International Airport, the Siem Reap International Airport and the Sihanoukville International Airport (SIA; now known as Sihanouk International Airport).[13]

Sihanoukville was established in the 1950s and has been identified by the RGC as forming one of the cornerstones of the country's tourism development along with Phnom Penh and Siem Reap.[14] The airport itself

[11] Ibid, p. 3.
[12] Ibid, p. 3.
[13] IFC (2007). *Cambodia Airport II: Environmental & Social Review Summary*. https://disclosures.ifc.org/project-detail/ESRS/25332/cambodia-airp-ii.
[14] Ibid.

was built in the 1960s, 15 km from Sihanoukville's city centre, and is a small airport with limited facilities.[15]

Financed and developed at the SCA's initiative, the RGC developed a master plan for the development of Sihanoukville to guide long-term development in the region through 2040.[16] The plan calls for the development of an international airport, which was intended to contribute to the expansion of logistical and port activity in Sihanoukville, and to the development of tourism along the coastal region.[17] This project would have had a significant impact on the Cambodian economy, as the RGC was aggressively promoting tourism in Cambodia, especially near the Sihanoukville coastline. Hence, the expansion of SIA was critical to the effort to grow the tourism industry. The RGC sought funding from the IFC as other sources of long-term limited resourcing financing were practically non-existent in Cambodia.[18]

In 2004, the IFC approved a USD10 million A loan to support the SCA's capital expenditure programme in Phnom Penh and Siem Reap. In 2006, the RGC expanded its airport concession with the SCA to include the development and operation of SIA. In 2007, the IFC approved a second project that reflected this change, and invested in it in 2008.[19]

The project itself was expected to cost USD40.1 million, and consisted of mandatory capital investments of USD7.5 million required under the concession for SIA for 2006 and 2007, and a future capital investment of USD10 million for the construction of a new runway at SIA in 2008–2010 if airport traffic increased in accordance with the SCA's projections.[20] In short, the project involved financing capital expenditures and runway investments for SIA.[21]

As part of the land acquisition process for SIA's expansion, the RGC issued a 'Land Freeze Sub-Decree' in March 2006, which prohibited

[15] Ibid.

[16] Ibid.

[17] Ibid.

[18] IFC (2007). *Cambodia Airport II: Summary of Proposed Investment*. https://disclosures.ifc.org/project-detail/SPI/25332/cambodia-airp-ii.

[19] Office of the CAO (2010). *Ombudsman Assessment Report: Complaint Regarding IFC's Cambodia Airport II Project*. www.cao-ombudsman.org/cases/document-links/documents/CambodiaAirportAssessmentReportFINALWebsite.pdf, p. 3; IFC, *Cambodia Airport II: Environmental & Social Review Summary*.

[20] Office of the CAO, *Ombudsman Assessment Report*, pp. 3–4; IFC, *Cambodia Airport II: Environmental & Social Review Summary*.

[21] CAO (2015). *Conclusion Report: Cambodia Airport II*. www.cao-ombudsman.org/cases/document-links/documents/Conclusion_Rpt_Sihanoukville_ENG.pdf, p. 1.

new construction and land transfers within 682 hectares of SIA, with the exception of land transfers to the RGC.[22] The RGC also appointed a Land Acquisition Committee (LAC) in April 2006 to deal with land acquisition. The SCA made an inventory of the buildings located in the area in January 2007, and the SCA would have had developed a Resettlement Framework – to be approved by the IFC – that outlined procedures to address any physical or economic displacement associated with airport expansion.[23]

USD10 million of the USD17.5 million loan remained undisbursed and was cancelled by the IFC in December 2009 because of the global financial crisis and the changing economic environment in Cambodia.[24]

The Pre-project Community Consultation Process

According to the complaint, the SCA did not provide detailed information or consult the complainants.[25]

According to the IFC's website, the LAC and local authorities, who were responsible for disclosing information about the project to the local community, held meetings to keep the public informed. One of the main concerns expressed at the meetings was the compensation price for land, which was at that point still under consideration by the LAC. The LAC also met with local authorities, government representatives, village chiefs and local representatives on a regular basis.[26] However, no details of the content of these meetings is available.

The IFC's website also stated that the SCA was required to set up appropriate grievance mechanisms or procedures to address complaints, and that the SCA would have had to develop its own community engagement programme to keep the local community informed and to express its concerns.[27] As part of the programme, the SCA would have organised meetings to discuss the positive and negative impacts of the project and how the negative impacts would be addressed; the SCA would have communicated with other stakeholders to ensure local residents were

[22] IFC, *Cambodia Airport II: Environmental & Social Review Summary.*

[23] Ibid.

[24] CAO, *Ombudsman Assessment Report*, p. 4; IFC, *Cambodia Airport II: Summary of Proposed Investment.*

[25] CAO (2009). *Complaint Regarding IFC's Cambodia Airport II Project.* www.cao-ombudsman.org/cases/document-links/documents/CambodiaComplaintforwebsiteredacted.pdf, p. 1.

[26] IFC, *Cambodia Airport II: Environmental & Social Review Summary.*

[27] Ibid.

aware of employment and other economic opportunities created by the project; and procedures would have been included to receive and respond to complaints.[28] However, no details of the implementation of this mechanisms is available.

The Community Complaint

A coalition of local and national non-governmental organisations (NGOs) filed a complaint with the Office of the CAO on behalf of seventy-nine families who live on or hold land adjacent to SIA in December 2009.[29]

The complaint raised concerns about 'improper land acquisition and compensation, loss of livelihoods, noise pollution, environmental impact to a national park, incorrect E&S categorisation by the IFC, lack of community consultation, and inadequate disclosure of project information to impacted communities'.[30] The complaint also stated that the SIA project was not compliant with IFC requirements, that many of the complainants lived in close proximity to SIA and many owned land.[31]

The complainants were told to move out without any further information. The complainants stated that they were willing to move, but would require fair compensation for their land.[32] The complaint noted that, despite the numerous complaints that had been filed to the SCA, Prime Minister Hun Sen and the local authorities over a four-year period, the issue still had not been resolved by the SCA.[33]

The relief requested by the complainants ranged from fair compensation to detailed project information, such as the timeline for land acquisition, the method of land appraisal and whether resettlement plans were being considered.[34] Of the seventy-nine complainants, the project would affect the houses of thirty-two families, the farmlands of forty-one families, and the house and farmlands of six families. The complainants, half of whom

[28] Ibid.
[29] CAO (n.d.). *Cambodia/Cambodia Airport II-01/Preah Sihanouk*. www.cao-ombudsman.org/cases/case_detail.aspx?id=155; CAO, *Ombudsman Assessment Report*, p. 3.
[30] CAO, *Conclusion Report*, p. 1.
[31] Ibid, p. 1.
[32] CAO, *Complaint Regarding IFC's Cambodia Airport II Project*, p. 1.
[33] Ibid, p. 2.
[34] CAO, *Ombudsman Assessment Report*, p. 3.

were headed by a female land owners, wanted a solution as soon as possible, and all desired cash compensation.[35]

The Ombudsman Assessment

The complaint was deemed eligible in January 2010, since it (1) pertained to an IFC project; (2) pertained to the CAO's mandate to address the social impacts of IFC investments; and (3) the complainant was potentially affected if the social impacts occurred. The Ombudsman assessment was initiated in the same month.[36] As part of the Ombudsman assessment, the CAO interviewed various stakeholders, including the complainants, NGO representatives, the SCA, the Inter-ministerial Resettlement Commission (IRC) and provincial government representatives to understand the basis for the concerns, the issues raised and whether the parties were willing to identify acceptable options to address the concerns.[37]

The Community's Concerns

According to the CAO's Assessment Report, the complainants supported the development of SIA and recognised the beneficial role it would play in rejuvenating Cambodia's economy, but took issue with the delayed land acquisition process, specifically the lack of clarity over the right to develop their land.[38]

This lack of clarity meant that the complainants could not exercise their rights over their land or make decisions about their future. Hence, their access to the land, its use and benefits were limited because of the process, which was exacerbated by the Land Freeze Sub-Decree and the fact that only four houses were built with durable materials, and none of the houses were linked to a water network.[39]

The complaints suffered from: the inability to expand or construct new structures; the inability to maintain or improve on existing structures; disincentives to invest in agriculture or other productive activities; disincentives to invest in community services, specifically permanent infrastructure (water, sewage, power, etc.); damage to land due to recurring saline water inflows as a result of damage to and non-maintenance of the

[35] CAO, *Complaint Regarding IFC's Cambodia Airport II Project*, p. 1.
[36] CAO, *Ombudsman Assessment Report*, p. 5.
[37] Ibid, pp. 5–6.
[38] Ibid, p. 6.
[39] Ibid, p. 6; IFC, *Cambodia Airport II: Environmental & Social Review Summary.*

dam; and deprivation from NGO or aid agency-funded development projects as they were not willing to invest in a community that may be resettled.[40]

The complainants' livelihoods were affected as a result of not being able to sell their land or put it to productive use, and they felt 'imprisoned in their land'.[41]

The complainants were also not clear who was responsible for land acquisition. Some complainants believed that the SCA was responsible for land acquisition and paying land compensation, but that responsibility was in fact specifically designated to the IRC, which in turn designated a sub-commission and a series of consultation divisions, which interacted with local representatives.[42]

The Cambodian Government's Perspective

The RGC and its LAC saw the delays in the acquisition process as being due to financial reasons. There were high fluctuations in land prices and speculative pressures on the coastal areas after 2006, resulting in increased demand for compensation and placed unexpected budgetary pressures on the LAC. Additionally, the global financial crisis diminished touristic activity in Sihanoukville, but also stabilised land prices, hence creating a situation where the expectations of all parties to the land negotiations were more likely to be met.[43]

The IRC had been verifying information with community leaders and had prepared detailed documentation for the land acquisition process beginning in 2006, but there had been challenges with verifying the information and communicating with landholders, as some of them did not reside on the land.[44]

Additionally, the CAO acknowledged that the IRC was willing to accommodate multiple types of land and landholding relationships in its considerations, that there were unidentified community members that may have been affected by the land acquisition process and hence were uncertain about their status, and that there were differences in negotiation positions relating to land prices and just compensation that had yet to be reconciled.[45]

[40] CAO, *Ombudsman Assessment Report*, p. 7.
[41] Ibid, pp. 6–7.
[42] Ibid, p. 8.
[43] Ibid, p. 7.
[44] Ibid, p. 7.
[45] Ibid, pp. 7–8.

The CAO found that all sides were willing to engage in a dialogue process, and there was a desire among all for a quick resolution to the problem, more clarity over and a timetable for the land acquisition process, predictability, transparency and fair compensation for the land.[46]

The Dispute Resolution Process

The CAO began the dispute resolution process after releasing the Assessment Report in August 2010.[47] The parties (the complainants and other affected community members, NGOs, various government representatives, the SCA and the IFC) agreed to try to resolve the issues through a CAO-convened collaborative dispute resolution process, but they were unable to all meet in a joint, multi-stakeholder dialogue forum. Therefore, the CAO employed a combination of separate meetings and 'shuttle diplomacy' to facilitate the dispute resolution process between the parties.[48]

During the CAO's monitoring of commitments, some complainants raised concerns about the SCA's modifications to the interior airport boundary wall, as it led to increased flooding and drainage problems along the airport fence where they lived. In response, the CAO encouraged the SCA and the affected complainants to work together and with the relevant authorities to come to a mutually acceptable resolution.[49]

In February 2015, the CAO held a final closure meeting with twenty-two of the original complainants and the NGOs that helped the communities throughout the process. They provided feedback on the dispute resolution process and confirmed that their issues were satisfactorily resolved.[50]

The Outcome

The issue was resolved and the case was closed in May 2015 after the CAO confirmed that the complaint had been resolved to the satisfaction of the complainants, the SCA and the RGC.[51]

[46] Ibid, pp. 7–8.
[47] CAO (2015). *Summary of CAO Cases, FY 2015*. www.cao-ombudsman.org/publications/documents/CAOAnnualReport_SummaryofCAOCasesFY2015-English.pdf, p. 4.
[48] CAO, *Conclusion Report*, p. 1.
[49] Ibid, p. 1.
[50] Ibid, p. 1.
[51] CAO, Summary of CAO Cases, FY 2015, p. 4.

Regarding the complainants' concern about the impact on their livelihoods and engaging in a fair land acquisition process, the IRC had completed a resettlement action plan (RAP), in which the RGC committed to comply with the IFC's performance standards (PSs) and the IFC was given the opportunity to comment during the drafting.[52] In total, 191 families were compensated: 157 families received financial compensation, and thirty-four families received financial compensation and were resettled.[53] The elected community representative of the new resettled Teuksap Meanchey community even told the CAO during a follow-up monitoring visit, 'We are very happy here. It is better than where we lived before.'[54] The RGC also implemented an income restoration programme in partnership with Green Goal, a Cambodian consulting firm assisting with the resettlement, and Conservation and Development on Cambodia (CDCAM), one of the NGOs that helped to file the initial complaint. The programme included health education for the community, vocational training, identifying types of businesses for income generation, holding regular community meetings, and implementing and managing a community development plan.[55]

Regarding the complainants' concern about access to project information and having a local community voice in decision making, the LAC of the Council of Ministers hired Green Goal to assist with the RAP implementation, specifically the income restoration programme. Green Goal in turn partnered with CDCAM to provide consultation services to prepare the affected families for resettlement, as well as joint community planning at the resettlement sites. Green Goal and CDCAM also conducted educational workshops on fresh water systems, community administration, credit, and planning, and livelihood restoration.[56] Informational leaflets on the RAP were made available at the airport, but parties preferred to communicate and stay informed via informal local channels – such as local government commune offices, NGOs, Green Goal and community meetings.[57] Furthermore, grievances regarding land ownership, compensation amounts and

[52] CAO, *Conclusion Report*, p. 2.
[53] Ibid, p. 2.
[54] Ibid, p. 2.
[55] Ibid, p. 2.
[56] Ibid, p. 2.
[57] Ibid, p. 2.

land use were addressed through consultation at three levels: the commune, the provincial government and the LAC.[58]

Lessons Learned

Involve All Key Stakeholders

The CAO realised early on the importance of involving all the key stakeholders. The complainants, SCA and IFC could not resolve the issues at hand without the RGC, who was in charge of the resettlement process.[59] The government is typically not a primary stakeholder, but often plays an important role in supporting the dispute resolution process and may have a role to play in identifying solutions and implementing outcomes.[60] In this case, the RGC was an important partner in addressing land acquisition and resettlement concerns.[61] The RGC was actively involved in the drafting of the RAP and provided assistance with resettlement and livelihood initiatives and support for income restoration programmes.[62] The CAO also found the NGOs who assisted with filing the complaint to be key stakeholders, as they were also involved in monitoring the project and advising the complainants; and provincial government representatives also had a key role to play as well.[63] Due to the interdependence of the stakeholders, everyone's cooperation and engagement was required for a successful outcome.[64]

Be Flexible with Dispute Resolution Options

The CAO also found it key to be flexible with dispute resolution options. Where some stakeholders were unable or unwilling to engage with each other directly, it was important to be prepared to assist with the dispute resolution process in a creative and flexible manner.[65] There was no formal mediation or dialogue processes in this case, instead, the CAO and the local

[58] Ibid, pp. 2–3.

[59] Ibid, p. 3.

[60] CAO (2015). *Annual Report 2015*. www.cao-ombudsman.org/publications/documents/CAO_Annual_Report_2015.pdf, p. 24.

[61] Ibid, p. 24.

[62] Ibid, p. 24. The RGC was also actively participating in the CAO dispute resolution process in relation to Phnom Penh International Airport and the Ministry of the Interior issued a letter of support for the CAO-facilitated dialogue process in relation to the impact of rubber plantations on local communities in the Ratanakiri Province.

[63] CAO, *Conclusion Report*, p. 3.

[64] Ibid, p. 3.

[65] Ibid, p. 3.

mediator employed separate meetings and 'shuttle diplomacy' through 'good offices' to facilitate indirect and informal communication.[66] According to the CAO, this method helped to 'clarify issues, explore topics of mutual concern, reduce tensions, and ultimately address the parties' most important needs'.[67] However, the CAO noted that shuttle diplomacy does have its limitations: it was slower, less efficient and made it harder to build trust, relationships and understanding between parties.[68]

Case 2: IFC/World Bank Mongolian Oyu Tolgoi Community–Investor Dispute

Overview

The IFC/World Bank Mongolian Oyu Tolgoi community–investor dispute case demonstrates the importance of pre-project consultation given that the lack of meaningful consultation was a driving factor leading to the complications that resulted. In assessing the outcome, it was found that had there been proper pre-project consultation giving greater weight to the herder's input, the entire dispute could have been avoided. The presence of local dispute resolution facilitators was also significant in achieving effective communication between the parties, given their local understanding of culture and language. Joint fact finding supported by independent third parties was likewise significant. Finally, the involvement of the local government, given its comprehensive perspective and access to planning resources, was critical to arriving at resolution.

Background: The Oyu Tolgoi Project

The Oyu Tolgoi project (the 'Project') was a USD12 billion investment for the development of a copper and gold mine at Oyu Tolgoi in the Southern Gobi region of Mongolia. Ownership over Oyu Tolgoi LLC is divided between Turquoise Hills Resources (THR), a Canadian public company, and Erdenes Oyu Tolgoi LLC, a Mongolian state-owned holding company. The former is the majority owner (66%), while the latter owns the 34% remainder.[69]

[66] Ibid, p. 3.
[67] Ibid, p. 3.
[68] Ibid, p. 3.
[69] Office of the CAO. (April 2013). *CAO Assessment Report: Complaint Regarding the Oyu Tolgoi Project (IFC #29007 and MIGA #7041), South Gobi Province, Mongolia.*

The proposed investment of the IFC, under the World Bank Group, was a USD400 million A loan for IFC's account and a USD1 billion B loan syndicated to international commercial banks as part of the proposed USD4.5 billion project debt financing. World Bank Group's MIGA also provided guarantee against the risks of expropriation, war and civil disturbance, and breach of contract for a USD1 billion parallel debt tranche.[70] Oyu Tolgoi is managed by Rio Tinto, the majority shareholder of THR. Construction of the mine began in 2010, and the first batch of copper from the mine was shipped on 9 July 2013.[71]

The Issues That Gave Rise to the Complaint

There were two complaints lodged by local nomadic herders and community members to the CAO in relation to the Project, one in October 2012 ('First Complaint') and the other in February 2013 ('Second Complaint'). The two complaints were bundled together for the purposes of resolution, and the handling and procedures that follow were addressed together (jointly referred to as the 'Complaint').

The First Complaint originated from issues[72] concerning the project's use of land and water, which allegedly posed a disruption to the livelihood activities of nomadic herders in Khanbogd Soum, the location of the Project; the compensation and/or relocation arrangements for the herders, which were alleged to be inappropriate or inadequate; the Project's due diligence, particularly regarding the sustainable use of water in and around that area.

The Second Complaint originated from issues revolving around the Undai River diversion component of the Project:[73] jeopardisation of the herders' nomadic lifestyle and livelihood; the fear of river diversion leading to the drying up of water systems, deterioration in pastureland

www.cao-ombudsman.org/cases/document-links/documents/CAOAssessmentReport_OT_April2013_ENG.pdf.

70 Ibid.

71 Oyu Tolgoi. (9 July 2013). *Press Release: Oyu Tolgoi Begins Concentrate Shipments: Significant Milestone for Company and Mongolia*. https://web.archive.org/web/20130831001122/http://ot.mn/en/media/press-release/090713.

72 Office of the CAO, *CAO Assessment Report: Complaint Regarding the Oyu Tolgoi Project (IFC #29007 and MIGA #7041), South Gobi Province, Mongolia* (April 2013).

73 Office of the CAO (July 2013). *CAO Assessment Report: Second (Oyu Tolgoi-02) Regarding the Oyu Tolgoi Project (IFC #29007 and MIGA #7041), South Gobi Province, Mongolia*. www.cao-ombudsman.org/cases/document-links/documents/OT-2_Assessment_Report_ENG.pdf.

yields and diminishment of water supply to forests; and cultural impact given the Undai River was viewed as sacred.

The Pre-project Community Consultation Process

Since the beginning of the Project's intensive exploration phase and before the complaint was lodged, two arrangements were made between Oyu Tolgoi and the herders in an effort to address the latter's concerns as to the Project's environmental and livelihood impacts, namely the 2004 relocation programme and the 2011 compensation without relocation programme.

The Community's Access to the Consultation

While pre-project consultation took place, there was limited information as to the nature of the consultation process, if any, and whether the negotiations resulted in an agreement and were conducted fairly and on a level playing field.

Regarding the 2004 'consultation', the complaints alleged that the herders were made to select new locations at short notice, and while many resisted relocation, they eventually acceded upon the local government's threat of forced eviction.[74] This suggests that consultation with the local community, if any, was likely a formality and lacked meaning.

The 2011 'consultation' faced a similar problem. While there was discussion between the parties on the compensation package, Oyu Tolgoi was criticised for refusing to hear the herders' concerns as to the impact quantification and the issues they suffered.[75] The complainants were also not clear about the actual methodology used to determine the level of impact on herders, pointing to a lack of transparency. Oyu Tolgoi allegedly pressurised the herders into signing compensation contracts, either by threatening no compensation or procuring older herders' signatures without explanation. The herders could only raise proposed changes to the contract provisions to the working group, in which they were under-represented and had no meaningful participation.

[74] Oyu Tolgoi-01 Letter of Complaint (redacted). (12 October 2012). www.cao-ombudsman.org/cases/document-links/documents/OyuTolgoiCAOComplaint_Oct122012_Redacted.pdf.

[75] Ibid.

The Community Complaint

The complaint concerned the grievances of a group of nomadic herders residing in Khanbogd Soum where the Project was located, whose livelihoods and culture were affected by the operation of the Project. The complaint was jointly lodged by three parties: (1) Khanbogd soum herders; (2) Gobi Soil, a local Khanbogd-based NGO; and (3) OT Watch, a national NGO (together referred to as the 'Complainant').

Four main issues in the complaint included: negative impacts and unsatisfactory implementation of the 2004 relocation agreement; inappropriate criteria used for determining impacts and compensation for the 2011 compensation agreement; impropriety of the 2004 and 2011 agreements as a response to stop and/or mitigate the negative impacts inflicted by the Project such as loss of income source, decreased livestock productivity and health, water depletion and degradation of pastureland; and inappropriate and improper implementation of the compensation agreed upon in the agreements, such as protecting and monitoring living standards and vocational training.[76]

The Legal, E&S Concerns

Legal

The Complainant submitted, as part of the Second Complaint, that local community consent and approval was required for the Undai River diversion, while Oyu Tolgoi contended that they had acquired all relevant legal permissions and rights to proceed with the diversion work within the mine license area.[77] As regards to the portion to be constructed outside the mine license area, Oyu Tolgoi claimed that since they had yet to obtain the local governor's approval, construction work outside the mine license area had not yet commenced at the time of the Complaint.

Oyu Tolgoi was also criticised by the Complainant for not recognising the herders' rights to the pastures that were affected by the Project, contrary to recognition under customary law. Oyu Tolgoi justified their

[76] Battsengel, L. (24 August 2013). *Information on the Negotiation Meetings between Khanbogd soum Elected Herder Representatives and Oyu Tolgoi Company*. www.cao-ombudsman.org/cases/document-links/documents/EHT-OTJointinfoflyer_Sep-2013_ENG.pdf.

[77] Office of the CAO, *CAO Assessment Report: Second (Oyu Tolgoi-02) Regarding the Oyu Tolgoi Project (IFC #29007 and MIGA #7041), South Gobi Province, Mongolia* (July 2013).

position on the ground that the herders were not an ethnic minority.[78] The Complainant also alleged that the Undai River diversion violated their human rights under Mongolian and international laws, specifically on their rights to water, pasture, livelihood, environmental protection, and historical and cultural heritage protection.[79]

Environmental

The Complainant raised concerns regarding environmental impact. There was purportedly a lack of demonstrated availability of water resources required for the Project, and the high concentration of mining projects in the region was worrying due to scarce water resources and damage to soil in the territory.[80] Particularly, diversion of the Undai River would cause multiple water systems to be dried out, inflicting irreversible damage to pastureland.[81]

Social

Considering themselves as indigenous to the area, the herders were concerned with the Project's endangering of their Mongolian nomad lifestyle, a deep-rooted ancient tradition. The compensation offered by Oyu Tolgoi was criticised for not including mitigation or remedy for the herders' loss of opportunity to carry out their traditional nomadic herding lifestyle, and ability to pass this tradition on to their descendants. The Second Complaint also highlighted the sacredness of the Undai River in Mongolian culture.[82]

The CAO Complaints Process: Dispute Resolution

Initial Meetings

From March 2013, CAO played an active role in facilitating the resolution of the complaint between the stakeholders. Trainings were provided to both sides of the dispute in negotiation, conflict resolution and communication skills.[83] For the purposes of the joint meetings and

[78] Oyu Tolgoi-01 Letter of Complaint (redacted).
[79] Oyu Tolgoi-02 Letter of Complaint. (3 February 2013). www.cao-ombudsman.org/cases/document-links/documents/UndaiRiverComplaint_Feb32013_ENG.pdf.
[80] Oyu Tolgoi-01 Letter of Complaint (redacted).
[81] Oyu Tolgoi-02 Letter of Complaint.
[82] Ibid.
[83] Office of the CAO (May 2020). *CAO Dispute Resolution Conclusion Report: Oyu Tolgoi 01 & 02/Southern Gobi*. www.cao-ombudsman.org/cases/document-links/documents/CAOMongolia_Conclusion_Rpt_2020-05-ENG.pdf.

negotiations, an elected herders team (EHT) was formed to represent the interests of the Complainant,[84] consisting of herder representatives from each Bagh democratically elected at large public community meetings.

The initial joint meetings were considerably successful. The parties exchanged their views on the impacts of the Project operations and followed up on the others' proposed actions in each subsequent meeting. Oyu Tolgoi accepted EHT's request and agreed to provide information on the E&S impacts of the Project, organise thematic meetings to address the issues at stake, and provide access opportunities to visit project sites.[85]

Independent Expert Panel

During the meetings, the parties mutually agreed to engage, and finalised the criteria and selection of an independent expert panel (IEP) as the first joint fact-finding effort. The IEP was tasked to assess the Project's impacts on important water sources including the Undai River, the herders' pastureland, access to water and water quality.[86] The validity of Oyu Tolgoi's information and analysis was also tested. The process emphasised stakeholder participation, mainly in the form of consultations with parties such as the herder community, local government representatives and Oyu Tolgoi compliance officers. To establish mutually credible information, IEP carried out the joint fact-finding while maintaining a high level of transparency and inclusivity, clear and culturally appropriate communication and neutrality in the substance of issues and evaluation of findings.[87]

The IEP published its findings in relation to the complaint in 2015, particularly noting the irreversible disturbance to nomadic livestock due to the loss of surface water and an intensifying trend of decreasing pasture productivity due to resettlement.[88]

[84] Battsengel, *Information on the Negotiation Meetings between Khanbogd soum Elected Herder Representatives and Oyu Tolgoi Company*.

[85] Ibid.

[86] Undai River Diversion Complaint Independent Expert Panel Final Work Plan and Methodology for Joint Fact Finding Process: Phase 1 (6 December 2013). www.cao-ombudsman.org/cases/document-links/documents/FINAL_IEPWorkPlanandMethodology_ENG.pdf.

[87] Ibid.

[88] Undai River Diversion Complaint Independent Expert Panel Executive Summary. (30 January 2015). www.cao-ombudsman.org/cases/document-links/documents/ExecutiveSummary_edit_Jan_30_2015-ENG.pdf.

Establishing a TPC

The parties agreed to request the participation of the Khanbogd Soum government (KSG) in the dispute resolution process in 2014, and subsequently decided to establish a Tri-partite Council (the TPC) equally composed of representatives of EHT, Oyu Tolgoi and KSG. The TPC operated on a Memorandum of Understanding (MoU) signed in June 2015, which set out its mandate of addressing proposals and recommendations on issues relating to, inter alia, herders, pasture and water raised in the complaints to CAO.[89] It oversaw the implementation process for allocated actions such as initiatives and recommendations, and the transparent exchange and dissemination of information including pond construction at the Ust Bag Mod Quarry hollow, and close liaison with the Umnugobi Almag government's Ministry of Food and Agriculture and Ministry of Mining on implementing IEP's recommendations.[90]

Second Fact-Finding Process

In its first meeting in July 2015, the TPC embarked on a second joint fact-finding process to assess the Project's impact on the herders' livelihoods and adequacy of Oyu Tolgoi's compensation.[91] A multi-disciplinary team (MDT) was established for the socio-economic study, which upon agreement on the selection criteria, resulted in a team of researchers from JSL Consulting, the University of Oxford and the Institute for Geography and Geo-Ecology of the Mongolian Academy of Sciences.[92] The MDT assessed changes in access to and quality of pasture and herd water; changes in herders' household livelihoods; evaluation of adequacy of Oyu Tolgoi's 2004 resettlement; and 2001 economic displacement compensation.

[89] Memorandum of Understanding Relating to the Establishment of a Tri-partite Council. (8 June 2015). www.cao-ombudsman.org/cases/document-links/documents/FinalSignedMoUwithAnnexures_ENG.pdf.

[90] Tripartite Council of Khanbogd Soum Herders, Local Government and Oyu Tolgoi Company (11 January 2016). *Summary Report on 2015 Activities*. www.cao-ombudsman.org/cases/document-links/documents/2015TPCReport_ENG.pdf.

[91] Tripartite Council of Khanbogd Soum Herders, Local Government and Oyu Tolgoi Company (1 July 2015). *Statement of Tripartite Council of Khanbogd Soum Government: Herders Representatives: Oyu Tolgoi LLC*. www.cao-ombudsman.org/cases/document-links/documents/1July2015-TPCStatement_ENG.pdf.

[92] Tripartite Council of Khanbogd Soum Herders, Local Government and Oyu Tolgoi Company (25 February 2016). *Joint Statement: Khanbogd Soum Tripartite Council*. www.cao-ombudsman.org/cases/document-links/documents/JointStatement-Feb2016-English.pdf.

The study was released in January 2017. After two days of negotiations, TPC reached unanimous agreement to accept and implement eighteen of the twenty-eight recommendations proposed by the experts.

Final Outcome

After years of effort, two final agreements were reached in resolution of the complaint and were signed on 9 May 2017 as the Herders' Complaint Resolution Agreements #1 and #2 (the 'HCR Agreements'). The HCR Agreements provided for the implementation of more than sixty action items related to water, pastureland, the Undai River and compensation to herders, mostly undertaken by Oyu Tolgoi. Among others, these included:[93] resolving issues related to the 2004 resettlement's inadequacy; TPC acting as a compensation claims committee to approve retrospective compensation claims; providing support and opportunities to affected herders in education, health services, vocational trainings and employment; and developing a Khanbogd Soum pastureland management plan and joint monitoring by local herders and OT Watch. Oyu Tolgoi would be responsible for the funding for implementation of HCR Agreements.[94]

As part of the CAO complaints process, the case proceeded on to a monitoring stage by the CAO to ensure that the HCR Agreements' terms were met.[95]

Lessons Learned

Importance of Pre-project Consultation

The lack of meaningful pre-project consultation and negotiation with the herders was a driving factor leading to the complaints and complications that followed. The fact that the dispute was able to be resolved collaboratively with a mutually beneficial outcome indicates that had there been more comprehensive and proper consultation before the Project, particularly with Oyu Tolgoi giving more weight to the herders' input, the

[93] Herders' Complaint Resolution Agreement #1 (9 May 2017). www.cao-ombudsman.org/cases/document-links/documents/OT1_ComplaintResolutionAgreement1_ENG.pdf; Herders' Complaint Resolution Agreement #2 (9 May 2017). www.cao-ombudsman.org/cases/document-links/documents/OT2_ComplaintResolutionAgreement2_ENG.pdf.

[94] Tripartite Council of Khanbogd Soum Herders, Local Government and Oyu Tolgoi Company (22 March 2017). *Joint Statement: Tripartite Council of Khanbogd Soum*. www.cao-ombudsman.org/cases/document-links/documents/JointStatementMarch2017_ENG.pdf.

[95] Office of the CAO, *CAO Dispute Resolution Conclusion Report*.

dispute could have been avoided altogether. Therefore, it would be in the interests of parties to a dispute to engage in in-depth consultation and discussion on any solutions before deciding to resort to a formal dispute resolution process.

Importance of Local Personnel and Input

Collaborative dispute resolution demands the building of trust and connection between the parties and the facilitator. The engagement of local dispute resolution facilitators was important due to their understanding of the local culture, context and languages,[96] helping the parties feel more comfortable in consultations rather than seeing them as an extension of an uninterested third party. Here, the work of a Mongolian mediator was instrumental in building rapport with local herders and catalysing the dispute resolution process. Regular stakeholder meetings also facilitated trust-building by providing a platform for acquiring input for solution-finding, but also room for local stakeholders to exchange ideas and foster a communal atmosphere.

Importance of Joint Fact-Finding Processes

As evident from this dispute, joint fact-finding was an essential tool for closing the gap between the conflicting parties, enabling them to find common ground. The impartiality accorded by the independent process strengthened the credibility of shared information obtained through scientific inquiry, reducing the parties' scope of disagreement.[97] Information acquired through such a method also proved useful to other relevant third-party stakeholders such as the local government. While this process took time, the search for appropriate long-term solutions was more beneficial than resorting to short-term measures.

Significance of Local Government Involvement

Disputes involving large-scale business interests are highly complex and generally cannot be resolved simply between two major parties. As in this case, the substantial environmental and compliance issues involved required the need for the local KSG's involvement. The value of government involvement lies in the inclusion of a comprehensive perspective,

[96] Ibid.
[97] Ibid.

offering access to expertise and resources, coordination with other ongoing policy plans and improving the credibility of outcomes.[98]

On the other hand, beyond this individual dispute, at the national level, while significant pre-project consultation with relevant government entities on the parameters of project scope, benefit sharing and fee-splitting arrangements may take place, at times, governments for a variety of domestic financial factors may disregard prior agreements and seek new cost-sharing arrangements that may affect overall project implementation.

Case 3: World Bank Indonesia PT WBN Project

Introduction

The World Bank Indonesia PT WBN project case demonstrates the significance of the lack of consultation and transparency on subsequent project delays and disputes. In this case, lack of engagement with all relevant stakeholders, both at the feasibility stage but also the decision-making stage, and lack of transparency about project risk resulted in the subsequent dispute.

Background

Co-owned by Singapore-based Strand Minerals Ltd and Indonesian state-owned mining corporation PT Aneka Tambang, PT WBN proposed the construction of a nickel and cobalt mine and a hydrometallurgical processing plant in Central Halmahera and East Halmahera Regencies, North Maluku Province.[99] On 11 August 2010, a guarantee of USD207 million was issued by MIGA to Strand Minerals (Indonesia) Pte Ltd for its investment in the PT WBN project. During the three years of coverage, USD230 million was invested for engineering and feasibility studies for the operation of the nickel cobalt mine with a hydrometallurgical processing plant. It was expected that the final investment decision would be made by the end of 2012.[100]

[98] Ibid.

[99] WBN Project: Response of PT Weda Bay Nickel to the CAO Complaint, p. 1.

[100] CAO Appraisal for Audit of MIGA: Case of MIGAs Guarantee Linked to the Engineering and Feasibility Phase of Developing the PT Weda Bay Nickel Project, p. 5. www.cao-ombudsman.org/sites/default/files/downloads/CAO_Appraisal_Report_C-M-R5-Y11-F146.pdf.

On 2 July 2010, civil society organisations, consisting of (1) Friends of the Earth (WALHI), (2) the Mining Advocacy Network (JATAM), (3) the Anti-Debt Coalition (KAU) and (4) the People's Coalition for Fisheries Justice (KIARA),[101] filed a complaint about the PT WBN project.

The mining concession covered an area of 76,280 hectares ± 72,775, of which (over 95%) were forests. The allegation was that WBN's plan to open mine nickel and cobalt mining operations by way of disposing of tailings in the deep sea would result in extraordinary harm to nature. The complaint alleged that, as a result, the livelihood of those who rely on local natural resources, such as the lakes and forests, would be destroyed and that Forestry Law No. 41/1999 would be violated if WBN engaged in open mining in the Abe Kobe protected forest.[102]

The complainant requested that the CAO conduct an investigation into the project, and that, until such results were released, MIGA postpone its approval for granting a guarantee of the feasibility phase of the PT WBN project study.

The Pre-project Community Consultation Process

Public consultation was held as part of the environmental assessment in May 2008 and April 2009. Local and national NGOs including Friends of the Earth Indonesia were invited and attended the meetings.[103]

Another round of consultations with local NGOs took place in June 2010. The North Maluku branch of Friends of the Earth Indonesia was invited.[104] The third round of consultation took place in the Cemara Hotel on 14 June 2010. Several national NGOs, including JATAM, KIARA, WALHI, ICEL (International Council of Environmental Law), KAU, AMAN (Association for Mass Advancement Network), FPP (Forest Peoples Programme), HUMA (Humanitarian Medical Assistance), Birdlife, WWF, LATIN (Lembaga Alam Tropika Indonesia), Forest Watch and Greenpeace, were invited. The national branch of Friends of the Earth Indonesia and some other NGOs chose to boycott the meeting and instead held a demonstration outside the hotel.[105]

[101] Complaint Letter by Civil Society Organization, p. 1.
[102] Ibid.
[103] CAO (2011). *Ombudsman Assessment Report: Complaint Regarding the MIGA*, p. 38. www.cao-ombudsman.org/sites/default/files/downloads/WBN_Assessment_FINAL_with_appendices_ENG.pdf.
[104] Ibid, p. 19.
[105] Ibid, p. 19.

The MIGA, in its response to the ombudsman Assessment Report, claimed that it had made a public written response to issues raised by the NGO community and held meetings with the interested parties in Washington, Ternate and Jakarta in June 2010.[106]

The Community Complaint

The complainants raised several issues including concerns surrounding social and environmental management, pollution prevention and abatement, land acquisition and involuntary resettlement, biodiversity conservation, Indigenous peoples, cultural heritage and information transparency.

Social and Environmental Assessment and Management Systems

The first concern focused on the PT WBN's ESIA documents failure to take into consideration various alternatives available for exploration. In addition, required phases of the project such as construction operations and decommissioning were not covered in the ESIA. There was inadequate information regarding biodiversity and sedimentation, resulting in an inability to assess its accuracy. The project, moreover, would potentially lead to forest destruction and a water crisis since nickel mining exacts total land clearance. It was foreseeable that more than 9,000 hectares of forest would be destroyed to build housing, roads and mine shafts. The impacts on the environment would be irretrievable and far-reaching.[107]

Pollution Prevention and Abatement

As far as the impact on deforestation and the use of other lands, the risks of sedimentation had not been identified, especially given that the project would operate in the vicinity of ecologically sensitive and protectable areas such as coral reefs and national parks. The project documents did not sufficiently identify the risks of pollution. In particular, sampling methods for the composition of solid residues, health threats stemming from asbestos, methods for estimating projected contamination of dirty water flow and air pollution from sulphuric acid production were

[106] MIGA's Memorandum: Response to Ombudsman Assessment Report #8113. www.cao-ombudsman.org/sites/default/files/downloads/2011-June28MIGAResponse_AssessmentReport.pdf.

[107] CAO, *Ombudsman Assessment Report: Complaint Regarding the MIGA*, p. 14.

inadequately evaluated and addressed. Sewage treatment, disposal facilities and residue storage facilities were also not sufficiently explored. The documents provided little basis for the statement that ground water would be replenished in limestone mines.[108]

The complainant expressed concern regarding tailings planned for disposal into the sea. Such a system would create pollution to the Weda Bay maritime ecosystem and destroy maritime organisms in Buyat Bay. Rock and heavy metals produced in the Santamonica mine shaft would contaminate local rivers and ground water through water flow from the mine shaft. This would deprive the Weda community, given their dependence on rivers, of clean water for their everyday needs.[109]

Land Acquisition and Involuntary Resettlement

The Tobelo Forest people who live in the area where construction work would take place would likely have had to leave their homes. This fact was inconsistent with the proposal's statement that 'it is hoped that there will be no physical dispossession of families from their homes' (V-1) and the claim that no moving or dispossession actions are needed.[110]

Biodiversity Conservation and Sustainable Natural Resource Management

The inaccuracy and insufficiency of basic information on biodiversity in the ESIA was another issue of concern. Almost half of the work area was protected forest under Forestry Law No. 41/1999, 'whose main function [was] to protect the life support systems for hydrology, prevent floods, control erosion, protect from sea water intrusion and guard soil fertility'. The ESIA failed to provide guarantees as to the protection of the critical habitat where species endemic to Halmahera or Maluku reside. No buffer zone was planned to cater to the protection of the national parks 4 km from the project area. Fragmentation of the habitat resulting from deforestation would damage the forest regions.[111]

While some rehabilitation and improvement exercises were proposed, the feasibility and practicability were not addressed properly. Projections that the natural forest would be able to be restored in twenty years lacked proof. The project was also criticised for being a 'commercial mining

[108] Ibid, p. 3.
[109] Ibid.
[110] Ibid, p. 4.
[111] Ibid, pp. 4–6.

operation', given that the wood from land clearing was to be on sale in the market.[112]

Indigenous Peoples

The complaint alleged that WBN should have designed a project in such a way as to prevent the relocation of Indigenous people from their community. It should have consulted with communities on relocation plans and documented the potential project impacts.[113]

Cultural Heritage

The complaint alleged that there was a duty on the part of the WBN, at the very least, to prevent substantial damage to cultural heritage. Any alterations, damage or removal of critical cultural heritage should be avoided. However, 'the project area has still not been fully mapped in detail and assessed for its tangible cultural heritage'. WBN, therefore, cannot be said to be 'responsible for the mapping and design of a project to avoid significant damage to cultural heritage' or to have protected the critical cultural heritage.[114]

The complainant also criticised WBN's approach to other issues, namely consultation and community involvement, transparency of information, and social, economic and political risks.[115]

Consultation and Community Involvement

The complaint expressed concern that a number of meetings were held with the civil society and some local NGOs, including the North Halmahera Friends of the Earth, however, these NGOs denied having such a meeting with them.[116]

Transparency of Information

The complaint also stated that until April 2020, documents relating to the project were not made available on MIGA's website. Members of the public found it difficult to access the relevant information.[117]

[112] Ibid.
[113] Ibid, p. 7.
[114] Ibid.
[115] Ibid.
[116] Ibid.
[117] Ibid, p. 8.

Social, Economic and Political Risks

The local community relied on forest resources for various everyday needs, and resource scarcity could give rise to conflict. In addition, perceived damage to the Batu Gua Lubang, a place sacred to the community, would trigger great resistance. The pollution arising out of mining operations would not only eliminate the clean water and sources of clean food in the area, but also damage their source of income, with no benefit to local communities.[118]

The Complaint Handling Process

The CAO received the complaint in July 2010. The CAO sought to clarify the issues and concerns raised in the complaint and reviewed the project documents, including MIGA, WBN and NGO files. They then conducted interviews and focus group discussions with the complainants, MIGA's project team, project sponsors and additional affected community members. They also made country missions and project site visits to North Maluku on three occasions (in October 2010, November 2010 and January 2011). The team subsequently planned to assist the parties in making a decision as to their various options resolving the complaint.[119]

Upon assistance from the CAO in exploring options for resolving the concerns raised in the complaint, in June 2011, the office concluded that the dialogue process might not be suitable for the parties involved. The case was then transferred to CAO's Compliance for appraisal.[120] The CAO Compliance appraisal sought to investigate whether the case should proceed to the stage of a Compliance audit, which would depend on whether the case involved substantial concerns with regards to social or environmental outcomes.[121] The CAO appraisal also determined the question of whether the MIGA 'has diligently reviewed and assessed the environment and social risk, and potential environment and social impacts, of the development of the WBN Project'.[122]

[118] Ibid, pp. 8–9.

[119] *Ombudsman Assessment Report: Complaint Regarding the MIGA PT Weda Bay Nickel Project (#8113)*, Halmahera Island, North Maluku, Indonesia, p. 7.

[120] Ibid.

[121] Ibid, note 2, p. 3.

[122] Ibid, p. 5.

Ombudsman Assessment Report

WBN expressed its willingness to take part in a dialogue process with the complainants and other local community members. However, upon discussion with the CAO team, the complainants decided not to engage in a dispute resolution or dialogue process convened by the CAO to protect community confidentiality. The complaint was thus transferred to CAO's Compliance for appraisal in accordance with the CAO Operational Guidelines.[123]

The CAO also offered to conduct a workshop for all stakeholders, including government representatives, local community members and WBN staff. Such a workshop, which sought to strengthen mutual understanding surrounding issues such as 'methods and approaches of dispute prevention and early response; grievance mechanisms and non-adversarial dispute settlement; and best practices for constructive stakeholder communication and interaction', attracted the support from both WBN and the complainants. According to the report, the CAO aimed to conduct the workshop within two months of the release of the report.[124]

The case was transferred to CAO Compliance for further action. Upon further review, the case was found to not merit an audit. The case was closed with no further action.

Lessons Learned

Pre-project consultation is central, particularly for projects that may have an impact on the environment and livelihood of residents. To understand the concerns of stakeholders, it is important that all interested parties engage in an open dialogue. Community engagement does not stop at consultation. Developers should involve the local community and relevant NGOs not only in the feasibility stage but also the decision-making stage of the project.

Transparency is another key factor. In this particular case, the complaint expressed concerns regarding the lack of open and complete information,[125] including information on environmental protection strategies, risks identified and mitigatory measures in a manner understandable to the general public.

[123] Ibid, note 21, p. 9.
[124] Ibid, p. 10.
[125] Ibid, note 1.

Case 4: ADB/IFC/EIB Bangladesh LSC

Introduction

In the ADB/IFC/EIB Bangladesh LSC case, a process of informed participation (a lower standard of engagement) rather than full and meaningful consultation, limited environmental, social and governance diligence standards and resettlement without prior full consent, inaccurate land documentation, limited external monitoring and limited engagement with local stakeholders resulted in the subsequent dispute. Ultimately, the land issue was referred to the local courts for resolution.

Background

A complaint was filed in relation to the LSC ('the Project'), a mining operation funded by the IFC together with the ADB, DEG – Deutsche Investitions and Entwicklungesellschaft MBH – EIB, the Arab Bangladesh Bank and Standard Chartered Bank, Bangladesh.

The Project involved the construction and operation of an integrated, dry process cement plant,[126] which was based in the Chhatak, Sunamganj district of Bangladesh. It also involved another limestone quarrying and crushing operation located in Meghalaya. The two operations were connected by an overhead conveyor belt.[127] In May 2005, an informal complaint was lodged and the IFC sent a review team comprised of four people. No report was ever released to the complainants as promised by the review team.[128]

Lafarge Surma Cement Ltd ('LSC or The Company') completed construction of a cement plant with a capacity of 1.2 million tons per year in north-east Bangladesh in 2006. A quarry operated by a subsidiary in the neighbouring Indian state of Meghalaya supplied the plaint with limestone via a 17-kilometer cross-border conveyor belt.[129]

The present complaint was filed by three individuals from Shella village, East Khasi Hills district in the State of Meghalaya, India, in January 2014.

[126] CAO Assessment Report regarding local stakeholders concerns in relation to IFC's project with Lafarge Surma Cement (#8035) in India dated May 2014, p. 5.

[127] Ibid.

[128] Complaint Letter: 'Indigenous Peoples' Land mortgaging, impoverishment, social chaos and ecological destruction in IFC support for Lafarge Surma Cement mining in Khasi Territory of Meghalaya' dated 6 January 2014, p. 1.

[129] CAO Appraisal Report: IFC Investment in Lafarge Surma Cement (IFC Project #8035), India, dated 14 October 2014, p. 1.

While the complainants requested dispute resolution, LSC claimed that it was not prepared to engage in a dispute resolution process.[130]

The Company published information outlining its position on the issues raised in the complaint. It asserted that it was in compliance with the laws of the land and the essential approvals were obtained under the Meghalaya Transfer of Land Act (1971). It also alleged that the durbars of Nongtrai and Shella Villages had approved their acquisition of the relevant lands in the Project.

Pre-project Community Consultation Process: The India Social Impact Assessment, the Indigenous Peoples' Development Plan and Consultation[131]

As required by the loan agreement, the Company commissioned a social impact assessment for the India components of the Project, which was reviewed and disclosed by IFC. The India social impact assessment found that the residents of the project area were almost exclusively Khasi tribe; tribal land in Meghalaya could only be transferred to a non-tribal person with government clearance and approval from the relevant durbar; the mine site was located in community land belonging to Nongtrai Village, and the conveyer belt crossed mostly private lands owned by people from Shella Village; and there was a need to acquire land from fifty-four families to build the conveyor belt track.

For consultation and disclosure, it was reported that the Project proponents engaged in stakeholder consultation on the India components of the project commencing in late 1998. Detailed discussions with landowners regarding the land required for the conveyor belt were held. Negotiations were conducted with Shella and Nongtrai durbars.

The India social impact assessment also set out the legal framework for land tenure in the project area, the grievance mechanism and internal and external monitoring measures. The social impact assessment included an Indigenous Peoples' Development Plan, which set out the allocation of funds and provision of technical assistance to the durbars in support of community development activities; the establishment of a health centre at the mine site; and the provision of an annual grant to Shella durbar for community development activities.

130 Ibid, p. 4.
131 Ibid, pp. 8–10.

The Community Complaint

According to the community complaint, the impacts of the Project could be categorised into two areas, namely land ownership and land alienation and institutional change.[132]

Land Ownership

With respect to the land ownership complaint, the Project was alleged to have infringed the ownership of the land in Shella and the Tynger village as it was carried out without any notice to or consent from the land owners. Mining was carried out while a conveyor belt was built through their lands, which operated from Shella village to Bangladesh. In addition, fencing was erected around the land and the land owners were forbidden to enter into their own lands.

Land Alienation and Institutional Change

Regarding land alienation, first it was alleged that the land of Shella and Tynger village was used by LSC without the owners' consent or knowledge. Second, some land of Shella village was sold by some individuals from the village without the villagers' consent. Third, the land bought by Lum Maushun Minerals Private Ltd (LMMPL) was transferred to Lafarge Umium Mining Private Ltd (LUMPL) and mortgaged eventually to the banks.

The issue of whether these purchase and leasing arrangements were legal under Schedule 6 of the Constitution of India, and whether Indigenous people's land could be transferred to non-Indigenous people or companies was discussed in the Guwahati High Court.

A further concern was that the land of the Shella and Tynger village was used by Lafarge without its consent. The Nongtrai village leased its land to LMMPL. Subsequently, Lafarge made an illegal transfer of the land that belonged to the people of Shella and Tynger village. It was only at the time of project construction that the real land owners realised their lands were being used.[133]

In addition, it was claimed that the land of Shella village was sold by some individuals from the village without the real land owners' consent. Therefore, the purchase of land by LMMPL for the conveyor belt was illegal. The so-called headman of Shella village, in collaboration with the

[132] CAO (2014). *Lafarge Complaint*, pp. 2–5. www.cao-ombudsman.org/sites/default/files/downloads/LafargeComplaintredacted.pdf.

[133] Ibid, pp. 3–4.

project authorities, granted land ownership certificates to eighty-nine villagers who were not the real owners of the land, without the endorsement of the Shella village court.

The purported headman was a shareholder of LMMPL and played a key role in acquiring land and mining rights for it. It was also alleged that he had no authority to exercise any right over the land of the village on the basis of letters written by the then-deputy commissioner of Khasi and Jaintia Hills in 1938 and 2006. Moreover, the notification of 7 June 1978 by the Special Secretary (Revenue Department) of the Government of Meghalaya prohibited any transfer of tribal land in the East Khasi Hills district. The complainants hence argue that the permission given by the purported headman was null and void.[134]

According to the complaint, LMMPL transferred the legal titles of the land leased and bought for mining and the conveyor belt to LUMPL, who further mortgaged it to the banks for loans. Based on the aforementioned notification, such transfer and mortgage in relation to the tribal land was alleged to be illegal. This was also in contravention to the traditional land transfer norms based on the Khasi people's traditional land holding system and the Sixth Schedule to the Constitution of India.

In addition, the complaint noted that the Project was mainly supported by outside consultants, while only a few Indigenous persons were hired. Coupled with the destruction of their sources of livelihood, many community members were compelled to migrate to nearby towns and cities, adding to the marginalisation of the Shella people.[135]

Small-scale limestone mining had been carried by the people of East Khasi Hills since the pre-British days. These activities were vital to the local subsistence economy. The Project was considered to be destructive not only to the local ecology but also to sustainable economic practices through heavy blasting and the use of modern technology.[136]

In addition, the complainants also enumerated several IFC policy and loan agreement violations, including: that the resettlement policy was not triggered until 2002; no monthly internal reports of resettlement implementation were provided from Lafarge until 2008; no reports as to annual external monitoring surveys were provided; social performance appeared to not be covered in annual monitoring reports; the implementation of the RAP relating to the conveyor belt was not carried out; there was no

[134] Ibid.
[135] Ibid.
[136] Ibid.

confirmation that the company had implemented the 'corrective action plan' including payment to all affected people; the company used/leased/acquired other land not in the original loan agreement; and the IFC took land titles of Indigenous people as mortgage without their consent.[137]

The Complaint Handling Process

In the CAO's assessment, it considered the complaint eligible and issued an Assessment Report dated May 2014.[138] It found that the key issues were the following.

Lack of Consultation and Information Disclosure

The complainants alleged that, as the owners of the land, they were never fully informed or consulted about the land acquisition process and the project.

Lack of Compensation

While LUMPL paid compensation to other landowners in Shella for the acquisition of land, the complainants alleged that some of them were never properly identified as land owners and thus received no compensation. It was their position that the land certification process was tainted with incorrect and fraudulent claims. They expressed willingness to share relevant documents showing their claim to ownership and entitlement of compensation.

Access to Land and Livelihood

The complainant noted that the projected deprived them of access to the land negatively impacting their livelihoods.

In response, LSC and LUMPL stated that a lengthy land identification and acquisition/leasing process was undertaken in the late 1990s, referencing the 6th Schedule of the Constitution of India, various other local/tribal laws, and other applicable customary practices. Effort was put into identification and compensation measures. There were no land records or land surveys in the majority of the State of Meghalaya. LUMPL therefore complied with the tribal customs to identify the ownership of land by working with a local entity recognised by law called durbar to identify land owners and settle land disputes among tribal members.

[137] Ibid, pp. 5–6.
[138] Ibid, pp. 6–7.

They paid rent/contribution to the durbars, which were later distributed as per their own customs and decisions.

LSC and LUMPL believed that due process was followed. They found no reason to take part in the dispute resolution process with the complainants given that they believed it has conformed to all legal and customary requirements. Given the voluntary nature of the dispute resolution process, the parties could not be compelled to participate. Therefore, the complaint was thus dealt with through the CAO Compliance process.

The Outcome

While the CAO found that the IFC did review its client's India social impact assessment as well as conduct site supervision visits, it queried the sufficiency of such supervision. Particularly, it was unclear whether the IFC adequately supervised its client's commitment to carry out a programme of independent external monitoring as set out in the India social impact assessment.[139]

Moreover, the CAO questioned whether the IFC's response to the issues raised by the complainants was sufficient. The IFC determined that it was inappropriate to respond to the complaints before the court's decisions were released. Grievances were to be expected in such situations, not least because the E&S review procedures required the IFC to assure itself that a client's response to complaints was consistent with its E&S requirements.[140]

While the IFC's supervision and preparation of the Project, particularly in the area of E&S, raised a number of questions, they were not found to be of sufficient systemic importance. Unless a complaint was received from a broader group of affected individuals, the CAO was reluctant to pursue an investigation. The case was therefore closed.[141]

Lessons Learned

CAO Compliance was tasked with determining whether the IFC prepared the project in accordance with its E&S requirements for the issues

[139] CAO (2014). *Compliance Appraisal Report (Report No. C-I-R6-Y14-F212)*, p. 10. www.cao-ombudsman.org/sites/default/files/downloads/CAOAppraisalReportLafargeOctober142014.pdf.

[140] Ibid.

[141] Ibid.

raised by the complaint. It was of the view that the relevant E&S requirements incorporated into its loan agreement in June 1998 might not have been sufficient to lend support to the approval of the Project in accordance with IFC policies in place at that time.[142] Here are some of the suggestions and lessons learnt.

Pre-investment Review

The IFC's review of the project started in early 1997. There was no specific reference to issues of land acquisition or to the impact of the project on Indigenous peoples in the summary of project information. However, the project environmental documents were made publicly available at the 'Office of Headman' in Shella Bazar, Meghalaya, India.

No expected adverse impacts from the Project were identified in the EA for the proposed mining site in India. While some of the impacts were acknowledged in the EA, including the cutting off of access to village-owned land used for fuel wood collection and plantation crops, certain remedial and compensatory measures were in place to offset the impact. The company was committed to reforesting two plots owned by Nongtrai village and using local labour for constructing and operating the quarry. It was also noted in the EA that the company made 'significant efforts to approach and inform the local communities . . . during project planning and implementation'.[143]

IFC Approval of the Project and Loan Agreement

The Project was approved in June 1998. The loan agreement was signed between the IFC and the company on 18 September 2001. It incorporated World Bank safeguard policies into its loan agreement for the project as required by its 1993 Procedure for Environmental Analysis and Review of Projects. Nonetheless, there was a lack of a full EA for the India side of the Project.[144] Deficiencies in the implementation of the involuntary resettlement and Indigenous peoples policy were found.

General Supervision

The IFC made efforts in supervision by reviewing annual monitoring reports submitted by the company and conducting periodic site supervision visits. The documentation indicated that the company's E&S performance was, on the whole, considered satisfactory. However, it appeared that

142 Ibid, pp. 5–8.
143 Ibid.
144 Ibid.

the IFC did not assure itself that the project completed an independent external monitoring programme as set out in the India social impact assessment. More supervision could have been exercised. While the complainants raised concerns as to land issues and requested that IFC conduct an inquiry the IFC's visit in May 2008, the IFC decided not to take a position on the issues until they were decided by the courts.[145]

Case 5: IFC Philippines: Mindoro Resources Project

Introduction

The IFC Philippines Mindoro resources project case demonstrates the importance of oversight of de-centralised consultative process involving local government authorities, company representatives and Indigenous populations. In this case, local community members were not provided with the higher standard of consultation (prior informed consent) or even free, prior and informed consultation given that the IFC standards were not yet updated to provide appropriate protections as members of an Indigenous group. Rather, even the lower standard of 'informed consultation' was not employed, as the community was not designated as Indigenous. Ultimately, the 'consultation' process was characterised by uni-directional decision making and fabricated consent. In addition, risks from lack of transparency, an ineffective social and economic audit, and obfuscation of facts resulted in the dissolution of trust between parties. Ultimately, the project was suspended.

Background

The project concerned mineral exploration and extraction in various identified sites in the Philippines, named the Agata Nickel project. This exploratory project was undertaken from 2000 by Mindoro Resources Ltd (MRL), a mining exploratory company that was listed on the Toronto and Australian stock exchanges.

The mining project was segmented into two major phases. The first involved the Agata Mineral Production Sharing Agreement (MPSA), MRL's main nickel laterite resource in the Agusan del Norte province.[146]

[145] Ibid, p. 10.

[146] CAO (2012). *CAO Compliance Appraisal of IFC (Report No. C-I-R5-Y12-F165)*, p. 5. www.cao-ombudsman.org/sites/default/files/downloads/CAOAppraisalofIFCMindoroResourcesOctober2012.pdfn 8.

Additionally, MRL drafted plans to undertake exploratory work in areas north of the Agata MPSA's tenements (the 'Tapian Extension'), in respect of which regulatory approval by the Philippines' National Commission of Indigenous Peoples (NCIP) was granted in November 2010.[147]

The IFC's equity investments began in July 2010 and amounted to CAD10 million. They were intended to support MRL's resource drilling, as well as other MRL operations, including exploration activities for various minerals. This included the purchase of MRL shares worth CAD4 million and CAD600,000 in July/November 2010 and January 2012, respectively.[148]

Issues

One of the core issues of MRL's exploratory projects was the location of its project sites. Both the Agata MPSA and the Tapian Extension were located adjacent to Lake Mainit, a primary source of drinking water for neighbouring Indigenous communities and an important site for biodiversity, particularly for the Mamanwa tribes of Dinarawan and Bunga, the complainants in the present instance. Another key concern of the complainants was that the sites were located on ancestral land that housed cultural heritage sites and were generally of spiritual importance to local communities. The grievances of the local communities in this respect were thus both environmental and sociological in nature.

Besides the locality of the project, the interactions between local Indigenous communities and MRL and local authorities also formed the subject matter of the complainants' grievances. The complainants claimed that MRL had manipulated and eroded the integrity of negotiations between it and local communities in order to satisfy the requirements of the NCIP by obtaining ill-informed and at-times fabricated consent from locals for its exploratory activities.

The Pre-project Community Consultation Process

The IFC PSs prescribe guidelines on how the IFC should appraise and mitigate the E&S risks associated with the projects that it financially supports. PS7 mandates that there be free prior informed consultations (FPICs) with communities living within affected areas where such

[147] Ibid, p. 5.
[148] Ibid.

communities are those of 'Indigenous peoples',[149] a term that is 'used in a generic sense to refer to a distinct social and cultural group' with characteristics such as 'collective attachment to geographically distinct habitats or ancestral territories in the project area' and '[c]ustomary cultural, economic, social, or political institutions that are separate from those of the mainstream society or culture'.[150] One key complaint regarding the consultation process concerns the improper designation of the affected communities in this case as being non-Indigenous, which purportedly diluted the quality of MRL's consultations.

The contents of the requirement for FPICs are case-specific, but generally mandate the involvement of representative bodies and organisations of the Indigenous communities, and the provision of sufficient time for the Indigenous peoples' decision-making processes.[151] Regardless of whether the development project in question concerned Indigenous peoples, the consultations to be conducted by the development company should be 'organised and iterative' and yield results that will inform the company's decisions as regards to any 'proposed mitigation measures, the sharing of development benefits and opportunities, and implementation issues' as per PS1.[152]

Administrative Order No. 3, Series of 2002 of the NCIP also prescribed steps for the FPIC process.[153] A 'preliminary consultative meeting' between the elders of the Indigenous communities, the company and any collaborating NGOs should be convened by the NCIP to allow all parties to articulate their provisional views on the project before the Indigenous elders conduct their own consultation meetings with their respective communities.[154] Subsequently, an NCIP-convened assembly should take place where Indigenous representatives announce their decision as regards the development project through a community-wide vote, to be accompanied with a Memorandum of Agreement containing the terms of the community's approval of the project or a document of

[149] IFC (1 January 2012). *Performance Standards on Environmental and Social Sustainability.* www.ifc.org/wps/wcm/connect/24e6bfc3-5de3-444d-be9b-226188c95454/PS_English_2012_Full-Document.pdf?CVID=jkV-X6h&MOD=AJPERES, p. 43.

[150] Ibid, p. 42.

[151] Ibid, p. 43.

[152] Ibid, p. 10.

[153] National Commission on Indigenous Peoples: Quezon City (2002). *NCIP Administrative Order No. 3, Series of 2002.* https://mgb.gov.ph/images/stories/NCIP_Dao3-2003.pdf.

[154] Ibid, pp. 14–15.

rejection that clarifies whether or not they will entertain alternative proposals, as the case may be.[155]

The Consultations Undertaken by MRL

According to various IFC documents, MRL was deemed to have fulfilled the FPIC requirement and conducted the necessary consultations with the Mamanwa tribes. The IFC's E&S Action Plan of June 2010 documents that MRL completed a '[c]omplete and document free prior informed consultation' with local Indigenous communities.[156] In its Environmental and Social Review Summary of 2008 (ESRS), the IFC documents that 'Free Prior Informed Consent was declared to exist by the NCIP' when MRL requested the NCIP to conduct a second assessment of the presence of Indigenous peoples in the MPSA in early 2008,[157] and that 'MRL has been engaging with these communities since 2006'.[158]

The ESRS explained that MRL adopted the practice of jointly developing 'Community Technical Working Groups' (CTWGs) with local authorities, comprising of representatives from, inter alia, Indigenous peoples, local government agencies, fisherfolk and farmers, local NGOs, and religious groups.[159] MRL purportedly used these CTWGs to harness the local communities' concerns with its projects, but that '[n]o major grievances have been registered to date'.[160] The ESRS also described the MRL's use of 'Soc-Envi Management Teams' to 'seek permission from the surrounding communities for the exploration ... [and] to ensure a positive working relationship between [MRL] and the community'.[161] The ESRS highlighted the obtainment of an 'Environmental Compliance Certificate' awarded by local environmental authorities after 'a series of public consultation exercises coordinated by the [awarding authority]' as evidence of sufficient community engagement.[162] It is worth noting that

155 Ibid, p. 19.

156 IFC (June 2010). *Environmental and Social Action Plan* (updated in June 2010), p. 1; Obtained from International Finance Corporation (2010). *IFC Project Information & Data Portal: Mindoro Resources Ltd.* https://disclosures.ifc.org/project-detail/ESRS/26987/mindoro-resources-ltd.

157 IFC (2010). *Environmental and Social Review Summary (ESRS)*, pp. 12–13. Obtained from International Finance Corporation, IFC Project Information & Data Portal: Mindoro Resources Ltd.

158 Ibid, p. 2.

159 Ibid, p. 11.

160 Ibid, p. 15.

161 Ibid, p. 14.

162 Ibid, p. 1.

this certificate was described as encompassing 'Direct Shipping of Ore' operations ('DSO Operations'), which is in addition to exploratory mining, and which was described by the CAO as potentially posing more extensive E&S impacts to local communities.[163] As will be seen later, the CAO regards the IFC's due diligence in respect of MRL as being insufficient to account for the implications of its DSO Operations.[164] Though not explicitly expounded, this purported lack of oversight may have materially impacted the quality and scope of the MRL's consultative exercises in relation to the needs of those affected by the DSO Operations.

Indeed, the only allusion to any deficiency in MRL's consultative process in the ESRS was that there was 'limited understanding of the scale of payment which [the indigenous peoples] could receive under future mining operations', a reference to the legal requirement that companies are required to pay 1% of its revenue royalty to Indigenous communities where its operations are to take place in areas officially recognised as being ancestral domain.[165]

It appears, therefore, that the Mamanwa tribes were granted access to MRL's consultations through their representation by their tribal elders or leaders at CTWG-related forums with MRL and other community actors. These consultations appear to have taken place prior to the DSO Operations, but well after the first tenement was granted in respect of the Agata MPSA in May 1999 and the requisite exploration permits were applied for in October 2000 and granted.[166] Local FPIC consultations were said to have been undertaken elsewhere in CAO documentation at the time of application of said permits,[167] although there were no substantive details on the process and contents of these consultations. There is no information on the discrete issues that formed the subject matter of either round of consultations.

The documentation by the CAO primarily consisted of the complaints of local Indigenous communities about the shortcomings of the consultation process. These will be explored in greater detail later.[168] At this juncture, it suffices to say that the local communities' account of the consultative process was that its apprehension and disapproval of the

[163] CAO, *CAO Compliance Appraisal of IFC (Report No. C-I-R5-Y12-F165)*, pp. 8–9.
[164] Ibid, pp. 8–10.
[165] IFC, *Environmental and Social Review Summary*, p. 13.
[166] CAO, *CAO Compliance Appraisal of IFC (Report No. C-I-R5-Y12-F165)*, p. 5.
[167] Ibid, p. 9.
[168] CAO (2012). *CAO Ombudsman Assessment Regarding Community and Civil Society Concerns*, pp. 10–12. www.cao-ombudsman.org/sites/default/files/downloads/AssessmentReport_MRL_May2012_ENG.pdf.

MRL project was 'not taken seriously'.[169] The Assessment Report states that there was an overall lack of consent from the Mamanwa tribes.

Other parts of the Assessment Report shed light on how the consultations were conducted. These include statements that there were 'repeated consultations, information sessions, and FPIC processes that [wore] down the community, and burden[ed] them in terms of time', at times sowing deep divisions in local communities.[170] The MRL alleged that the consultations were in fact conducted primarily by the NCIP – and consequently, that local dissatisfaction with the consultative process was misdirected towards MRL[171] – and that local NGOs violated FPIC regulations by both disrupting private consultations amongst local communities and generally fabricating dissent against MRL's presence through falsified signatures and untruthful statements to derail productive consultations.[172]

The Community Complaint

The complaint by the local Indigenous communities can be summarily characterised as one of spanning environmental, socio-legal, economic and procedural concerns.

Environmental Concerns

The main environmental complaint lodged by the Mamanwa tribal communities was the pollution of the nearby Lake Mainit. Both the Tapian Extension and the Agata MPSA border Lake Mainit.[173] As mentioned, the lake is a critical site for biodiversity, and an important water source for these communities. Many attribute such importance to these environmental assets that they expressed the view that no mining activity of any kind should take place within the exploratory sites of MRL.[174]

Some were also concerned about the decrease in fish populations within the lake, affecting livelihoods. Other concerns were expressed regarding pollution to surrounding habitats, including forests and

169 Ibid, p. 10.
170 Ibid, p. 11.
171 Ibid, p. 12.
172 Ibid, p. 14.
173 Ibid, pp. 7–8.
174 Ibid, p. 10.

other protected areas surrounding Lake Mainit,[175] as well as soil erosion threatening nearby farmland.[176]

Socio-legal Concerns

The Mamanwa tribes contended that the mining operations were 'not compatible with their traditional ways of life and the care and respect they have for lands they consider their ancestral domain', including disturbances to land, water and trees, which are themselves regarded as sacred manifestations of their ancestors,[177] and may also constitute disturbances to traditional burial grounds that fall within the exploration zone.[178] The complainants also argued that MRL's presence in the area also posed challenges to tribal unity and cohesion. As previously mentioned and as will be expounded in discussions about flaws with the consultation process later, the local communities regarded interactions with MRL as being intrinsically divisive, and that in-fighting and familial divisions, which at times culminated in violence, have already occurred.[179]

Of particular concern was the fact that the communities were not legally recognised by the local authorities as Indigenous peoples, thus leading to their presence not being brought to MRL's attention. This fact was evidently recognised by the IFC and MRL in the ESRS, which noted, contrary to the communities' contention that MRL was unaware of their presence, that the NCIP 'did not identify any IP's living in the area', though the extent to which this fact was relied upon to justify MRL's continued presence was not clearly articulated in the ESRS. It appears that the IFC did not explicitly rely upon NCIPs categorisation to classify MRL's project as being of a lower E&S risk ('Category B'),[180] and that, in any event, MRL elected to engage in FPIC consultations with the local communities.[181]

[175] Ibid, p. 5.
[176] The Office of the CAO (September 2011). *Complaint Letter from Alyansa Tigil Mina, September 16, 2011.* www.cao-ombudsman.org/cases/document-links/documents/MindoroComplaintforWeb_Sept16_2011.pdf at p. 3.
[177] CAO, *CAO Ombudsman Assessment Regarding Community and Civil Society Concerns*, p. 11.
[178] Ibid, p. 11.
[179] Ibid, p. 11.
[180] CAO, *CAO Compliance Appraisal of IFC (Report No. C-I-R5-Y12-F165)*, p. 8.
[181] Ibid, p. 8.

Economic Concerns

The community also raised economic concerns regarding the loss of their ancestral domain and environmental pollution, as mentioned earlier, as harming their sources of livelihood.

Procedural Concerns

The Mamanwa tribes made clear their dissatisfaction concerning both the consultative process with MRL and other alleged conduct designed to undermine the legitimacy and productivity of dialogue between the parties. Although complaints of this nature were primarily directed at MRL, some also implicated the local authorities.

Complaints Concerning the Consultation Process Itself

The consultation process, along with information sessions and FPIC processes, was described as being overly repetitive by design, as mentioned earlier, so as to 'wear down' the consulted communities by attrition through a 'divide-and-conquer' mechanism. Concerns about a lack of adequate information about the mining project was also raised by representatives of local concern groups, who stated that MRL never expressly asked for the communities' consent.[182]

There were also concerns that the consultation process oversaw the conclusion of agreements with individuals who were not legitimate community leaders.[183] This clearly amounted to a violation of the NCIP's aforementioned regulations on the FPIC process, which mandates that the interests of local communities should be represented by recognised elders or leaders of the community in company-facing consultation meetings, and to whom community individuals should relay their concerns in private meetings.[184]

[182] Ibid, p. 10.

[183] Ibid, p. 11.

[184] Ibid, p. 14. The NCIP Administrative Order, No. 3, Series of 2002 requires that '[t]he participants to the preliminary consultative meeting are: the identified council of elders or leaders, the representatives from the proponent, the NCIP, the representatives from collaborating NGOs and the civil society operating in the concerned area', and that '[w]ithin a period of fifteen (15) days after the termination of the last and final preliminary consultative meeting/s, the Elders/Leaders shall complete the conduct of their own consultative meetings with their members in complete the conduct of their own consultation meetings with their members in the community employing their own traditional consensus building processes in order to further discern the merits and demerits of the proposal as presented in the preliminary consultative meeting'.

The CAO has also noted that as regards to consultations for drilling activities in the Tapian Extension, for which regulatory approval was granted at a later stage, they were beyond the scope of the IFC's original due diligence review, rendering the IFC's description of the FPIC consultations being 'completed' by the MRL as being 'potentially misleading'.[185]

Alleged Conduct by MRL beyond the Consultation Process

According to the complainants, MRL also exerted undue pressure and influence over community leaders, including co-opting them with the promise of personal benefits, calling on local representatives to pressure these leaders and attempting to fabricate 'parallel leadership structures' within the Mamanwa tribes that covertly answer to the MRL instead.[186]

MRL was also accused of using illegitimate signatures to substantiate communal consent to their projects – conduct that MRL instead attributed to local NGOs.[187] The Mamanwa tribal representatives consistently highlighted the overarching feeling of being 'disrespected' throughout the consultation process and through other interactions with MRL.[188]

The Complaint Handling Process

As mentioned previously, the CAO's complaint handling process corresponded roughly with its three roles, as well as with the willingness of the complainants and the relevant counterparties to engage in a settlement or dispute resolution procedure.

The question in this case triggering the CAO's intervention was 'whether IFC exercised due diligence in its review and supervision of environmental and social (E&S) aspects of the Project', particularly as they relate to issues concerning flaws in MRL's consultation process.[189] The complaint handling process was therefore focused on the objective of providing complainants with suitable means of redress, but also reforming the IFC's internal practices to pre-empt similar cases in the future.

[185] CAO, *CAO Compliance Appraisal of IFC (Report No. C-I-R5-Y12-F165)*, p. 13.

[186] CAO, *CAO Ombudsman Assessment Regarding Community and Civil Society Concerns*, p. 11.

[187] Ibid.

[188] Ibid, p. 12.

[189] CAO, *CAO Compliance Appraisal of IFC (Report No. C-I-R5-Y12-F165)*, p. 5.

Meetings with MRL representatives were intended not only to procure information on the project itself (including relevant licenses and permits, and any technical challenges),[190] but presumably to relay the communities' concerns to MRL and offer the company a chance to explain its position (seeing as the concerns raised by MRL correspond with the complaints mentioned earlier). For instance, MRL submitted that the convoluted FPIC process was largely conducted by NCIP and that it had 'complied with the process to the best of their ability', and that as MRL saw it, there was in fact 'widespread acceptance' of the company's projects given the reports of 'cordial and collaborative relationships' from the NCIP and the 'engagement' the projects would bring to the local communities.[191] In response to complaints about environmental pollution and the legal recognition of Indigenous peoples, MRL also submitted that it had instituted remedial environmental programmes, and reaffirmed its recognition of the communities' status as Indigenous peoples through the provision of a '1% gross royalty despite the fact that the Sitio Coro community does not have a Certificate of Ancestral Domain Title'.[192]

Facilitating Settlement or Compliance appraisal

In this case, the CAO noted that the complainants were unwilling and uninterested in pursuing any form of dispute resolution. Therefore, the ombudsman referred the case to the CAO's Compliance division for 'initial appraisal' to examine whether there was a prima facie case for an investigation into or audit of the CAO's internal procedures,[193] thereby adopting the 'Compliance' role.

The substantive results of the initial appraisal are explored in the following section. For the purposes of evaluating the effects, if any, of the complaint handling process on dispute resolution, it suffices to acknowledge here that the Appraisal Report considers the grievances of the communities as 'unaddressed', and that the 'CAO reserves the right in line with its Operational Guidelines, to reconsider [the] decision' to review the IFC's involvement in the project should it progress in a deleterious manner.[194]

190 CAO, *CAO Ombudsman Assessment Regarding Community and Civil Society Concerns*, p. 12.
191 Ibid, p. 12.
192 Ibid, p. 13.
193 Ibid, p. 14.
194 CAO, *CAO Compliance Appraisal of IFC (Report No. C-I-R5-Y12-F165)*, pp. 14–15.

The Outcome

As mentioned earlier, the complaints by the Mamanwa tribal communities were not directly resolved. The initial appraisal involved an examination of the IFC's procedural shortcomings in vetting MRL's operations and facilitating a robust consultative process. The CAO 'questioned' whether the IFC sufficiently accounted for the Tapian Extension and the DSO Operations in its due diligence reviews of the projects' E&S impacts, including through vehicles such as the ESRS.[195] The 'immediate focus' of MRL on 'exploration and other small footprint activities' and the likely prospect of larger-scale projects in the future warranted, in the CAO's view, a more cautious approach that it opined was not necessarily demonstrated by the IFC's classifying the project as 'Category B',[196] a category reserved for projects with 'limited adverse social or environmental impacts that were few in number, generally site specific, largely reversible and readily addressed through mitigation measures'.[197]

After these findings, the CAO decided that, despite the significant social impacts of extractive industry projects, the aforementioned conclusions were 'unlikely to be materially advanced by the conduct of a compliance audit at present'.[198] In other words, an audit was unlikely to realise better social and environmental outcomes in the MRL project. In particular, the CAO found that any immediate risk of this nature was 'mitigated by MRL's decision to suspend exploration in the contested area',[199] while longer-term risks were also reduced by subscription agreement covenants negotiated by the IFC with MRL designed to 'prevent MRL from proceeding with operations in the contested area absent a waiver from IFC'.[200]

Lessons Learned

The consultation process adopted by MRL was evidently flawed, given that, even when one takes MRL at its best and barring any consideration of procedural allegations raised by the Mamanwa tribal communities, its process was deficient in the transparent sharing of information. Further

[195] Ibid, p. 9.
[196] Ibid, p. 10.
[197] Ibid, p. 8.
[198] Ibid, p. 14.
[199] Ibid.
[200] Ibid.

development of the IFC and the CAO's powers to ensure that both institutions have the requisite information and enforcement capacity to implement solutions that directly safeguard the environmental, social and legal interests of all affected communities could be considered. This is particularly relevant for Indigenous communities whose undefined legal status may serve as either a convenient excuse or the basis of a bona fide mistaken belief for either the company or relevant local authorities to be subject to a lower level of accountability in their obligations to the affected communities.

Focusing solely on the practices of the IFC and MRL, key lessons include: the need for contractual mechanisms, oversight of the decentralised consultative process, and the question of whether local authorities or the company should conduct consultations.

The Need for Contractual Mechanisms

Irrespective of the veracity of the communities' concerns and complaints, a core issue with the IFC's management of the MRL project was that it was never in a position to proactively vet and scrutinise the project's progress to ensure its compliance with the IFC's own PSs and to assess the actual environmental and social impacts of the project in real time so as to continually determine the justifiability of the IFC's endorsement of such projects. Part of this can be attributed to a lack of information about the project. The CAO's Appraisal Report itself notes that the IFC 'relied primarily on assertions of its client in assuring itself that the investment was being executed in compliance with the Performance Standards'.[201]

Thus, contractual mechanisms are needed to (1) ensure that information regarding various parameters pertinent to the PSs are *regularly* adduced, recorded and relayed to the CAO; (2) expressly and unequivocally articulate the IFC's right to pre-emptively vet and approve or disapprove future expansions or extensions of any projects (which is especially relevant to exploratory projects like that of MRL that are intended to materialise into full-fledged resource extraction operations); (3) codify the PSs themselves into contractual language instead of allowing the standards to remain as non-binding guidelines; and (4) to ensure that, in the event of any change in the corporate structure or operation of

[201] Ibid, p. 13. The report notes that 'CAO questions whether this provided an adequate basis on which to: (a) evaluate the status of its client's compliance with the Performance Standards in practice, and (b) decide if the client needed additional support to carrying out its work in accordance with the Standards'.

the company (such as a joint venture), the company remains liable to the aforementioned obligations and undertakes the distinct obligation to inform the other corporate entity(ies) of these obligations as well.

Point (2) in the preceding paragraph is derived in part from the Appraisal Report's finding that the IFC covenanted with MRL to mandate the latter to seek approval before engaging in further expansionary work.[202] This was, however, a reactive measure that cannot pre-empt any damage already inflicted upon the local communities. Point (4) is again particularly relevant to exploratory projects or projects that are otherwise experimental and fiscally uncertain. The high infrastructural costs and barriers to entry of many such projects are also conducive to frequent corporate developments. For instance, it was revealed that MRL was in discussions with another junior exploration company, TVI Pacific, with a view to forming a joint venture.[203] MRL was also in the process of acquiring a 40% stake in a junior miner, Red Mountain.[204] Both deals occurred roughly one year after IFC first acquired an interest in MRL.[205] As part of the Red Mountain deal, MRL stated that 'in addition to E&S warranties contained in the existing purchase agreement, Red Mountain would consider issuing a separate letter indicating its commitment to the IFC Performance Standards'.[206] While this was a step in the right direction, and informed the Appraisal Report's conclusion that a further investigation into the CAO's internal practices were unnecessary, the exact contents of the 'E&S warranties' are unknown, and there was evidence that such covenants originate not from the benevolence and self-discipline of MRL but from a systematic policy at the IFC to require the inclusion of such covenants.

Challenges Overseeing MRL's De-centralised Consultative Process

The IFC's ESRS documented MRL's use of CTWGs and 'Soc-Envi Management Teams' to facilitate the consultative process with the local communities. In effect, MRL de-centralised the consultative process by gathering opinions on and objections to the project through multiple, smaller-scale platforms and forums.

202 Ibid, pp. 8–10.
203 Ibid, p. 11.
204 Ibid, p. 11.
205 Ibid, p. 11.
206 Ibid, p. 11.

The problem with this practice was that many of the issues that MRL itself identified as hampering the effectiveness of the consultation process could be attributed to this outsourcing. An instructive example of this was the fact that MRL claimed its consultations suffered from interference by local NGOs.[207] An outsourced consultative process may be prone to such interferences since it may be difficult to monitor. The same can be said of the apparent dissonance between MRL's perception of how well-received its project was, and the communities' complaints that the CAO has enumerated in its documentation. It may have been difficult to ensure consistency in the practice of the various CWTGs and consultation forums, or to ensure that the results of each were accurately passed on to MRL, leading to a mismatch between MRL's understanding of the results and the actual opinions of those engaged in the consultations.

The Question of Whether Local Authorities or the Company Should Conduct Consultations

According to MRL, the NCIP was largely in charge of the consultations with the Mamanwa tribes, with the Appraisal Report noting that 'MRL emphasises that the FPIC process is conducted by NCIP, and not by the company, and often there is a misunderstanding about this distinction'. The respective roles of each are such that 'the company engages with the community and its leaders as designated by the NCIP'.[208] It is also worth noting that the NCIP prescribes procedures in its administrative orders for the conduct of these consultations, as previously mentioned.[209]

This arrangement was problematic for several reasons. Firstly, the government's initiating role does not bode well for public faith in the consultation process, as the public may be inclined to perceive authorities like the NCIP as working in tandem with the company to premeditatively engineer the makeup of the consultation so as to maximise its chance of success for the company. In particular, the legally ambiguous status of Indigenous peoples and any associated political controversies or agendas may inhibit the relevant local authorities' willingness or capacity to engage sufficient and legitimate representation from the potentially affected communities to partake in a consultation that identifies these authorities as the lead actor. Besides questions of engagement,

207 CAO, *CAO Ombudsman Assessment Regarding Community and Civil Society Concerns*, pp. 13–14.

208 CAO, *CAO Ombudsman Assessment Regarding Community and Civil Society Concerns*, p. 12.

209 Ibid, p. 13.

there are also ancillary shortcomings of the government-led consultation process in the MRL case, including the feasibility of involving multiple other relevant government authorities that represent specific facets of the local communities' interests (in this case, for instance, the Department of Environmental and Natural Resources) in the organisation of the consultations.[210]

A more effective means of conducting the consultation process would empower the company to present its case more directly to a wider cross-section of the Indigenous communities in question, with the government playing a mediative role. This approach would place greater responsibility of ascertaining the potential scope of affected individuals on the company, and afford local communities greater autonomy in deciding how to convey their objections or suggestions to any proposed projects. This approach would also place a greater degree of constructive knowledge on the company as to the potential effects of its project on local communities, which may serve as a legal basis for public interest litigation or enforcement action should the project progress in an unsafe or exceedingly adverse manner.[211]

Governments should still be involved in the pre-consultation stage through the verification of technical information concerning the project itself and arrive at least a provisional view on the potential E&S impacts of the project before consultations commence. This allows governments to better dispense their mediatory role so as to check against any inaccurate representations made by the company during the consultations, and also to position authorities to nudge and steer the consultations in the direction they believe are of particular interest or concern to the local communities whilst preserving both their impartiality and the company's ability to present transparent information.[212]

Case 6: IFC/World Bank PNG SEZ Project

Overview

The IFC/World Bank PNG SEZ project case demonstrates the need for genuine multi-directional rather than 'uni-directional' consultation and thorough ESIA. Significantly, uni-directional 'consultation' consisting in one party informing another party of its plans in the absence of mutual

210 Ibid, p. 13.
211 Ibid, p. 13.
212 Ibid, p. 13.

decision making is not a substitute for genuine consultation. Compounding the lack of genuine consultation, insufficient environmental planning resulted in the subsequent dispute.

Background

The Government of PNG (GoPNG) decided to incorporate the concept of SEZs into its overall development strategy, and in 2008, GoPNG asked the IFC for assistance in developing the strategy and legislative framework for establishing SEZs in PNG.[213] Special economic zones are geographically delimited areas set up with conditions conducive to investment, such as by providing incentives to startup businesses through simplified processes, and by supplying infrastructure and labour.[214]

The Pacific Marine Industrial Zone (PMIZ) was to be the first SEZ established by GoPNG. It aimed to cluster a range of tuna catching and processing facilities to take advantage of PNG's considerable tuna stock, with the goal of promoting investment in onshore processing of regionally caught tuna. The PMIZ project was led by the PNG's Department of Commerce and Industry (DCI).[215] In April 2009, the IFC approved the project as part of its Advisory Services (ASs),[216] and entered into discussions with the DCI.[217] The initial components of the project were: legal and regulatory advice; policy and regulatory framework to ensure access to global markets; and commercial viability and site assessment.[218]

[213] Office of the CAO (n.d.). *Papua New Guinea/PNG SEZ-01/Madang Province*. www.cao-ombudsman.org/cases/case_detail.aspx?id=175; CAO (2012). *Ombudsman Assessment Report: Complaint Regarding the Special Economic Zones Advisory Services Project*. www.cao-ombudsman.org/cases/document-links/documents/AssessmentReportPNGSEZ.pdf, p. 5; CAO (2014). *Ombudsman/Dispute Resolution Conclusion Report: Papua New Guinea Special Economic Zone*. www.cao-ombudsman.org/cases/document-links/documents/PMIZ_Conclusion_Rpt_FINAL.pdf, p. 1.

[214] CAO, *Ombudsman Assessment Report*, p. 5.

[215] Ibid, pp. 5 and 7.

[216] CAO, *Papua New Guinea/PNG SEZ-01/Madang Province*.

[217] CAO, *Ombudsman Assessment Report*, p. 5.

[218] CAO (2014). *CAO Appraisal Report: IFC Advisory Services to Government of Papua New Guinea (Special Economic Zones)*. www.cao-ombudsman.org/cases/document-links/documents/CAOAppraisal-IFCASProjectPNG-SEZ_08-29-14.pdf, p. 4.

The Government of PNG subsequently took the lead in selecting the site in Madang Province.[219] Therefore, the IFC revised the project scope in June 2010 to focus only on advice in relation to the national legal framework for SEZs.[220]

After June 2010, the IFC drafted a legal model that provided a general legislative framework for the development and operation of SEZs in PNG and submitted the model legislation to the DCI for consideration.[221] The IFC did not support any of the activities related to the proposed PMIZ other than facilitating the initial June 2009 meeting of the PNG SEZ Taskforce held in Madang.[222] The IFC formally completed project implementation in May 2011, but post-implementation activities continued until June 2012.[223]

The Pre-project Community Consultation Process

According to the community complaint and the Office of the CAO Assessment Report, the complainants stated that there was inadequate consultation with landowners. When project designers and promoters met with them, itwas only to inform them of the PMIZ rather than to consult them on their concerns and insights regarding it. Additionally, even when 'consultations' took place, tensions were high and people were too scared to speak up.[224]

The Community Complaint

In July 2011,[225] the Bismark Ramu Group, a local NGO, filed a complaint to the CAO on behalf of several villages in Madang Province near the

[219] CAO, *Papua New Guinea/PNG SEZ-01/Madang Province*; CAO, *Ombudsman Assessment Report*, p. 6.

[220] CAO, *CAO Appraisal Report: IFC Advisory Services to Government of Papua New Guinea (Special Economic Zones)*.

[221] CAO, *Papua New Guinea/PNG SEZ-01/Madang Province*; CAO, *Ombudsman/Dispute Resolution Conclusion Report*, p. 1; CAO, *Ombudsman Assessment Report*, p. 6.

[222] CAO, *CAO Appraisal Report: IFC Advisory Services to Government of Papua New Guinea (Special Economic Zones)*, p. 4.

[223] Ibid, p. 4.

[224] CAO (2011). *Letter of Complaint*. www.cao-ombudsman.org/cases/document-links/images/Complaintletterpage1_071211.jpg, p. 1; CAO, *Ombudsman Assessment Report*, p. 8.

[225] CAO, *Papua New Guinea/PNG SEZ-01/Madang Province* states that the complaint was filed on 12 July 2011, but it is inconsistent with CAO, *Ombudsman Assessment Report*, which states that the CAO found the complaint eligible for further assessment on 8 July 2011.

PMIZ site.[226] The complaint had 105 local signatories[227] and the support of an elected representative.[228]

The complaint raised concerns about the IFC's role in supporting the PMIZ establishment and impact on the livelihood of local populations and the surrounding environment.[229] The main issues were the lack of community consultation with landowners in the area, lack of environmental planning, impacts on fish populations, reefs and lagoons, and wider social and environmental impacts.[230]

The complaint stated that there was no proper consultation, and the landowners were simply informed of what was going to happen.[231] The complaint also noted that an SEZ focused on tuna processing would deplete fish populations.[232] It referred to the community's experience with RD Tuna, a branch of a Filipino company that ran a tuna cannery in the Madang Vidar area since 1997, which resulted in damage to the reef, foul smells, unsanitary conditions and negative social ramifications. The tuna cannery was fined for violating PNG laws of the sea and was shut down by the European Union for unsatisfactory and unsanitary conditions.[233] There was an ongoing court case against the National Fisheries Authority over the PMIZ over the E&S implications.[234]

Therefore, since the complainants believed that the PMIZ would not benefit most people nor was it in the interest of the environment, and the IFC was involved in advising GoPNG and assisted in drafting legislation for the SEZs, the complainants requested an investigation of the proposed PMIZ and the IFC's involvement in the project, especially

[226] CAO, *Ombudsman Assessment Report*, p. 6; CAO, *CAO Appraisal Report: IFC Advisory Services to Government of Papua New Guinea (Special Economic Zones)*, p. 4.

[227] CAO, *Papua New Guinea/PNG SEZ-01/Madang Province*; CAO (2011). *List of Complainants and Villages*. www.cao-ombudsman.org/cases/document-links/documents/Complaint_NamesVillagesList_071211.pdf.

[228] CAO, *Ombudsman Assessment Report*, p. 6; CAO, *Ombudsman/Dispute Resolution Conclusion Report*, p. 1.

[229] CAO, *Ombudsman Assessment Report*, p. 5; CAO, *CAO Appraisal Report: IFC Advisory Services to Government of Papua New Guinea (Special Economic Zones)*, p. 4.

[230] CAO, *Papua New Guinea/PNG SEZ-01/Madang Province*; CAO, *Ombudsman/Dispute Resolution Conclusion Report*, p. 1.

[231] CAO, *Letter of Complaint* (2011), p. 1.

[232] CAO, *Ombudsman Assessment Report*, p. 6; CAO, *CAO Appraisal Report: IFC Advisory Services to Government of Papua New Guinea (Special Economic Zones)*, p. 4.

[233] CAO, *Letter of Complaint* (2011), p. 1; CAO, *Ombudsman Assessment Report*, p. 6.

[234] CAO, *Letter of Complaint* (2011), p. 1.

regarding the IFC's role in paving the way for the establishment of the PMIZ and its impact on local populations and the environment.[235]

The Complaint Handling Process

The Ombudsman Assessment

The CAO found the complaint to be eligible for further assessment in July 2021,[236] as it related to an IFC project, the issue was within the CAO's mandate to address the E&S impacts of IFC investments, and the complainant was or would be affected by the project. Thus, the CAO began assessing the opportunities for resolving the issues.[237]

Summary of Issues

The CAO identified the primary issues based on the original complaint and further stakeholder discussions.

The first issue was how community benefits could be maximised for those affected by the PMIZ SEZ. The main concern was that the PMIZ did not benefit the majority of those who were affected by it. In response, GoPNG acknowledged that maximising community benefits was vital to the PMIZ's success. During interviews with stakeholders, some referenced two landowner companies that were created to represent and manage the interests of two broad groupings of landowners, and that received capital from the DCI. Based on this, the CAO found that there were potential opportunities for broader community consultation on how these companies could use seed capital.[238]

The second issue was how the negative environmental impacts from development in the PMIZ might be mitigated or avoided altogether. The main concern was that the PMIZ's focus on tuna would deplete other fish populations and have a negative effect on the overall marine ecosystem. This was based on the complainant's previous experience with existing tuna factories, which caused foul smells, environmental damage to reefs and unsanitary conditions. The complainants claimed that the environmental planning for the PMIZ was unsatisfactory.[239]

[235] Ibid, p. 2; CAO, *Ombudsman Assessment Report*, p. 6.
[236] CAO, *CAO Appraisal Report: IFC Advisory Services to Government of PNG (Report No. C-I-R5-Y14-F214)*, pp. 5–6.
[237] CAO, *Papua New Guinea/PNG SEZ-01/Madang Province*; CAO, *Ombudsman Assessment Report*, p. 5.
[238] Ibid, p. 7.
[239] Ibid, p. 8.

The third issue was how all parties could ensure meaningful community consultation and engagement during all stages of the development and implementation of the SEZ. The main concern was the poor level of consultation with landowners. The complainants stated that when project designers and promoters met with the community, it was only to inform them of the PMIZ rather than consult them on their concerns and insights regarding the project. For instance, villagers from Rempi lost access to a significant mangrove area, which served as an important food source for them without being able to give any input. Additionally, even when 'consultations' took place, tensions were high and people were nervous or too scared to speak up. As a result, the complainants desired a constructive way to handle disagreements and to identify and resolve issues related to the PMIZ.[240]

Finally, the fourth issue was how concerned parties could clarify land rights and titles and resolve any land disputes in a mutually satisfactory manner. The stakeholders involved had some confusion and disagreement over certain land rights related to the PMIZ project site. In CAO meetings, the community members described their traditional and historical connection to the land, and their understanding of the transfer of land titles between communities, the Church and GoPNG. Additionally, even where the legality of titles was not in question, the community members sought to have a voice in the land title transfer process.[241]

Conclusion and Dispute Resolution Steps

The complainants and GoPNG agreed to undertake a collaborative and voluntary dispute resolution process to resolve the issues in the complaint with the CAO's assistance.[242] The CAO would encourage the parties to draw on previous experiences of managing community disputes and apply the lessons learned in a constructive way to the PMIZ dispute.[243]

IFC's Response to the CAO Assessment Report

The IFC's response was dated 11 April 2012.[244] As a reply to the Assessment Report, the IFC stated that it had stepped back from direct

240 Ibid, p. 8.
241 Ibid, p. 8.
242 Ibid, p. 9; CAO, *Papua New Guinea/PNG SEZ-01/Madang Province*; CAO, *Ombudsman/ Dispute Resolution Conclusion Report*, p. 1.
243 CAO, *Ombudsman Assessment Report*, p. 9.
244 IFC (2012). *IFC Response to CAO Ombudsman Assessment Report: Complaint Regarding the Special Economic Zones Project in Papua New Guinea*. www.cao-ombudsman.org/

involvement in the PMIZ project when it became clear that GoPNG had already selected a site and wanted to develop the zone before the site and viability assessment could have been completed.[245] Additionally, the IFC's PNG SEZ project was closed once the commitment of assistance with a basic, best practice legislative framework for the development of SEZs in PNG had been met.[246]

The Dispute Resolution Process

Between February and September 2012, the CAO held multiple separate meetings with stakeholder groups to determine the best way forward. In October 2012, the CAO convened a multi-stakeholder meeting, where over 100 participants discussed options for resolution.[247]

Agreement (MoU), Action Plan and Joint Communiqué

During the October 2012 multi-stakeholder meeting, an MoU was signed by all parties – including GoPNG representatives – and an action plan was agreed upon.[248]

The mutual understanding was that the parties wanted the PMIZ project to proceed without hindrance to the benefit of impacted communities and Madang as a whole. The parties committed their resources, time and best efforts to make the action plan successful. They agreed to talk through any differences and find mutually acceptable solutions, seek national and provincial Government funding, and encourage the State and all parties involved in the environmental court case to consider a settlement.[249]

Furthermore, a joint communiqué was released by the Minister for Trade Commerce and Industry, the President of Karkar LLG, a Rempi Impact Community representative and a Kananam (a town in Madang Province) impact community representative following consultations and discussions held at the Madang Resort Hotel on 19 December 2012. In the Joint Communiqué, they recognised and accepted the issues raised by

cases/document-links/documents/IFCresponsetoCAOassessmentreport-PNGSEZ564427.pdf.

245 Ibid.

246 Ibid.

247 CAO, *Ombudsman/Dispute Resolution Conclusion Report*, p. 1.

248 CAO, *Papua New Guinea/PNG SEZ-01/Madang Province.*

249 Bai, D., Wangad, J., Masai, H., et al. (2012). *Memorandum of Understanding between PMIZ Stakeholders*. www.cao-ombudsman.org/sites/default/files/downloads/Signed_MoU_16-Oct-2012.pdf, p. 1.

the parties, acknowledged the effort and commitment to resolving the complainants' issues, and recognised the MoU reached between the PMIZ stakeholders on 16 October 2012.[250]

Philippines Study Tour

In May 2013, the DCI agreed to sponsor a study tour for two of the plaintiffs in the community court action taken to halt the PMIZ project. The study tour was a visit to a similar industrial zone in the Philippines, which took place in May/June 2013. There, the participants viewed and learnt first-hand how the zone was managed and development impacts.[251]

Settlement of Court Case

A counsellor from Kar Kar Island (northwest of the PMIZ site) and a community leader from Rempi village (directly adjacent to the PMIZ site) filed a court action[252] to halt the PMIZ project, citing community concerns around environmental damage and social impacts. This action was later withdrawn around mid-2013 after the plaintiffs accepted GoPNG's assurances that their concerns would be addressed during PMIZ implementation, but the plaintiffs reserved the right to refile if it did not happen.[253]

Aftermath: CAO Monitoring

During the CAO's monitoring of the agreement implementation, the community members and MPG noted that the Ministry of Commerce and Industry were not following through with their part of the agreed actions. The CAO enquired with the Ministry and requested meetings, but did not receive any response. Therefore, the CAO was unable to continue with the dispute resolution process and its monitoring role.[254]

Since the agreements were not fully implemented as a result of disagreements around the MoU implementation, the CAO transferred the case to the CAO's Compliance function for appraisal on 31 July 2014.[255]

250 Maru, R., Wamm, B., Don, F. K., & Gem, F. (2012). *Joint Communiqué*. www.cao-ombudsman.org/sites/default/files/downloads/JointCommunique.pdf, p. 1.

251 CAO, *Ombudsman/Dispute Resolution Conclusion Report*, p. 2.

252 PMIZ: WS No. 440 of 2011: *Bagar Wamm* v. *NFA & 2 Ors*. No information could be found online about this court action.

253 CAO, *Ombudsman/Dispute Resolution Conclusion Report*, p. 2.

254 CAO, *Papua New Guinea/PNG SEZ-01/Madang Province*.

255 Ibid; CAO, *Ombudsman/Dispute Resolution Conclusion Report*, p. 2; CAO, *CAO Appraisal Report: IFC Advisory Services to Government of PNG (Report No. C-I-R5-Y14-F214)*, p. 1.

The Outcome

Since the implementation of the MoU was not fully completed and the CAO closed the case, the issue was not resolved. However, one agreed item was implemented – the establishment of the Madang Environmental Office, which would act as the monitoring agent on environmental concerns.[256]

The PMIZ project never got off the ground. The primary outputs were an access road, a fence and a gate that cost USD1 million at the site as of 2019.[257] However, GoPNG recently indicated that it will be developed in two phases (as of 5 August 2024).[258]

Lessons Learned

In complex dispute resolution cases, it is not uncommon to have some change in leadership within one or more stakeholder groups during the process, such as changes in community management or ownership, community representatives, NGO leaders or GoPNG officials. As a result, at times, the involvement of new decision makers who were not involved from the beginning of the process can be disruptive.[259]

In this case, PNG's national elections were held in mid-2012, after which the initial Minister and DCI Secretary were replaced by acting officials, who were subsequently replaced by a new Minister and Secretary in 2013. As a result of this turnover, the implementation of the MoU was disrupted and the CAO was unable to get any response from the Ministry after the turnover.[260] There were also deficiencies in the process of appointing and constituting the local umbrella organisations (LUOs) such that that there were no representation in choosing and appointing the leadership of the LUOs, giving rise to mismanagement and community disenchantment.[261]

[256] CAO, *Papua New Guinea/PNG SEZ-01/Madang Province.*

[257] Blades, J. (2019). Madang marine project lives another day, *RNZ*. www.rnz.co.nz/international/pacific-news/385373/madang-marine-project-lives-another-day; Smith, G. (2018). The Belt and Road to nowhere: China's incoherent aid in Papua New Guinea, *The Lowy Institute*. www.lowyinstitute.org/the-interpreter/belt-and-road-nowhere-china-s-incoherent-aid-papua-new-guinea; Post-Courier (2017). Govt splurges k4 million 'only' on gate. https://postcourier.com.pg/govt-splurges-k4-million-gate/.

[258] Post-Courier (2021). NFA ready to implement PMIZ. https://postcourier.com.pg/nfa-ready-to-implement-pmiz/.

[259] CAO, *Ombudsman/Dispute Resolution Conclusion Report*, p. 2.

[260] Ibid, p. 3.

[261] Ibid, pp. 1–2.

In hindsight, the parties could have discussed how to manage potential changes in representation including mechanism to assist the parties through turnover in the GoPNG stakeholders.[262]

This case also demonstrates that uni-directional 'consultation' consisting in one party informing another party of its plans in the absence of mutual decision making is not a substitute for genuine consultation. While project implementing teams may pursue such an approach for the sake of expedience, ultimately, this results in higher costs due to stalled or even cancelled projects including multiple post-dispute conflict resolution sessions.

Compounding the lack of community consultation with landowners in the area, the lack of environmental planning and examination of impacts to fish populations, reefs and lagoons, and wider social and environmental impacts[263] resulted in the subsequent dispute. Villagers from Rempi lost access to a significant mangrove area, which served as an important food source.[264]

Conclusion

The pre-2013 cases under conditions of lax pre-project diligence and consultation standards highlight the risks and dangers of insufficient attention to community consultation. The necessity of maintaining relationships with new decision makers that emerge over the course of a project life cycle, the need for genuine multi-directional rather than 'uni-directional' consultation and the importance of thorough prior ESIA are highlighted. Of the six cases examined, four were cancelled or stalled, one proceeded to court litigation and one was closed. The cases highlight the risks of insufficient attention to community consultation, the necessity of maintaining relationships with decision makers that emerge over the course of a project life cycle, the need for genuine multi-directional rather than 'uni-directional' consultation and the importance of thorough prior ESIA.

The IFC/World Bank Cambodia Airport II project demonstrates the importance of involving all key stakeholders at the outset of a project, the need for awareness of external constraints and providing scope for parties to weigh various options for resolution. The IFC/World Bank

262 Ibid, p. 3.

263 CAO, *Papua New Guinea/PNG SEZ-01/Madang Province*; CAO, *Ombudsman/Dispute Resolution Conclusion Report*, p. 1.

264 Ibid, p. 8.

Mongolian Oyu Tolgoi community–investor dispute case demonstrated how the lack of meaningful pre-project consultation was a driving factor that led to subsequent dispute. In assessing the outcome, it was found that had greater weight been given to the herder's input, the entire dispute could have been avoided. The presence of local dispute resolution facilitators was also significant in achieving effective communication between the parties given their local understanding of culture and language. Joint fact finding, supported by independent third parties and agreement on relevant facts was likewise significant. Finally, the involvement of the local government was critical to arriving at resolution. The World Bank Indonesia PT WBN project similarly demonstrated the dangers of a lack of consultation and transparency on subsequent project progression. The ADB/IFC/EIB Bangladesh LSC case, implementing lower standards of 'informed participation' rather than full consultation or consent, resulted in inaccurate land documentation, limited external monitoring and limited engagement, resulting in the subsequent dispute. Ultimately, the land issue was referred to the local courts for resolution. Finally, the IFC Philippines: Mindoro resources project demonstrated the importance of oversight of de-centralised consultative process involving local government authorities, company representatives and Indigenous populations. Risks arising from lack of transparency, ineffective social and economic audits and obfuscation of facts resulted in the dissolution of trust between parties. Ultimately, the project was suspended. Overall, these cases highlight the significance of meaningful pre-project consultation standard for the long-term success of infrastructure projects.

6

Mandated Pre-project Community Engagement Cases in the Asia Pacific

Overview

Building on Chapter 5, which examined six infrastructure development cases in the Asia Pacific prior to the implementation of increasingly mandated community engagement policies including heightened diligence and pre-project consultation standards, this chapter explores continuities and developments after standards for pre-project consultation were raised in 2013.

The six cases examined in this chapter (see Table 5), funded by multilateral and national development banks operating in the Asia Pacific region after heightened community engagement policies were introduced, underscore a number of key insights. After increasingly mandated community engagement practices were introduced starting in 2013, a number of continuities and advancements were identified in dispute emergence. The post-2013 cases broadly demonstrate a number of key improvements including greater rigour in consultation and diligence mechanisms, heightened precision in identifying issues of community concern, higher pre-project diligence and screening standards, ongoing environmental and technical monitoring, the presence of locally trained mediators, skill development for consultation participants, a longer-term view of community welfare and responsive grievance remedies. Shortcomings persisted in some cases, including instances of duress, lack of information disclosure, fraud, limited access to consultation mechanisms and environmental harm leading to project cessation in two cases when the adverse social impacts were seen to outweigh potential benefits. On the whole, corresponding with an overall trend towards more rigorous community consultation and diligence standards, during this phase, the number of stalled/cancelled and litigated cases declined by 33%, the percentages of cases brought to court declined by 16%, and the number of cases pursuing party agreement through

Table 5 *Phase 2: post-2013 multilateral development bank models of community engagement and resulting challenges.*

No	Name	Country	Sector	Stakeholders	Issues	Year	Result
1	International Finance Corporation (IFC)-funded Adjaristsqali Georgia Power Plant project	Georgia	Construction of hydroelectric power plants	Local villagers/ population	Lack of detailed geological study, disregard for safety of local population and potential environmental damage, loss of water, biodiversity damage, increased frequency of landslides and harvest failures	2017	Community dialogue and assistance from the company and government led to the establishment of a 'Natural Disasters Fund'; the last phase of the project was cancelled
2	IFC-funded Azerbaijan TANAP Natural Gas Pipeline project	Azerbaijan	Construction of a natural gas supply route	Landowners	Contested compensation for land lease, partial compensation for crops, duress; loss of profits due to payment delays/ currency devaluation, inadequate consultation; fraudulent issuance of ownership documents by the municipality	2018	Compensation provided to municipality; the Compliance Advisor Ombudsman (CAO) decided not to proceed with further investigation as issues relating to resettlement occurred before the loan guarantee

3	Asian Infrastructure Investment Bank (AIIB)/World Bank-funded Amaravati project	India	Urban development	Landowners, farmers	Farmers forced to pool land into a land pooling scheme (LPS) or lose their land without compensation, limited resettlement framework, lack of analysis of project alternatives; limited environmental impact review, limited consultation	2014	Project cancelled after the World Bank withdrew support due to adverse social impacts; in June 2024, it was re-started
4	Chinese Bank Consortium (China Development Bank, Export–Import Bank of China (EXIM), Silk Road Fund)/IFC World Bank Karot Hydropower project	Pakistan	Hydropower plant (HPP)	Labour union	Labour/management: denied access to the project site, lack of communication and unavailability of individuals with authority to resolve labour-related issues, denied referendum for reaching collective bargaining agreement (CBA)	2016	Mediation is ongoing; the current challenge is lack of jurisdiction over government entity to compel participation

Table 5 (*cont.*)

No	Name	Country	Sector	Stakeholders	Issues	Year	Result
5	IFC/World Bank, AIIB, African Development Bank (AfDB), Nubian Suns project in Benban Solar Park (BSP)	Egypt	Solar plant construction	Employees, local villagers, government	Labour practices; lack of labour grievance mechanism, intimidation, limited local access to employment; lack of accessible grievance offices, lack of consultation prior to filing of complaints	2022	Most complaints filed were set to be resolved through a CAO-facilitated dispute resolution process
6	Asian Development Bank (ADB)-funded Ulaanbaatar Urban Services Case	Mongolia	Multi-tranche financing facility for urban development	Individual complainants	Lack of social impact assessment, insufficient consultation, insufficient information disclosure	2018	Case resolved through Office of the Special Project Facilitator (OSPF)-facilitated mediation process; ninety-three out of 110 claims resolved in favour of the complainants

mediation or negotiation increased by 50% compared with ad-hoc discretionary consultation practices prior to 2013.

Case 1: IFC-Funded Adjaristsqali Georgia Power Plant Project

Introduction

The IFC-funded Adjaristsqali Georgia Power Plant project case demonstrates the importance of government involvement in facilitating community access to information and participation,[1] and participant skill development prior to the mediation process[2] to ensure the process was inclusive.[3] While the parties ended the mediation process without a final agreement, there were some partial outcomes, including[4] ongoing community support from the company and the government; the establishment of a 'Natural Disasters Fund' and continued engagement through the Working Group.[5] Given the economic and environmental risks and lack of community support, the final phase of the project was cancelled.

Background

The Adjaristsqali Georgia LLC (AGL or 'the Company') project, developed by AGL,[6] was a joint venture between India's Tata Power, Norway's Clean Energy Invest and the IFC. It involved constructing a cascade of hydroelectric power plants in the Adjaristsqali region, Adjara, Georgia.[7] The project was financed by the ADB, the IFC and the European Bank for Reconstruction and Development (EBRD). Apart from IFC's financing, the project was issued a guarantee by the Multilateral Investment Guarantee Agency (MIGA) covering an equity investment of Tata Power International Pte. Ltd of Singapore.[8] Originally, the project was designed to proceed in phrases. Ultimately, AGL did not pursue the final scheme in light of economic and environmental risks.[9]

[1] Ibid.
[2] Ibid.
[3] Ibid.
[4] Ibid.
[5] Ibid.
[6] A special-purpose company established to implement a cascade hydropower project.
[7] CAO Assessment Report Regarding Complaint in Relation to Adjaristsqali Georgia LLC (AGL), p. 5.
[8] Georgia: AGL/Makhalakidzeebi-01 Dispute Resolution Conclusion Report – October 2020, p. 1.
[9] Ibid., p. 2.

The CAO received a complaint filed by seventeen residents of the Rabati District of the Makhalakidzeebi village, Shuakhevi Municipality in the Autonomous Republic of Adjara, Georgia.[10] They represented twenty-two households in the village of Makhalakidzeebi.[11] The project sought to build two dikes and a number of derivation tunnels from different tributaries of the Acharistskali river, one of which was on the territory adjacent of the complainants' village. The project involved some drilling and explosion work.[12]

The group of residents' first complaint letter to the bank management in August 2017 requesting response to the hazards arising from the project and endangering existence of their village was met with no reply.[13]

Pre-project Community Consultation Process

A series of meetings were held with stakeholders, including the local government, AGL and the Ministry of Energy.[14] The company signed a memorandum with village dwellers under which it would compensate for any damages arising out of the construction work in 2014.[15]

Community Complaint

In the complaint letter, the complainants alleged that[16] the company's representative played down the disturbance of the impulses (shocks) during the meetings between parties; the company started the construction work without a prior detailed geological study and mitigation works, which represented a violation of the IFC's requirements; the company showed a disregard for the safety of the population in the area and potential damage to the natural and social environment, including the effect on drinking and irrigation water; the project would damage rivers, leaving only 10% of the river water available, and change the microclimate of the village, resulting in more frequent landslides and rockfalls;

[10] CAO Assessment Report Regarding Complaint in Relation to Adjaristsqali Georgia LLC (AGL), p. 5.
[11] Georgia: AGL/Makhalakidzeebi-01 Dispute Resolution Conclusion Report – October 2020, p. 2.
[12] Complaint Letter from Rabati District of the village of Makhalakidzes' of Shuakhevi Municipality to Compliance Mechanism of International Financial Corporation, P.1
[13] Ibid.
[14] Ibid, p. 2.
[15] Ibid, p. 1.
[16] Ibid, pp. 1–2.

after the construction phase, the community lost its portable water and trout and fish species, experienced rockfalls and landslides more frequently and suffered decreased harvest. Survival in the village became impossible. Over the last two years as at the letter of complaint, that is, 2017–2018, geologists assessed the village and published reports confirming the disastrous geological conditions caused by drilling and explosion works of the project; and without a formal assessment of the damage in accordance with the standards set out in Article 2.7 of the memorandum of understanding (MoU) between the company and the village, the government of Autonomous Republic of Achara simply offered them 25,000 GEL as compensation.

Community members alleged that AGL failed to attend to the geological and social risks of the project and to abide by the agreement entered between the Government of Adjara and village residents in 2014, which governed the provision of compensation in case of damage arising from construction activities.[17]

It was the complainants' claim that they were not compensated for the damage and harm arising out of the project. They claimed that in 2014, the Government of Adjara entered into an agreement with the Makhalakidzeebi village that they would 'provide resettlement to households that were destroyed or damaged as a result of a natural disaster'. Under the agreement, the company would also 'remediate any damages to private property and to the water supply attributable to the [p]roject, and to survey the water supply in the village'. The complainants said that while the regional government did offer to pay some compensation, this was rejected by the community because the amount was deemed disproportionately low.

The complainants indicated that the biodiversity of the Adjaristsqali river suffered harm because of the construction activities. Some endangered fish species have since disappeared from the river.

The community demanded that[18] the company conclude a property inventory of the Rabati district dwellers and define individual compensation packages; and that the IFC conduct a compliance assessment of Shuakhevi HPP project, and its environmental and social (E&S) impacts in light of the bank's E&S policy.

In response, the company noted that[19] it had engaged with the local community in the early stages of the project and made timely response to

[17] CAO Assessment Report Regarding Complaint in Relation to Adjaristsqali Georgia LLC (AGL), p. 5.

[18] Ibid, p. 7.

[19] Ibid, pp. 7–8.

their requests and opinions. They claimed that more than thirty meetings with the community were held to facilitate communication. A public information centre and a company-based grievance mechanism, which handled more than thirty complaints from the community in relation to house deformation and groundwater loss, was established in 2013.

The Complaint Handling Process

The complaint was found to be eligible for further assessment in April 2018. The CAO facilitated a dispute resolution process between the company and the complainants.[20]

The complainants also filed a complaint with the Project Complaint Mechanism (PCM) of the EBRD and the OSPF of the ADB because they were co-financiers of the project along with IFC.[21] When the complaint was being assessed, the parties agreed that the CAO and PCM would facilitate the dialogue process jointly, while the OSPF would act as the observer.[22]

A parallel dispute resolution process was conducted by the CAO, PCM and OSPF. The three parties liaised with each other to determine the way forward. The complainants and the company agreed to a dialogue process so the complaint was handled by the CAO's dispute resolution function.[23]

As part of the assessment, the CAO conducted desk reviews of project documents, calls with parties, and meetings and phone calls with project teams. In June 2018, the CAO and PCM held meetings with the complainants and the company. Issues such as the agenda, meeting structure and ground rules were discussed. The first few meetings were tense because of the complainant's urgent need for assurances. The parties, in the first mediation joint meeting, signed a Framework Agreement for the dialogue process, which set out the roles of participants, the format of meetings, and the rules concerning decision making, confidentiality and communications. Both parties agreed that the local municipality administration, represented by the Mayor of Shuakhevi, was an important stakeholder who should be invited to take part in the mediation process. The complainants indicated that the landslides, rockfalls and decreases in the water supply were the top issues. In response, the company denied responsibility on the basis that the issues related to pre-existing

[20] Ibid, p. 5.
[21] Ibid, p. 1.
[22] Ibid, p. 1.
[23] Ibid, p. 8.

geological characteristics of the local environment rather than the construction work.[24]

After the first joint meeting, parties began exploring viable solutions and engaged in negotiations. In September 2018 at the second joint meeting, a Working Group composed of representatives of the complainants, the company and the Shuakhevi municipal government was formed to provide a constructive space for co-operation and action planning.[25]

The third joint meeting was held in December 2019. A representative from the Adjara regional government was invited to join the mediation process and participate in a fourth joint meeting.[26]

At the fourth joint meeting in June 2019, parties agreed on the establishment of a Joint Programme for Community Safety and Development and coordinate the existing governmental eco-migration programme. While the parties originally agreed that the programme would be implemented in 2020, they were not able to agree on the specifics of the programme by July 2020. The main disagreement revolved around the requirement that community members register for the eco-migration programme before they could benefit from the company's support.[27]

The fifth joint meeting was held online due to Covid-19 restrictions on 14 July 2020. The parties were not able to overcome their disagreements and find common ground. The CAO solicited feedback and questions from the parties and explained the next steps.[28]

The Outcome

Over the span of two years from June 2018 to June 2020, the CAO and PCM encountered a number of challenges, including 'the need to allocate time to develop the [p]arties' capacity to engage in the mediation, the involvement of the government as a key stakeholder, and the restrictions brought by Covid-19'.[29]

The parties ended the mediation process without a final agreement in relation to the issues raised in the complaint. The complaint, hence, was

[24] Ibid, pp. 7–8.
[25] Ibid.
[26] Ibid.
[27] Ibid.
[28] Ibid.
[29] Ibid, p. 1.

transferred to the CAO Compliance team for appraisal of the IFC's and MIGA's performance related to the project.[30]

Despite the fact that a final settlement agreement was not reached, there were some positive outcomes, including, among others:[31] the creation of a space for dialogue; assistance from the company and the government; and the establishment of a 'Natural Disasters Fund'.[32]

Lessons Learned

The parties in this case were involved in the design of the structure and ground rules of the dialogue, which strengthened the building of trust.[33] The involvement of the government was also helpful in enhancing the parties' access to information about existing government programmes.[34] It was important that the mediators identified capacity gaps and skills requiring development through the mediation process[35] and ensure the process was inclusive of men and women in the community.[36] While full resolution was not reached, some support was introduced. The benefits of the final phase of the project were deemed not to outweigh its risks, and was therefore cancelled.

Case 2: IFC-Funded Azerbaijan TANAP Natural Gas Pipeline Project

The IFC-funded Azerbaijan TANAP Natural Gas Pipeline project case demonstrates the risks associated with fraudulent issuance of ownership documents, limited disclosure of relevant facts, duress and unequal bargaining power leading to imbalanced terms. Had there been adequate pre-project consultation instead of a top-down notification process, the issues giving rise to the dispute could have been avoided.

30 Ibid, pp. 7–8.
31 Ibid.
32 Ibid.
33 Ibid, p. 8.
34 Ibid.
35 Ibid.
36 Ibid.

Background

The Trans-Anatolian Natural Gas Pipeline (TANAP) project and South Caucasus Pipeline Expansion (SCPX) project was part of the Southern Gas Corridor programme for the construction of a natural gas supply route spanning from Middle Eastern and Caspian regions to Europe, with the aim of reducing dependency on Russian gas and diversifying energy sources. Among the programme's three pipelines is TANAP, which transports natural gas extracted from the Shah Deniz field in the Caspian Sea in Azerbaijan to Turkey and Europe.[37] The particular section of the TANAP project complained of in this case was the construction of the SCPX.

On 27 June 2018, the World Bank Group's MIGA agreed to issue guarantees amounting to USD780 million and €286 million (approximately USD331 million) for a loan provided by multiple commercial banks to the Southern Gas Corridor Closed Joint-Stock Company (CJSC), an Azerbaijani joint investment company with control over the TANAP project through majority ownership, in order to finance its share of the project.[38] Meanwhile, British Petroleum (Shah Deniz) Limited (BP) served as the technical operator of SCPX.

Community Complaint

The community complaint centred on land compensation and consultation concerns during the construction work of SCPX, which passed through and affected pieces of land in Azerbaijan under the de facto ownership of nine individuals (the 'complainants'). While the project commenced after 2013, the earlier exploratory phase of the project took place prior to the application of heightened diligence standards contributing to the issues giving rise to the complaint.

The complainants were relocated by the local municipality in 2007 to neighbouring farmlands due to the SCPX construction.[39] While the

[37] AIIB (7 December 2016). *Project Document of the Asian Infrastructure Investment Bank – Republic of Azerbaijan Trans Anatolian Natural Gas Pipeline (TANAP) Project*. www.aiib.org/en/projects/approved/2016/_download/trans-anatolian/document/tanap-project-document.pdf.

[38] Office of the CAO (August 2019). *CAO Assessment Report: Regarding Concerns in Relation to MIGA's Investment in Trans-Anatolian Natural Gas Pipeline (TANAP) Project # 13661, in Azerbaijan*. www.cao-ombudsman.org/cases/document-links/documents/CAOAssessmentReportTANAP-02Azerbaijan-ENG.pdf.

[39] Ibid.

municipality issued new ownership documents for the land concerned, BP, as SCPX's operator, allegedly contested ownership over the land as the ownership documents were fraudulent and lacked specific coordinates. While the complainants successfully challenged the documents' issuance with government entities and courts, which were then cancelled, they were subsequently only permitted to possess the affected lands without being issued official ownership documents for such.

On that basis, BP denied compensation for the leasing of the affected lands to the complainants, but instead paid compensation to the municipality as the formal owner. The complainants also claimed that BP paid only partial compensation due to contested land coordinates. This position matched BP's practice of signing non-binding MoUs with each lawful land owner, and its reliance on the relevant information provided by the State for compensation calculation (e.g. ownership documents, official on-site survey photos and satellite images).[40]

Allegedly, BP delayed compensation payments by eight months, resulting in a loss of income due to the devaluation of the Azerbaijani Manat during the period. The expression of the terms in the local currency was criticised as a bad-faith tactic, while BP explained that the alleged delay was stipulated in the lease agreements, and that Azerbaijani legislation prohibited contracting in USD when both contracting parties are locals.[41]

Pre-project Community Consultation Process

During the course of the TANAP project, a total of sixty-three public participation meetings were held to inform the affected communities about the project and gather feedback and suggestions,[42] while three consultations with local and international non-governmental organisations (NGOs) were held pursuant to Turkish legislation requirements. Compensation-related issues and grievance redress mechanisms (GRMs) were recurring themes in the meetings.

In the context of SCPX and the complainants, the Garajemirli village community in Azerbaijan's Shamkir region was invited by BP in 2014 to

40 Ibid.

41 Ibid.

42 AIIB, *Project Document of the Asian Infrastructure Investment Bank*; World Bank (22 July 2016). *TANAP Project's Executive Summary of ESIA and Supporting Environmental and Social Safeguard Documents*. https://documents1.worldbank.org/curated/en/937361470850514706/pdf/EXECUTIVE-SUMMARY-ENG-No-Memo-07262016.pdf.

a meeting informing them about SCPX's construction work that would pass through and affect their village.[43] It was further submitted to the CAO by BP that a second consultation session was held in 2015 to provide information on the pipeline and discuss the compensation rates.

The Community's Access to the Consultation and Relevant Process

While the complainants' community had access to consultation through the 2014 information sessions, the complainants claimed that there was insufficient information about the SCPX project, and they were pressured into signing the lease agreements.[44] Notably, the complainants accused BP of telling them that if they refused the agreements' terms, their land would be used regardless, and they could only seek redress elsewhere. Such alleged duress was arguably reflected in the thirteen restrictions on the complainants' use of land upon installation of the SCPX pipeline,[45] which BP contends was consensual.

Regarding the second consultation session in 2015, BP emphasised that land owners were not obliged to enter into the lease agreements, nor to accept the proposed compensation rate predetermined by an independent evaluator. Some land owners rejected the proposed compensation. It was further stated by BP that it had a complaints mechanism accessible to the affected community. It was reported by BP that multiple complaints were received and handled during the consultation process via such a mechanism.[46]

For the land owners that signed the lease agreements, including the complainants, the contractual terms, compensation rates and payment dates were formally agreed upon. The issues raised in the complaint only surfaced when the SCPX construction was underway.

Formal Complaint

The complaint concerned grievances by nine individual complainants, who were residents of Garajemirli village of the Azerbaijan's Shamkir region. The complaint was lodged with the support of the Oil Workers' Rights Protection Organisation Public Union and comprised of claims of inadequate and/or inappropriate land compensation and consultation.

[43] Office of the CAO, *CAO Assessment Report*.
[44] Ibid.
[45] Ibid.
[46] Office of the CAO, *CAO Assessment Report*.

Four main issues were raised:[47] no compensation for lease of the land; only partial compensation for crops on the land; duress to sign the lease agreements and loss of profits due to payment delays and currency devaluation; and inadequate consultation.

Legal, E&S Concerns

Legal

As previously discussed, the official recognition of legal ownership over the complainants' land was a disputed issue between BP and the complainants.[48] While the fraudulent issuance of ownership documents was successfully challenged before government entities and courts, the complainants' subsequent mere right to possess the affected lands posed a legal impediment to them demanding full compensation in accordance with their land use. It was therefore in the complainants' interest to obtain official ownership recognition from the municipality.

Environmental

The TANAP project involved a number of significant environmental concerns such as species conservation and protection of ecologically sensitive areas along the project route,[49] an issue later addressed in a Biodiversity Action Plan. However, for purposes of the complaint, no environmental issues were raised.

Social

The main social concern identified in the environmental and social impact assessments (ESIAs) was a potential misalignment between the project impacts and benefits and timely and full compensation.[50] While the scale of the TANAP project necessitated acquisition of enormous areas of land for pipeline construction, no physical displacement was required.[51]

The CAO Complaints Process: Assessment

The CAO determined on 19 November 2018 that the three eligibility criteria were satisfied by the complaint, on the basis that MIGA

[47] Ibid.
[48] Ibid.
[49] AIIB, *Project Document of the Asian Infrastructure Investment Bank.*
[50] Ibid.
[51] Ibid.

considered the South Caucasus Pipeline as an associated facility to TANAP. The CAO then proceeded on to the assessment stage.[52]

While the complaints expressed willingness to engage in a dispute resolution process, BP preferred the complaint to be handled through Compliance.[53] As dispute resolution requires consensus between the two parties, the complaint was referred to CAO Compliance for appraisal of the IFC's performance.

Compliance

MIGA's guarantee was prepared before the backdrop of its 2013 Policy on Environmental and Social Sustainability (the 'Policy') and Performance Standards (the 'Standards'), while the 2013 Environmental and Social Review Procedures Manual (the 'Manual') served as internal guidance on E&S due diligence and monitoring.[54] The underlying principles were that a project does no harm to people and the environment, and a mitigation hierarchy be designed to anticipate, avoid and minimise adverse impacts.[55]

Where MIGA's guarantee holder (i.e. the client) is a lender that does not control the project enterprise, as in this case for the multiple bank lenders, the client is nevertheless required by the Policy to enforce covenants requiring compliance with MIGA's E&S standards.[56] Meanwhile, MIGA itself bears responsibility for reviewing the client's third-party risk identification and must determine mitigation requirements on a case-by-case basis.

Due Diligence Review

The CAO found that MIGA relied on an E&S due diligence review conducted by the World Bank Group's International Bank for Reconstruction and Development (IBRD) prior to MIGA involvement.[57] The review

[52] Office of the CAO, *CAO Assessment Report.*

[53] Ibid.

[54] Office of the CAO (16 March 2020). *Compliance Appraisal: Summary of Results: Trans-Anatolian Pipeline (IGA Project # 13661), Complaint 02 Azerbaijan.* www.cao-ombudsman.org/cases/document-links/documents/CAO-Compliance-Appraisal_TANAP-02_.pdf.

[55] MIGA (1 October 2013). *Policy on Environmental and Social Sustainability.* www.miga.org/sites/default/files/archive/Documents/Policy_Environmental_Social_Sustainability.pdf.

[56] Ibid.

[57] Office of the CAO, *Compliance Appraisal.*

categorised SCPX as an 'associated facility' of TANAP with a safeguard policy waiver approved by the IBRD's Board of Executive Directors dispensing with a reasonable expectation in access to all project documentation and negotiating a legal framework allowing the IBRD to exercise remedies in the event of non-compliance.[58] The IBRD concluded that SCPX generally complied with its safeguard procedures and no significant compliance issues were identified.[59] MIGA's own E&S due diligence confirmed IBRD's conclusion that the land acquisition and social impacts were acceptable.[60]

However, the CAO had reservations as to the robustness of MIGA's analysis in concluding that there was no prospect of exerting influence on SCPX to leverage outcomes consistent with the Performance Standards and other E&S requirements through the stakeholder institutions.[61] This was evident from MIGA's lack of engagement with SCPX and TANAP shareholders as part of its due diligence, and failure to provide analysis of manageable third-party risk conditions.

The CAO noted that MIGA undertook a variety of actions to monitor the project, including a regular monitoring programme for business activities via the client's Annual Monitoring Report and updates on the E&S Action Plan.[62] MIGA also conducted a site visit to the TANAP project in Turkey in October 2018, finding satisfactory management of E&S risks.

The Outcome

The CAO noted that the issues raised by the complainants, particularly economic displacement and compensation, had potential substantial material livelihood impacts on a large number of households.[63] It also noted the shortfalls in MIGA's E&S due diligence and analysis, questioning MIGA's conclusion of a purported lack of operational control and influence over SCPX, and thus inability to extend its E&S requirements accordingly.

58 Ibid.

59 World Bank (22 November 2016). *Azerbaijan and Turkey: Trans-Anatolian Natural Gas Pipeline Project (P157416) Project Appraisal Document.* https://documents1.worldbank.org/curated/en/224911483470754491/pdf/PAD1665-REVISED-OUO-9-P157416-PAD-Main-Final-12012016.pdf.

60 Office of the CAO, *Compliance Appraisal.*

61 Ibid.

62 Ibid.

63 Office of the CAO, *Compliance Appraisal.*

Nonetheless, upon weighing the relevant factors, the appraisal stage concluded that a CAO Compliance investigation was an inappropriate response to the complaint given that the resettlement process giving rise to the complaint took place before MIGA's provision of a guarantee for the TANAP project; MIGA's guarantee was cancelled in August 2019 after CJSC repaid the loan obtained from the lender banks; and the IBRD received from its Board of Executive Directors the safeguard policy waiver for SCPX as a TANAP-associated project.

Accordingly, the case of the complaint was closed following the CAO's decision not to proceed on to investigation following compliance appraisal.

Lessons Learned

Importance of Pre-project Consultation

The issues raised in the complaint could be consolidated as stemming from two main problems: different interpretation of ownership recognition accorded by the municipality as a 'third party'; and the complainants' lack of understanding and bargaining power in reaching the terms of the lease agreements. Notably, it is likely that the two problems could have been addressed sufficiently had there been adequate pre-project consultation.

The discrepancy in interpreting ownership over the affected lands arose as a result of the fraudulent issuance of ownership documents by the municipality that caused the complainants' predicament, and it was understandable for BP to instinctively rely on official, government-provided information as a basis for its compensation. However, the mismatch in understanding causing the compensation dispute could have been resolved had there been adequate pre-project diligence and consultation, particularly emphasising an exchange of information instead of a top-down meeting that merely served a notifying function.

Case 3: Amaravati Project

Introduction

The Amaravati case demonstrates an approach to project suspension where a project is found to be both sufficiently detrimental to local affected communities and lacking community support. This is exemplified by the case of the Amaravati project. The cancellation of disbursements is generally an option of last resort applied only in exceptional or 'unusual'[64] circumstances, and the World Bank, ADB and AIIB generally prefer to adopt other approaches to redressing grievances, including dispute resolution and compliance investigations.[65]

In this case, though the management detailed thorough pre-project consultation mechanisms, proper implementation was lacking. Community complaints viewed the consultation mechanism as flawed due to concerns about coercive behaviour on the part of officials and limited follow up. The issue of the land resettlement policy underscored the need for a principled regulatory framework. The project was suspended in 2019. After a five-year hiatus, and following further legislative and community deliberation and policy re-formulation, the project resumed in 2024.

The case illustrates the growing attention multilateral development banks (MDBs) place on the quality of the prior project consultation in assessing the existence of support from affected communities in the vicinity of project's sites. Such considerations factor into the bank's evaluation of its continued assistance of and involvement in such projects. Although these more 'extreme' measures are yet to be fully reflected in regulatory literature, the project case demonstrates a greater focus on the efficacy and transparency of independent accountability mechanisms (AMs), a greater appreciation for the temporal aspects of these grievances (including any long-term societal risks or harms of the project, a commitment to community welfare post-withdrawal of funding, and the use of contractual safeguards for community welfare that allow for withdrawal to occur at an earlier stage), and a community-oriented approach to remedying grievances in response to the particular facts of each case.

Background

The Andhra Pradesh Reorganization Act 2014, which came into effect on 2 June 2014, provided for the reorganisation of the existing state of Andhra Pradesh. The State Cabinet meeting of 1 September 2014 passed a resolution 'to locate the Capital City in a central place of the state,

64 Guardian News and Media (12 January 2016). World Bank cancels funding for Uganda road amid sexual assault claims. *The Guardian*. www.theguardian.com/global-development/2016/jan/12/world-bank-cancels-uganda-road-sexual-assault-claims.

65 Ibid.

around Vijayawada, and to go for decentralised development of the state with 3 Mega Cities and 14 Smart Cities'.[66]

The Amaravati Capital City has an area of 217.23 km^2 and is spread across twenty-five villages in three mandals (Thulium, Mangalagiri and Tadepalli) of Guntur district. The twenty-five villages in the Capital City area have a population of about 100,000 people.[67] The Project Development Objective of the proposed Amaravati Sustainable Capital City Development Project (ASCCDP) was to provide select urban infrastructure in designated locations of Amaravati Capital City, and to support the initial development of its institutional and governance structure.[68] The key institutions involved in the implementation of the ASCCDP are the Andhra Pradesh Capital Region Development Authority (APCRDA) and the Amaravati Development Corporation (ADC), both governed by the Department of Municipal Administration and Urban Development (MA&UD) of the Government of Andhra Pradesh.[69]

Although the World Bank pledged to support the project with a funding of USD300 million, given the ongoing community conflicts, on 15 July 2019, the Government of India withdrew its request to the World Bank for financing, followed by withdrawal of funding from the AIIB.[70] The project was controversial and, although it has created a strong public reaction,[71] officially, there was only one complaint registered with the Inspection Panel at the World Bank, detailed here.

Pre-project Consultation

Thousands of consultation events took place since 2014 following each phase of development of the project, starting with the preparation of the Master Plan.[72] Consultations have taken many forms – in the early days, they were informal, door-to-door conversations in the villages and

66 APCRDA (August 2018, revised in November 2024). Environmental and Social Assessment for the Amaravati Integrated Urban Development Program (P507508). https://documents1.worldbank.org/curated/en/099112524143524033/pdf/P507508-3e96f044-3f97-423a-9f92-584637a7066e.pdf, [1].

67 Ibid, [2].

68 Ibid, [3].

69 Ibid, [9].

70 www.livemint.com/news/india/asian-infrastructure-investment-bank-withdraws-funding-to-amaravati-project-1563946400320.html.

71 https://thefederal.com/explainers-2/amaravati-farmers-protest/.

72 APCRDA (August 2018). Environmental and Social Assessment, p. 70, note 66.

community meetings, which evolved after the start of the LPSs, into well-planned, documented consultations with hundreds of stakeholders.[73] Project information centers (PICs) were set up in every village to allow for continuous consultations to take place, on demand, when sought out by the residents of the project.[74] The PICs were well-staffed and open to the public.[75] Grievance logs and documentation were maintained, including descriptions of the project. Documents informing on safeguards were made available for consultation at the PICs as well as online once the safeguard instruments were finalised.[76]

Consultations were conducted in person, in writing and on the phone, in English and in Telugu.[77] This was coupled with a communications campaign that made extensive use of printed materials, newspapers, radio, videos, the internet and social media.[78] Pre-LPS consultations started in September 2014, and hundreds of distinct events were carried out by APCRDA to inform residents of the Capital City area of the development of the new city.[79] Efforts were made to organise consultations at different times (day and evening), and to have meetings in neighbouring cities (e.g. Bangalore).[80]

Numerous consultations with farmers and landless workers took place during the process of joining LPS, while layouts for returnable plots were agreed upon. A total of 30,000 farmers joined the LPS as of mid-2018, and were consulted at different periods in time.[81]

As part of the land acquisition process for capital city development under the Right to Fair Compensation and Transparency in Land Acquisition, Rehabilitation and Resettlement Act, 2013 (LARR Act 2013), the district administration conducted consultations and public hearings on village-specific social impact assessments in affected villages.[82] Consultations were held by independent consultants.[83]

Additional rounds of consultations were carried out as the World Bank project was prepared, and more specifically as the safeguard instruments

[73] Ibid.
[74] Ibid.
[75] Ibid, [60].
[76] Ibid.
[77] Ibid, [54].
[78] Ibid.
[79] Ibid, [56].
[80] Ibid.
[81] Ibid, [57].
[82] Ibid [58].
[83] Ibid.

were finalised. Separate consultations were held with multiple stakeholders, in preparation of the Environmental and Social Management Framework (ESMF), the Environmental Impact Assessment (EIA) and associated Environmental Management Plans (EMPs) for the roads and the flood management works.[84] Consultations were held primarily throughout 2017 and 2018.[85]

A robust GRM for the overall Capital City was set up by APCRDA. The GRM provided multiple avenues, covering physical, web-based and telephonic channels for registering and seeking redress of grievances.[86] Every Monday, a grievance redressal meeting to attend public grievances was held at APCRDA offices.[87]

The Complaint

The complaint for inspection was submitted by landowners from the area known as Amaravati in Andhra Pradesh, India (the 'Requesters') and included twenty-two attachments of project-related reports, media articles and court documents (the 'Request').[88] The Requesters alleged harm from the LPS in assembling lands required for the proposed city and for activities related to the proposed project.[89] The Requesters also claimed harm related to their livelihoods, environment, food security, resettlement and lack of consultation as a result of the Bank's non-compliance with its E&S standards.[90]

The Requesters noted that some of the proposed project activities would be implemented on lands assembled under the LPS.[91] They claimed that many landowners and farmers were intimidated and economically coerced to participate in the LPS.[92] They stated that farmers who had not consented to joining the LPS were forced to either pool their land under the LPS or their land would be acquired by the government under the Land Acquisition Act.[93] In their view, neither option provided

[84] Ibid, [62].
[85] Ibid, [64].
[86] Ibid, [52].
[87] Ibid.
[88] Inspection Panel at the World Bank (12 June 2017). *Notice of Registration re Proposed Amaravati Sustainable Capital City Development Project (P159808)*, [8].
[89] Ibid.
[90] Ibid, [21].
[91] Ibid.
[92] Ibid.
[93] Ibid.

adequate compensation to restore livelihoods or purchase comparable replacement land.[94]

The complaint argued that the Bank used its Resettlement Policy Framework (RPF) rather than a full Resettlement Plan, despite Bank documents suggesting that the 'zone of impact of subprojects' could be determined.[95] The Requesters claimed that the Bank did not accurately assess the nature and magnitude of the proposed project in relation to displacement, nor did it ensure that land acquired through the LPS complied with the Bank Policy on Involuntary Resettlement.[96]

The Request raised concerns regarding food insecurity, since the Amaravati area contained 'multi-crop irrigated land that produces 120 types of crops'.[97]

The Requesters noted that Component 2 of the proposed project would affect the Kondaveeti Vagu river and claimed that the fields adjacent to the riverbed are wetlands not adequately addressed in the Strategic Environmental and Social Assessment and ESMF (SESA-ESMF).[98]

The Requesters claimed that only one consultation was held in January 2017 on the draft SESA-ESMF and draft RPF, and that only 150 persons out of an estimated 127,505 potentially affected people (APs) attended this consultation and five online comments were submitted. They alleged that there was intimidation at the consultation meeting from security forces and that some participants were forcibly turned away.[99]

Complaint Handling Process

The Complaint was submitted to the Inspection Panel at the World Bank under the 2014 operating procedures.[100]

The Request was found not to be frivolous as it was submitted by two or more landowners and farmers in the proposed project area in Andhra Pradesh, India.[101] As part of its due diligence, the Inspection Panel met

94 Ibid.
95 Ibid, [10].
96 Ibid.
97 Ibid, [11].
98 Ibid, [12].
99 Ibid, [13].
100 Inspection Panel at the World Bank (April 2014). *Operating Procedures.*
101 *Notice of Registration*, [16].

with management on 24 May 2017.[102] On 12 June 2017, the Inspection Panel registered the Request.[103]

Summary of the Management Response

The management response referred to the optional nature of the LPS and stated that the APCRDA carried out an extensive information and consultation campaign to allow landowners to make an informed decision on their compensation options, and consent was confirmed by each landowner on at least six separate occasions during the LPS process.[104] The management response emphasised that the proposed project was still under preparation.[105]

Management noted the concerns about food security resulting from the large-scale conversion of agricultural land to urban land in the SESA-ESMF, which 'determined that the crops in the Amaravati City were predominantly crops that were not used for daily consumption by people. Transformation of agricultural land to urban land would, therefore, not significantly impact the production of food in the state.'[106] The management response stated that the Bank would work closely with the APCRDA to ensure that the scope of the environmental assessment was adequate, including for the Kondaveeti Vagu river and the surrounding wetland areas.[107]

Management acknowledged that 'a more extensive program of consultation and information on the proposed Project needed to be carried out, which could result in adjustments in project design'.[108]

As the proposed project was currently under preparation by the Bank, the loan amount was not yet disbursed.[109]

Inspection Panel's Observations and Recommendation

The Inspection Panel noted that the most current draft RPF referred to the LPS as 'a voluntary scheme'.[110] The Inspection Panel observed that once the area of Amaravati was decided, all people living within it

102 Ibid, [19].
103 Ibid, [21].
104 Inspection Panel at the World Bank (27 September 2017). *Report and Recommendation on a Request for Inspection re Proposed Amaravati Sustainable Capital City Development Project (P159808)*, [17].
105 Ibid, [19].
106 Ibid, [20].
107 Ibid, [21].
108 Ibid.
109 Ibid.
110 Ibid, [54].

(excluding those in urban villages) would have to, sooner or later, provide their lands through either the LPS, negotiated settlement or land acquisition in accordance with the 2013 LARR Act.[111] In this regard, the LPS was a choice within an overall involuntary situation; it represented one option in the context where the choice of keeping one's lands did not exist, and therefore it qualifies as involuntary resettlement.[112]

The Inspection Panel therefore recommended carrying out an investigation into the alleged issues of harm and related potential non-compliance with Bank policies, especially relating to involuntary resettlement (OP/BP 4.12).[113] The investigation primarily focused on resettlement aspects of the Bank's proposed Project, as well as environmental concerns and issues related to consultation, participation and disclosure of information as they pertained to the Bank's financing and Bank policies and procedures.[114]

While the Inspection Panel acknowledged the many positive steps taken by management to address issues of concern since the Inspection Panel's first Report and Recommendation of 27 September 2017, including clarification by management that all resettlement and land acquisition mechanisms, where applied to land within the Bank-financed project, were subject to the Bank's Involuntary Resettlement Policy,[115] it also included all the 21,374 landless labourer households in the capital city area as people affected by the Bank project.[116] The Inspection Panel also recognised that this project, with an LPS at a scale not previously experienced anywhere in the world, may establish a model for future similar initiatives elsewhere.[117] Based on its analysis of available documentation and information, the Inspection Panel had concerns regarding the Bank's due diligence and project design approach in relation to the Bank's Involuntary Resettlement Policy.[118] The Inspection Panel therefore recommended carrying out an investigation into the alleged issues of harm and related potential non-compliance with livelihood restoration requirements of the Bank's Involuntary Resettlement Policy (OP/BP 4.12).[119]

[111] Ibid.
[112] Ibid.
[113] Ibid, [58].
[114] Ibid.
[115] Inspection Panel at the World Bank (29 March 2019). *Third Report and Recommendation on a Request for Inspection re Proposed Amaravati Sustainable Capital City Development Project (P159808)*, [76].
[116] Ibid.
[117] Ibid.
[118] Ibid, [77].
[119] Ibid, [78].

Withdrawal from the Project

In July 2019, the World Bank announced its withdrawal from the Project, which was swiftly followed by a further withdrawal by the AIIB. Both institutions cited the 'adverse environmental, social, economic and financial implications of the new capital city developmental model',[120] and noted as their rationale the corresponding opposition from interested parties, including 'environmentalists, farmer groups, retired government officials' and others.[121] The potential adverse impacts to the environment were of particular concern given that the project's progression threatened to submerge Amaravati under floodwater from the neighbouring river Krishna, and posed further challenges to neighbouring forests and water bodies.[122]

The World Bank noted specifically the lack of community support in addition to the adverse environmental impacts the project posed. Many members of the affected communities in Amaravati took issue with the project resettlement policy. The World Bank's Inspection Panel[123] highlighted the 'considerable risks of a rural-to-urban transition at a large scale through the building of a new city supported by a Bank project'.[124] The project featured a 'land-pooling scheme', which saw landowners giving their farmland for the city's development, and receiving smaller urban serviced plots of higher value in return.[125] Both the legality of this scheme and the potential for it to decrease the net worth of individuals subject to the scheme and those dependent on their land for their livelihood were brought under scrutiny.[126]

This project was notable for the significant remedial actions that the World Bank and the AIIB took. Indeed, it was 'the first time that [the Panel] of world bank (sic) recommended an investigation into a project that has not yet been approved by the World Bank Board'.[127] The severity of this sanction, and the standards the World Bank applied in evaluating the social equity of the project was further illuminated by the fact that the

[120] Aggarwal, M. (18 August 2019). Amaravati Capital City project: From utopia to an uncertain future. *The Wire*. https://thewire.in/urban/amaravati-capital-city-project-from-utopia-to-an-uncertain-future.
[121] Ibid.
[122] Ibid.
[123] APCRDA (August 2018). Environmental and Social Assessment, p. 24.
[124] Inspection Panel of the World Bank, *Third Report and Recommendation on a Request for Inspection*, §77.
[125] Aggarwal, Amaravati Capital City project, §44.
[126] Ibid.
[127] n 3.

implementing agency for the project, the APCRDA, had declared earlier in January 2019 that it had developed solutions to many of the aforementioned issues pursuant to the World Bank's ESMF. These solutions purportedly included 'strategies for public consultation', 'plans for the capacity-building of key stakeholders' and 'plans to monitor the implementation of environmental and social safeguards' devised pursuant to the ESMF.[128]

This case demonstrates that the World Bank in particular had begun to adopt a more stringent approach to scrutinising not only the E&S issues raised by complainants, but also the efficacy of any purported safeguards including community consultation processes designed to address these issues.[129] There was in that statement an absence of community-oriented solutions designed to improve the project's transparency and facilitate healthier interactions with the local affected communities. Despite the aforementioned promise of improving the public consultation mechanisms for the project, the APRCDA merely signposted this without elaborating on its plans.

The solutions put forward in the disclosure statement were predominantly aimed at allaying environmental and socio-economic concerns raised by members of the affected communities, with little consideration of the project's relationship with the communities. Although the plan included programmes aimed at specific groups of people, including offering skills training to 'vulnerable and landless households'[130] and a recognition of the risk of 'gender-based violence for 'economically displaced female landless agricultural workers',[131] there were nonetheless no solutions put forward designed to fundamentally improve communications between affected communities and the project's stakeholders.

While the APRCDA did put forward a GRM, which featured online platforms, 'call centres', mobile applications and 'zonal offices' that made the process of conveying grievances to the authorities easier and more accessible,[132] nonetheless, the GRM was considered insufficient by

[128] The World Bank (18 January 2019). *Combined Project Information Documents/ Integrated Safeguards Datasheet (PID/ISDS): Amaravati Sustainable Infrastructure and Institutional Development Project (P159808).* https://documents1.worldbank.org/curated/en/531461548085838033/pdf/Project-Information-Document-Integrated-Safeguards-Data-Sheet-Amaravati-Sustainable-Infrastructure-and-Institutional-Development-Project-P159808.pdf, p. 18.

[129] Ibid, pp. 20–21.

[130] Ibid, pp. 21–22.

[131] Ibid, p. 23.

[132] Ibid, pp. 22–23.

the World Bank and the Panel because it did not detail how these grievances would be processed or evaluated, nor did it prescribe any procedural safeguards to guarantee the fairness of the redress process.

Following the withdrawal of the request for financing of the project by the Government of India, the Inspection Panel updated its Report and Recommendation not to recommend an investigation, since the project was no longer under consideration by the Bank.[133]

Lessons Learned

A number of lessons can be learned from this case. First, even though the management detailed thorough pre-project consultation mechanisms, the challenge remains in its implementation. Given the complaints by the Requesters, the implementation of the pre-project consultation mechanism was flawed due to concerns about coercive behaviour on the part of officials and limited pre-project consultation and redress follow up.

Second, the issue of the land resettlement policy underscored the need for a principled regulatory framework. The Inspection Panel expressed concern that the land resettlement or the LPS's framework under the LARR Act 2013 in itself likely contravened the Bank's Involuntary Resettlement Policy.

After a five-year hiatus following the project withdrawal in 2019, and after further legislative and community deliberation and policy re-formulation, the project resumed in 2024.

Case 4: Karot Hydropower Project in Pakistan

The Karot Hydropower project ('the Project') case in Pakistan demonstrates the importance of access to onsite grievance mechanisms and relevant government agency support in order to effectively address employment related claims during the course of a dispute.

The Karot Hydropower project was an initiative to construct, operate and maintain a 720 MW run-of-the-river HPP on the Jhelum river located in Punjab, Pakistan.[134] The Project was completed on

[133] Inspection Panel at the World Bank (16 July 2019). *Updated Third Report and Recommendation on a Request for Inspection re Proposed Amaravati Sustainable Capital City Development Project (P159808)*, [4].

[134] IFC (n.d.). *Karot Hydro*. https://disclosures.ifc.org/project-detail/SII/36008/karot-hydro.

29 June 2022[135] and is expected to generate 3,1743 GWh of electricity annually.[136] All the electricity is sold to the National Transmission and Despatch Company Limited (NTDC), through the Central Power Purchasing Agency (CPPA)[137] under a thirty-year power-purchase agreement.[138] The Government of Pakistan owns 88% of NTDC[139] and 100% of CPPA.[140]

The IFC(a member of the World Bank Group) committed an equity investment of USD125 million to the Project's sponsor, China Three Gorges South Asia Investment Limited (CSAIL) in November 2014[141] and an A-loan of up to USD100 million to the Karot Power Company Limited (KPCL)[142] on 25 November 2016.[143]

The Project was estimated to cost USD2 billion and funded with an 80-20 split of debt-to-equity ratio.[144] The debt financing was provided by a consortium of Chinese banks led by the China Development Bank, EXIM, and the Silk Road Fund to KPCL for USD1.29 billion, with the IFC contributing an additional USD100 million. Associated Technologies Private Limited and CSAIL own 7% and 93% of the shareholdings of KPCL, respectively.[145]

[135] CPEC Secretariat. (n.d.). *720MW Karot Hydropower Project, AJK/Punjab*. Ministry of Planning, Development, & Special Initiatives. https://cpec.gov.pk/project-details/16
[136] IFC, 'Summary of Investment Information', *Karot Hydro*.
[137] The National Electric Power Regulatory Authority (2 April 2015). *Tariff Petition for EPC Stage Reference Tariff for Karot Power Company (PVT.) Ltd 720 MW Karot Hydropower Project*. Karot Power Company (Private) Limited. https://nepra.org.pk/tariff/Tariff/Petitions/2015/Tariff%20Petition%20-%20Karot%20Hydropower%20Project.pdf.
[138] Ibid.
[139] The Pakistan Credit Rating Agency Limited (June 2020). *Rating Report: National Transmission & Despatch Company Limited*. www.pacra.com/summary_report/RR_2008_10528_13-Aug-22.pdf.
[140] www.cppa.gov.pk/central-power-purchasing-agency-cppa-g.
[141] IFC, 'Environmental and Social Review Summary', *Karot Hydro*.
[142] Office of the CAO (2023). (rep.). *CAO Assessment Report Regarding the Seventh Complaint Received in Relation to IFC's Investment in Karot Power Company Ltd (IFC #36008)*. www.cao-ombudsman.org/sites/default/files/downloads/Karot%2007_CAO%20Assessment%20Report_May%202023_2.pdf.
[143] AidData (n.d.). *Project ID: 37233 CDB, China Eximbank, and Silk Road Fund provide $1.292 billion USD in debt financing for the 720 MW Karot Hydropower Project. (Linked to Project ID#54012, #53675, and #54317) (BRI, CPEC, IPP)*. CHINA.AIDDATA.ORG. https://china.aiddata.org/projects/37233/
[144] IFC, 'Summary of Investment Information', *Karot Hydro*.
[145] AidData, *Project ID*.

Project Complaint

A labour management-related complaint was filed with the CAO by the complainant on 13 August 2022,[146] labelled as Karot Hydro (the 'Complaint'). The complaint was deemed to have satisfied the three eligibility criteria on 26 August 2022.[147] The Complaint was referred to the IFC at the complainant's request. The complainant expressed dissatisfaction with the IFC's complaint handling process since no action was taken despite direct engagement with the IFC and KHPP.

The complainant was the President of a local labour union named the Social Hydro Labour Union (SHU) at KHPP. The union was registered with the Registrar of Trade Unions (RTU) at Rawalpindi, the local authority regulating union matters, on 30 August 2019.

The Complaint concerned labour management issues related to alleged union busting. There were three components to the Complaint: (1) denial of access to the project site; (2) lack of communication and unavailability of individuals with authority to resolve labour-related issues; and (3) denial of a referendum for reaching a CBA.

Barred Access to Project Site

The Complaint claimed that KHPP relied on its Covid-19 entry protocol as a reason to deny access to the project site. However, the complainant informed the CAO that he had been granted access on 23 and 28 February and 2 April 2023 to the project site after KHPP had lifted the Covid-19 access protocol.[148] Nevertheless, the complainant was only provided with one-day passes instead of a permanent pass.

It was indicated to the CAO by KHPP that all Covid-19 restrictions had been lifted and Covid testing was no longer required for visitors. Still, KHPP followed a specific entry protocol in which all employees and visitors were required to present their ID cards and have basic information recorded. It was claimed by KPCL that no permanent pass would be granted due to the high-security protocol. Everyone, including employees

146 Office of the CAO (12 August 2022). *Pakistan: Karot Hydro-07/Jhelum River: CAO Data Hub*. www.cao-ombudsman.org/cases/pakistan-karot-hydro-07jhelum-river.

147 Ibid.

148 CAO, *CAO Assessment Report Regarding the Seventh Complaint Received in Relation to IFC's Investment in Karot Power Company Ltd (IFC #36008)*, p. 7.

and visitors, would have to provide details of their visit to the security department, claimed KHPP.[149]

The Pakistani army, instead of KHPP, was responsible for the security of the project site since it fell within the China–Pakistan Economic Corridor.[150] By correspondence, KPCL indicated that it had instructed the security office of KHPP to allow labour union secretaries to move freely at the project site, including the complainant.

The CAO noted the situation and indicated that it would follow up on the complainant's access to the project site in the capacity of the labour union president.

Lack of Communication and Person with Authority to Address Labour Issues

The complainant claimed he began labour union work in 2017 following a perceived lack of communication between labourers and KHPP on management, salary, bonus and health and safety issues at the project site. The complainant claimed KHPP denied that he had authority to negotiate labour issues even though the SHU was registered with the RTU in August 2019.[151] As of January 2022, the complainant claimed 90% of the workers had already left their job.[152]

It was claimed by KPCL that it had implemented nineteen labour policies in line with Pakistani law and IFC performance standards. These policies were reviewed and accepted by the IFC. These policies 'related to anti-reprisal, Covid-19, freedom of association, and freedom of movement, among other issues'.[153] It was also indicated by KPCL that KPHH had implemented an internal grievance mechanism, which resolved complaints received in 2022 and further indicated its willingness to adopt corrective actions.[154]

Blocked Referendum

The complainant claimed that KPCL and the RTU were collaborating to delay holding a referendum between the two unions at KHPP (i.e. SHU

[149] Ibid.
[150] Ibid.
[151] Ibid.
[152] Ibid.
[153] Ibid.
[154] KPCL did not specify what corrective actions will be adopted.

and Awami Labor Union; ALU), which would have enabled the selected union to become the default advocate for workers to decide on a CBA with KHPP.[155] The date of the referendum was to be set by the RTU, but the complainant claimed it had been postponed multiple times.

It was claimed by KPCL that it had been in regular contact with the SHU and ALU, and that it had held in-person meetings with the complainant between March 2022 to April 2023 at the project site. It was also claimed by KPCL that it was in regular contact with the RTU and was informed that RTU had requested the SHU's annual return and proceedings for election for office bearers, to which the complainant allegedly did not comply. It was indicated by KPCL that the referendum was the responsibility of the RTU, and KPCL only served as a facilitator at the request of RTU. It was mentioned by KPCL that it had to comply with RTU's rules and could not make decision for the referendum on its own.[156]

Outcome and Lessons Learned

In March 2023, the complainant indicated his interest in participating in a CAO-facilitated dispute resolution process and KPCL indicated a similar interest. The case was transferred to the CAO's dispute resolution function and mediation has been ongoing as of 5 May 2023.[157]

The challenge in the present case was the lack of jurisdiction by the CAO to compel parties including the RTU to participate in the fact-finding or dispute-resolution process. The complainant alleged the RTU, a Pakistani governmental body, delayed the referendum. Yet, KPCL claimed that RTU's rescheduling of the referendum was caused by the complainant's non-compliance. Both perspectives may not be mutually exclusive, but highlight the CAO's inability to ascertain the full picture behind the Complaint, especially when the CAO had limited access to the full facts.

Despite the RTU having a significant bearing on the resolution of the Complaint, it was neither interviewed nor invited to participate in the mediation. This limited the extent of the agreement that both parties were able to reach.

155 Ibid, p. 7.
156 Ibid, p. 8.
157 Ibid, pp. 3–4.

Case 5: Nubian Suns Project in BSP, Egypt

The Nubian Suns project case in BSP, Egypt, demonstrates that grievance channels, such as the CAO office, offer an effective avenue to address systemic issues regarding working conditions and terms of employment.[158] In general, the existence of an independent AM provides bargaining power to vulnerable groups affected by project mismanagement. In the present case, the contractor was willing to increase the complainants' salaries after the latter had filed a CAO complaint and similarly agreed to complainants' additional labour-related demands to prevent further involvement of the CAO. Finally, the fact that the complainant could bring the Benban Solar Developers Association (BSDA) to the table for mediation despite losing a case in the Egyptian Courts demonstrates that grievance mechanism provided by the CAO expand avenues of redress available to complainants.

Introduction

Project Nubian Suns ('the Project') was an initiative to construct and operate thirteen solar power plants in BSP in Aswan, Egypt.[159] It was funded by the World Bank and AIIB along with a consortium of MDBs. The issues raised in the project were similar to the previous case, largely employment-related and for the most part addressed through the World Bank's CAO office.

The aim of the BSP project was to house thirty-two solar plants with a total capacity of 1.65 GW.[160] It is the largest solar power project in Africa,[161] occupying 37 km^2 of land and housing over 7 million photovoltaic panels.[162]

The Project is part of the Egypt solar power programme. The Egyptian Government aims to introduce international and private investments into the country[163] to support its 'goal of generating 20% of its electricity from renewable resources by 2022'.[164] All output generated in BSP is

158 Ibid, p. 6.

159 British International Investment (n.d.). *Winnergy for Renewable Energy Projects SAE.* www.bii.co.uk/en/our-impact/investment/winnergy-for-renewable-projects-s-a-e/.

160 Ibid.

161 United Nations (12 April 2021). *Solar Projections.* https://unfccc.int/blog/solar-projections.

162 AfDB (19 August 2020). *Infrastructure Fund AFRICA50 Helps Egypt's Solar Power Sector Take Off.* www.afdb.org/en/news-and-events/infrastructure-fund-africa50-helps-egypts-solar-power-sector-take-36247.

163 Ibid.

164 IFC (n.d.). *IFC-Led Consortium Invests $653 million to Support the World's Largest Solar Park in Egypt.* https://pressroom.ifc.org/all/pages/PressDetail.aspx?ID=17490.

'sold to the Egyptian Electricity Transmission Company under a 25-year Power Purchase Agreement'.[165]

The project developers 'formed the Benban Solar Developers Association ("BSDA") to manage the entirety of the Solar Park. BSDA hired a facility management company, Health and Safety Home ("H&SH"), to manage the operation and maintenance of the Solar Park and address environmental and social (E&S) and other relevant issues for the entire park'.[166]

The IFC (a member of the World Bank Group) led a consortium of nine international banks to provide USD653 million for thirteen private companies to construct and operate the solar plants,[167] of which IFC provided USD225 million.[168] The consortium included 'the Africa Development Bank; the Asian Infrastructure Investment Bank; the Arab Bank of Bahrain, CDC of the United Kingdom,[169] Europe Arab Bank, Green for Growth Fund, FinnFund, ICBC, and OeEB of Austria'.[170] In addition, the EBRD has invested over USD1.1 billion in BSP since 2012[171] as part of a consortium led by International Development Finance (IDF).

Project Complaints

According to the CAO,[172] as of 2023, there were seven complaints concerning BSP (hereinafter referred to as Benban Solar: 01-7).[173] All

[165] AIIB (n.d.). *Egypt: Egypt Round II Solar PV Feed-in Tariffs Program: Projects.* www.aiib.org/en/projects/details/2017/approved/Egypt-Egypt-Round-II-Solar-PV-Feed-in-Tariffs-Program.html.

[166] Office of the CAO (8 June 2022). *Egypt: Benban Solar-01: CAO Data Hub.* www.cao-ombudsman.org/cases/egypt-benban-solar-01.

[167] Raven, A. (29 October 2017). *A New Solar Park Shines a Light on Egypt's Energy Potential.* IFC World Bank Group. www.ifc.org/en/stories/2010/benban-solar-park-egypt.

[168] CAO (2023). *CAO Assessment Report Regarding the First Complaint Received in Relation to IFC Investments and MIGA Guarantees in Benban Solar Park*, p. 6. www.cao-ombudsman.org/sites/default/files/downloads/Benban%2001_CAO%20Assessment%20Report_Final_Jan%202023_English%20%281%29.pdf.

[169] The investment was made before the CDC Group changed its name to British International Investment.

[170] Ibid, p. 6.

[171] Zgheib, N. (4 November 2022). *How the EBRD Became Egypt's Leading Partner for Renewable Energy.* EBRD. www.ebrd.com/news/2022/how-the-ebrd-became-egypts-leading-partner-for-renewable-energy-.html.

[172] CAO (June 2023). *CAO Public Disclosure: Monthly Case List* [Data set]. www.cao-ombudsman.org/sites/default/files/2023-07/CAO%20Public%20Disclosure%20-%20Monthly%20Case%20Status%20Update%20-%20June%202023.pdf.

[173] Office of the CAO (13 June 2022). *Egypt: Benban Solar-02: CAO Data Hub.* www.cao-ombudsman.org/cases/egypt-benban-solar-02.

complaints, except for Benban Solar-04 were related to labour practices of the private companies involved in the construction or management of BSP (Benban Solar Labour). Benban Solar-04 is mainly related to community health and safety issues (Benban Solar Health).

Labour-Related Complaints

The labour-related complainants raised four main issues regarding their working conditions, namely: (1) poor quality of food provided; (2) insufficient water; (3) lack of working electricity generators; and (4) lack of air conditioning on buses.[174] The issues of insufficient water and air conditioning were resolved by direct negotiations between the complainants and the BSDA. The issue of food quality was unresolved and the electric motor issue was only partially resolved.

The complainants raised concerns with the BSDA's compensatory practices, which were tied to the complaints about food quality.[175] During the direct negotiation between the complainants and BSDA, the complainants suggested cash allowance should be provided in lieu of meals. However, the BSDA rejected the proposal after consulting with the Labour Office,[176] which did 'not recommend substituting food with cash compensation' due to potential violation of Egyptian laws.

The BSDA counter-proposed to the complainants an increase in salary to address the food allowance issue. The BSDA increased the contract value granted to H&SH (the subcontractor of SWAT Security and Guards Company, i.e. the employers of the complainants) and requested the salary of the security guards be increased by 15% in November 2022 and 7% in January 2023 (for a total increase of 22%).[177] The complainants agreed to the proposal but claimed that the 7% increase was yet to be applied, rendering the issue partially resolved.

The complainant in Benban Solar-02 raised concerns with H&SH regarding (1) nepotism concerning benefits, promotions and salary

[174] CAO, *CAO Assessment Report Regarding the First Complaint Received in Relation to IFC Investments and MIGA Guarantees in Benban Solar Park*, pp. 7–8.

[175] Ibid, pp. 7–8.

[176] The definition of the Labour Office is not mentioned in the source. It could (but not necessarily) refer to the labour department in the Egyptian Government as Labour Office was referred to as 'Government Labour Office' in another CAO complaint assessment report – ibid, p. 8.

[177] Ibid, pp. 8–9.

increases; and (2) the 'absence'[178] of a labour grievance mechanism for H&SH.[179] A complaint of a similar nature was filed with the Egyptian Government Labour Office ('Labour Office'). Afterwards, the complainant received an email from the Director of Human Resources of H&SH indicating that the company was prohibited from dealing with his complaint due to the involvement of the Labour Office.[180] The BSDA, responding on behalf of BSP, did not address this part of the complaint in the CAO's assessment report.

Intimidation or Retaliation for Raising Grievances

The complainants in the Benban Solar Labour complaint expressed concerns that they were asked not to escalate their complaints to the CAO[181] during direct negotiation with the BSDA and IFC.[182] In the CAO's assessment report, the BSDA explained that they were only trying to 'educate the workers about the Grievance Mechanism of BSDA and H&SH at the Solar Park' and it was not their intention to 'intimidate the "complainants" or stop them from filing complaints with CAO'.[183]

Community-Related Complaints

The complainant raised concern as to the difficulty of raising grievances by the local community. The complainant stated that the headquarters of BSP and the grievance office were located 50 km from the village. The distance posed a great obstacle to submitting and following up on grievances.[184] He requested the BSDA establish grievance offices in villages that BSP aims to assist to facilitate direct communications.

The BSDA indicated that H&SH, acting as the facility management company for BSP, sends out grievance officers regularly to villages to communicate with locals and 'to make sure CSR projects are properly

[178] Although the wording used in the CAO's Assessment Report was 'absence', it seemed that the complaint was directed to the ineffectiveness of the existing grievance mechanism rather than the absence of such mechanism.

[179] Ibid, p. 6.

[180] Ibid.

[181] IFC (n.d.). *IFC/MIGA Independent Accountability Mechanism (CAO) Policy*. www.ifc.org/content/dam/ifc/doc/2023/ifc-miga-independent-accountability-mechanism-cao-policy.pdf.

[182] CAO, *CAO Assessment Report Regarding the First Complaint Received in Relation to IFC Investments and MIGA Guarantees in Benban Solar Park*, p. 7.

[183] Ibid, p. 9, note 166.

[184] Ibid, p. 7.

implemented'.[185] However, the BSDA had not addressed the proposal to establish outreach grievance offices in local villages in the CAO assessment report.

Lack of Consultation with the Local Community

The complainant alleged representatives from BSP had promised to provide a development plan and consult the local community but never followed up until September 2022 when BSP hosted a public hearing session inviting community members from villages in Benban.[186] The hearing session was held *after* the complaint was filed.

During the hearing session, representatives of BSP shared information on the scope of its Corporate Social Responsibility (CSR) programmes and the projects planned for all four villages in the Benban area, as well as answered inquiries. It was indicated to the participants by BSP that the CSR projects are expected to last more than twenty-five years.

Despite having participated in the hearing session, the complainant maintained that the BSDA should further consult the local community and amend its development plan to adapt to the long-term needs of the community.

While the complainant acknowledged that some projects funded by BSP in the CAO's assessment report such as providing food and a carpet weaving centre are useful, he maintained that issues important to local communities remained unaddressed, such as education, health and sanitation.

Employment and Education

The complainant also alleged that BSP has been 'bringing outside labour for positions that could be filled by locals from the Benban area'.[187] It recommended that training should be provided to local youth to integrate villagers into BSP and provide job opportunities.

The BSDA did not address the allegation of hiring outside labour over locals in the CAO's assessment report. Instead, it mentioned BSP's *planned* community projects relating to livelihood, which include projects supporting 'agricultural value-chain development, direct and indirect economic opportunities, employment creation, entrepreneurship, women's empowerment and livelihoods improvement'.[188]

[185] Ibid.
[186] Ibid.
[187] Ibid, p. 7, note 185.
[188] Ibid, p. 7, note 185.

The BSDA also stressed that over 40% of its CSR programmes relate to the promotion of education. Its *planned* CSR education projects aim to promote 'access to education, safe school facilities, girl's empowerment, access to water, students' cognitive and physical development, career guidance for students, awareness raising program and enhancement of solar energy education.'[189]

Complaint Handling Process

The various complaints were resolved through the CAO's involvement. The labour-related complaints are currently undergoing mediation[190] and pending results. Some of the issues have been resolved through referral to outside labour organisations, or direct negotiation including a change in supervision and management and new contract terms.[191]

The health and safety complainant expressed interest in participating in a CAO-facilitated dispute resolution process to discuss how BSP's CSR programme could be adapted to local needs. The BSDA was open to discussing the complainant's concerns.

Lessons Learned

This case demonstrates that grievance channels, such as the CAO office, offer an avenue to address systemic issues regarding working conditions and terms of employment.[192] In general, the existence of an independent AM provides bargaining power to vulnerable groups affected by project mismanagement. In the present case, the BSDA was willing to increase the complainants' salaries after the latter had filed a CAO complaint and similarly agreed to complainants' additional labour-related demands to prevent further involvement of the CAO. Finally, the fact that the complainant could bring the BSDA to the table for mediation despite losing a case in the Egyptian Courts demonstrates that grievance mechanisms provided by CAO expand avenues of redress available to complainants.

[189] Ibid.
[190] Ibid, p. 7, note 185.
[191] See n 27.
[192] Ibid, p. 9.

Case 6: Ulaanbaatar Urban Services Case

The Ulaanbaatar Urban Services case demonstrated the importance of a consistent presence by the mediator who was familiar with the local culture, NGO support, periodic capacity building and anticipating delays in implementation due to change in management personnel.

Background

The Government of Mongolia and the ADB signed a loan agreement to implement the Ulaanbaatar Urban Services and Ger Areas Development Investment programme (the 'Project').[193] The Project aims to improve the living conditions in Ulaanbaatar through a network of liveable, competitive and inclusive subcentres in the Ger areas.[194] It involved financing core urban infrastructure and basic services in priority road sections, investments in socioeconomic facilities based on communities' needs, and the improvement of service providers' operation management. It also supported (1) community participation, awareness and empowerment; (2) urban planning and subcentre development; (3) extensive on-the-job training in project management and implementation; and (4) sector reform initiatives to support policy development.[195] With about 1,400 households affected, the investment programme was categorised A for involuntary resettlement.[196]

Pre-project Consultation

According to the 2023 Social Monitoring Report by Urban Future Planning Consultancy LLC, which was engaged to support the external land acquisition and resettlement monitoring process for Mongolia and the ADB,[197] during the period of Tranche 1 project implementation, a total of eighty consultation meetings with APs and more than 5,000 individual meetings were held. According to the report, at least 72% and at most 93% of the participants engaged in the project monitoring survey reported that they attended one to three consultation meetings related to

[193] ADB (January 2019). *Problem-Solving Report of the Special Project Facilitator*, [1].
[194] Ibid.
[195] Ibid.
[196] Ibid.
[197] ADB (January 2023). *Social Monitoring Report*, [80].

the project. A small subset of APs who responded that 'they did not participate in any meeting' received compensation.

In the first two quarters of 2020, the team organised a total of fifteen meetings at subcentre locations for the affordable housing project with 317 residents. This was followed by a total of forty-five public meetings with 1,473 residents of Bayankhoshuu and Selbe subcentres, of which 56.82% were female.

The most common channels through which the APs received information were either through public meetings (Bayankhoshuu subcentre, 76.5%; Selbe subcentre, 58%) or individual meetings (Bayankhoshuu subcentre, 66.3%; Selbe subcentre, 68%).[198] However, the majority of the APs (150 or 82.9%) of Selbe subcentre named the most effective information channel as being printed/published materials rather than consultation meeting (150 or 82.9%). The most efficient sources of information were 'neighbours' (Bayankhoshuu, 30 or 15.3%), (Selbe, 66 or 36.5%), 'khoroo employees' (Bayankhoshuu, 32 or 16.3%; Selbe, 72 or 39.8%), while (6 or 3.1%) APs of Bayankhoshuu subcentre and 19 (10.5%) of Selbe subcentre received information through NGO employees.[199] A total of twelve APs, or 6.4%, responded that they received information from the project's web page and/or Facebook.[200]

On review, it was reported that information dissemination and consultation meetings conducted under Tranche 1 were organised meaningfully, including provision of information on the ADB's Safeguard Policy Statements and documented with signatures and photos of the meeting participants.[201]

The Complaint

A group of thirty-one APs supported by Oyu Tolgoi Watch, Zurgaan Buudal and Land Acquisition and Citizens' Rights and Interests submitted a Complaint to the ADB[202] through the OSPF on 28 March 2018. The complainants requested problem-solving under the ADB's AM Policy.

The complaint consisted of five parts involving inadequate information disclosure, lack of consultation, inappropriate timing of land

198 Ibid, [86].
199 Ibid.
200 Ibid.
201 Ibid.
202 ADB, *Problem-Solving Report of the Special Project Facilitator*, [3].

valuation and lack of meaningful oversight.[203] The first complaint was lack of social impact assessment and meaningful consultation in the process of developing the project and announcement of land acquisition notice without due preparation. According to the complainants, the

> first announcement of land acquisition and advice not to build new buildings, start new economic/business activities, sell or otherwise change current status was made in 2012 and stalled our lives for 6 years. Later in 2016 an official notice was issued still without timeline and status of the project. The process of land and property valuation started in October 2017. While the PMO (project management office) reports that series of discussion were carried out, true information about potential negative impacts on our livelihoods was not given and our support for the project was gained through promoting the project's benefits.[204]

The second complaint consisted of lack of consultation on the methodology of valuation. The complainants had various complaints in this regard, including that at the time the Selbe subproject began, there was no consultation with the owners and tenants of their khashaas.[205] The complainants further argued that the assets and homes were being arbitrarily undervalued. The third issue involved information not being disclosed, not accessible or misleading. Here the complainants raised concerns about how full information about the Project was not available and that officials had been misleading citizens to get their consent. Further issues included the use of intimidation and provocation of conflict amongst neighbours. The fourth complaint involved land acquisition being carried out in winter. Here the issue was that the land acquisition unit started the land and property valuation work in October 2017, which the complainants argued was in violation of the policies relating to safety and security of citizens. Finally, the complainants argued that the Oversight Committee (UN Habitat) responsible for protecting its interest was not fulfilling its mandate.

Complaint Handling Process

The AM relied on the OSPF as its complaint-redressal mechanism.[206]

203 The details of the complaint can be found online at: https://aconsole-static.s3.amazonaws.com/media/public/cases/mon-45007-004-complaint-form.pdf.

204 Ibid.

205 A fenced-in land of up to 0.7 ha with house and/or ger dwellings of owners and their extended family.

206 The SPF mechanism is detailed on the ADB website at: www.adb.org/who-we-are/accountability-mechanism/problem-solving-function.

To determine eligibility of the complaint, the OSPF undertook a desk review of the Project documents and the Special Project Facilitator (SPF) conducted an initial fact-finding mission from 7 to 9 April 2018.[207] The Project area, including the road alignment that affects many of the complainants, was visited and meetings were held with complainants, other community members affected by the Project who volunteered to provide feedback on the Project impacts, ADB Project staff from the East Asia Department and Mongolia Resident Mission, Municipality of Ulaanbaatar City (MUB), NGOs who signed a formal complaint on behalf of the complainants, and the Project Management Office (PMO).[208] The SPF determined that the complaint met the AM Policy eligibility criteria and was declared eligible for problem-solving on 12 April 2018.[209]

A local mediation facilitator was recruited on 17 April 2018 as part of the OSPF team to facilitate day-to-day activities.[210] The names of the complainants were released to the PMO and other project stakeholders on 19 April 2018. Although the formal complainants were the thirty-one signatories to the complaint letter, during the review and assessment stage, there was an increase in complainants to 110 households. This was due to additional complainants' claims submitted to the NGOs requesting to be included in the original complaint. At the outset, ground rules were agreed to between the key stakeholders for case-by-case household negotiations including identifying the issues, ways to convene the negotiation meetings, clarifying the roles of representatives for the complainants and preparing official representation letters.[211]

A Review and Assessment Mission was undertaken by OSPF in Ulaanbaatar from 27 April to 3 May 2018.[212] The objectives of the Mission included: (1) exploring the detailed history of the complaint and better understanding the issues submitted by the complainants; (2) confirming the key stakeholders, identifying additional issues, exploring parties' individual and shared interests; (3) mapping out perspectives and exploring stakeholders' readiness for joint problem-solving and facilitated dialogue; and (4) recommending next steps and a course of action.[213] The review and assessment also included: (1) documentation

[207] ADB, *Problem-Solving Report of the Special Project Facilitator*, [5].
[208] Ibid.
[209] Ibid.
[210] Ibid, [6].
[211] Ibid.
[212] Ibid, [7].
[213] Ibid.

review; (2) one-on-one and group interviews with the complainants and the PMO; (3) workshops; and (4) a round table discussion. The workshops were organised to consult and inform communities in Selbe and Bayankhoshuu areas on the safeguard policies and Mongolian law on land valuation.[214] The round table discussion included representatives from the ADB Project staff, MUB working group and the PMO.

The MUB, in principle, agreed to the proposed measures to address the key issues from the complainants, such as: (1) options for replacement land for non-land owners; (2) partial land acquisition with partial viability for residents; (3) options for replacement land for title holders with small plots and non-title holders; (4) livelihood restoration; and (5) a process for revaluation of land and assets.[215] It was decided that these issues would be further fleshed out in detail together with all the stakeholders and built into an MoU between the ADB Project team, complainants, MUB, NGOs and the PMO. Moving forward, it was agreed that the OSPF local mediation facilitator would facilitate the joint meetings among stakeholders to flesh out the MoU and provide support on a day-to-day basis in the complaint resolution process.[216]

A series of round table discussions were held between key stakeholders facilitated by the OSPF. An MoU was signed on 2 July 2018 by the ADB Project team, complainants, NGO representatives, MUB and the PMO outlining the various actions to be implemented, including the responsible parties to resolve the concerns raised by the complainants.[217] The MoU served as the guiding document for the case-by-case negotiations facilitated by OSPF between parties, initiated on 15 June 2018 and concluded 14 September 2018. The MoU specified the amounts to be paid per unit of land under varying circumstances, general agreements to be applied to all case-by-case negotiations, the timeline for the mayor's order issuance, contracting and compensation payments to the complainants, vacating land, implementing livelihoods restoration programme, training programmes on collaborative problem-solving and communication skills, and provision of comparable land to non-title holders who live on the same land plot with title holders who are complainants.[218] Follow-up activities included capacity building by the ADB and case-by-case negotiations.[219]

[214] Ibid.
[215] Ibid, [8].
[216] Ibid.
[217] Ibid, [10].

From 110 complainants, ninety-three claims were resolved in favour of the complainants through direct negotiations. This means that an agreement was reached on land and asset values for compensation. Twelve complainants were identified as being non-affected, four refused to sell their land because of land legacy and/or unreasonable demands for compensation packages higher than agreed in the MoU, and one passed away.[220]

Upon completion of the general and individual negotiation meetings, implementation and monitoring plans were jointly developed by the parties with OSPF facilitation. These included timelines for actions leading to payment of compensation comprising: (1) ordinance issuance, (2) concluding contracts, (3) payment of compensation to the complainants, and (4) official hand-over of the comparable land to the nontitle holders (thirty-six complainants).[221]

Follow-up review meetings were held between the ADB project team, small-scale technical assistance (SSTA) consultants, NGOs and the PMO to discuss expectations, objectives and outcomes of the SSTA on livelihood restoration. Several recommendations were adopted for further development of the programme based on SSTA report findings.[222]

Monitoring

During an OSPF Mission from 21 to 25 August 2018, the OSPF learned that some of the critical deadlines stipulated in the MoU and negotiation agreement, most notably involving compensation payments, were not met in a timely fashion.[223] In consultation with stakeholders, corrective actions were agreed, and an implementation and monitoring plan was prepared in September 2018. On the basis of an agreed follow-up plan prepared in November, it was agreed that the problem-solving process for this case had reached its final stage.[224]

220 Ibid, [11].
221 Ibid, [12].
222 Ibid, [13].
223 Ibid, [14].
224 Ibid.

Lessons Learned

This case demonstrated the importance of a consistent presence by the mediator who was familiar with the local culture, NGO support, periodic capacity building and anticipating delays in implementation due to change in management personnel.[225]

First, the continuous presence of a dedicated local mediation facilitator was essential for maintaining constructive dialogue among stakeholders. This gave the complainants confidence that they were being listened to and had access to assistance when and where needed, and, in particular, achieved a consistent, systematic approach to community and household-level negotiations. Similarly, the support to the complainants by the two NGOs strengthened the complainants' collective and individual voice and their understanding of their rights and options. The NGOs were also instrumental in flagging emerging issues to the OSPF so that timely responsive actions could be taken.

Second, providing periodic capacity building and training for various stakeholders, including project implementation staff and consultants on dispute-resolution skills helped to improve the flow of information and reduce misunderstandings. Based on feedback provided by participants from government agencies who attended OSPF capacity-building workshops, it was suggested that the participation of key decision makers and project management authorities in such trainings would likewise be beneficial.

Finally, changes in management led to several halts in the handling of grievances and this disrupted the implementation of the MoU. The lesson learned is the importance of supporting continuous oversight of the implementation process to maintain management's follow through in the overall problem-solving process.

Conclusion

The six cases examined in this chapter after more rigorous community engagement policies were introduced in 2013 underscore a number of key insights.

After increasingly mandated community engagement practices were introduced starting in 2013, a number of continuities and advancements were identified in dispute emergence. The post-2013 cases broadly

[225] Ibid, part III.

demonstrate a number of key improvements including greater rigour in consultation and diligence mechanisms, heightened precision in identifying issues of community concern, higher pre-project diligence and screening standards, ongoing environmental and technical monitoring, the presence of locally trained mediators, skill development for consultation participants, a longer-term view of community welfare and responsive grievance remedies. Shortcomings persisted in some cases, including instances of duress, lack of information disclosure, fraud, limited access to consultation mechanisms and environmental harm leading to project cessation in two cases when the adverse social impacts were seen to outweigh potential benefits. On the whole, corresponding with an overall trend toward more rigorous community consultation and diligence standards, during this phase, the number of stalled/cancelled and litigated cases declined by 33%, the percentage of cases brought to court declined by 16%, and the number of cases pursuing party agreement through mediation or negotiation increased by 50% compared with ad hoc discretionary consultation practices prior to 2013.

PART III

Community Engagement Developments in the BRI Region and Beyond

7

Dispute Prevention and Resolution Regimes in the Belt and Road Initiative and Beyond in the Context of Sustainable Development Goals

Introduction

The Belt and Road initiative (BRI), formally known as the One Belt, One Road Initiative, is a global development initiative initiated by the Chinese Government[1] that is arousing significant academic and policy interest.[2] Since 2005, China has completed close to USD2.3 trillion in foreign projects, with 41% (USD966 billion) financing infrastructure projects and an even larger amount (USD1.4 trillion) towards investment in foreign assets – port facilities, mining and energy assets, and acquisitions of foreign firms.[3] This chapter reviews the role of the BRI in infrastructure development, including its contributions and challenges in advancing sustainable development alongside efforts at engagement with local communities.

A number of approaches to addressing BRI disputes have emerged at the pre- and post-dispute stage. These include both formal and informal dispute mitigation and resolution mechanisms. Conversations with project coordinators highlight the importance of neutrality and relationship preservation. Systems are emerging to increase community access to grievance mechanisms including China's mediation and consultation mechanism for the mining industry.

1 Nedopil, C. Countries of the Belt and Road Initiative (BRI), *Green Finance & Development Center, FISF Fudan University*. https://greenfdc.org/countries-of-the-belt-and-road-initiative-bri/.

2 G7 Summit: Leaders detail $600bn plan to rival China's Belt and Road initiative, *BBC News*. www.bbc.com/news/world-asia-61947325 (Partnership for Global Infrastructure and Investment [PGII]).

3 Oi, J. C., Walder, A. G., & Kuik, C. C. (July 2024). China's global economic footprint: The Belt and Road Initiative and beyond. *AAS-in-Asia 2024*.

Aspirations and Challenges in Contributing to Sustainable Development

A growing body of literature has explored the contributions and challenges in the achievement of Sustainable Development Goals (SDGs) by BRI-funded infrastructure projects. Reference has been made to policy objectives outlined in the SDGs and the 2030 Agenda for Sustainable Development and the Chinese Government's Belt and Road Ecological Plan (2017).[4] The United Nations (UN) Development Programme has also jointly explored issues of sustainability with the Chinese government and host countries.[5]

China's outbound financed projects include a mix of both energy-efficient and carbon-generating projects. This includes smart eco-cities aiming to reducing carbon footprint and energy efficiency[6] alongside heavy carbon-generating projects including coal processing. One study conducted in over sixty countries participating in the BRI found some positive impacts on sustainability, with varied results between countries.[7] Another study examining eighty participating countries found that green development in selected jurisdictions increased from 2010 to 2018,[8] however, again, development varied across regions.[9] Similar conclusions were reached by Huang and Li, finding that the BRI has had some positive impacts on green development in participating countries[10] with the potential to aid in sustainable development.[11]

Specifically, green infrastructure investment and the introduction of green technologies has been the focus of a number of projects. Jiang and others, in a quantitative study, found strong evidence of the energy savings

4 Ferguson, R. J. (2021). *Greening China's New Silk Roads: The Sustainable Governance of Belt and Road*. Cheltenham: Edward Elgar Publishing, p. 72.

5 Ibid.

6 Ibid.

7 Xiao, H., Cheng, J., & Wang, X. (2018). Does the Belt and Road Initiative promote sustainable development? Evidence from countries along the Belt and Road. *Sustainability*, *10*(12), 4370. https://doi.org/10.3390/su10124370.

8 Xue, H., Zhang, Q., Liang, H., & He, Z. (2023). Assessment of the green development level for participating countries in the Belt and Road Initiative. *Annals of Operations Research*, 326, 125. https://doi.org/10.1007/s10479-021-04440-2.

9 Ibid.

10 Huang, M., & Li, S. (2020). The analysis of the impact of the Belt and Road Initiative on the green development of participating countries. *Science of the Total Environment*, *722*, 137869. https://doi.org/10.1016/j.scitotenv.2020.137869.

11 Yin, W. (2019). Integrating Sustainable Development Goals into the Belt and Road Initiative: Would it be a new model for green and sustainable investment? *Sustainability*, *11*(24), 6991. https://doi.org/10.3390/su11246991.

and emissions reduction effects of BRI projects.[12] Gu and Zhou, conducting a study of thirty-six renewable energy projects in BRI countries found a 49.68 million tonnes of carbon dioxide emission reduction.[13] Geng details a comprehensive list of renewable energy projects initiated under the BRI, including investments in hydropower, wind energy and solar energy.[14]

The focus of green BRI projects has varied between regions. Under the China–Pakistan Economic Corridor (CPEC),[15] a significant emphasis has been placed on job creation and economic growth[16] as well as connecting rural cities with industrial centres.[17] The Lahore Metro, for example, a mass transit system, is said to be an example of investment in green technology as it aims to reduce the local population's reliance on fossil fuel-consuming vehicles.[18] Li and others found that investment in renewable energy in Pakistan has created 8,905 jobs and USD39.8 million production value.[19] In Thailand, the Kunming–Singapore Rail Network[20] alongside investments in Cambodia have led to an increase in road and rail networks, energy production and port development.[21]

12 Jiang, Q., Ma, X., & Wang, Y. (2021). How does the One Belt One Road Initiative affect the green economic growth? *Energy Economics*, *101*, 105429. https://doi.org/10.1016/j.eneco.2021.105429.

13 Gu, A., & Zhou, X. (2020). Emission reduction effects of the green energy investment projects of China in Belt and Road Initiative countries. *Ecosystem Health and Sustainability*, *6*(1), 1747947. https://doi.org/10.1080/20964129.2020.1747947.

14 Geng, Q. (2021). The Belt and Road Initiative and its implications for global renewable energy development. *Current Sustainable/Renewable Energy Reports*, *8*(1), 40–49. https://doi.org/10.1007/s40518-020-00172-2.

15 National Assembly of Pakistan. *About CPEC*. https://na.gov.pk/cpec/?q=about.

16 Menhas, R., Mahmood, S., Tanchangya, P., Safdar, M. N., & Hussain, S. (2019). Sustainable development under Belt and Road Initiative: A case study of China–Pakistan economic corridor's socio-economic impact on Pakistan. *Sustainability, 11* (21), 6143. https://doi.org/10.3390/su11216143.

17 Ibid.

18 Imran, M., Ali, M., & Janjua, M. S. (2021). Urban development challenges under the China–Pakistan Economic Corridor (CPEC). In S. Sintusingha, H. Wu, W. Lin, S. S. Han & B. Qin (Eds.). *International Perspectives on the Belt and Road Initiative: A Bottom-Up Approach*. London: Routledge, p. 94.

19 Li, R., et al. (2022). China's investments in renewable energy through the Belt and Road Initiative stimulated local economy and employment: A case study of Pakistan. *Science of the Total Environment*, *835*, 155308. https://doi.org/10.1016/j.scitotenv.2022.155308.

20 Sintusingha, S. (2021). Establishing the BRI in Thailand contrasting 'desire lines' in the delivery of two high-speed rail projects, in Sintusingha et al., International Perspectives on the Belt and Road Initiative, p. 119.

21 Han, S. S., & Lim, Y. (2021). China's Belt and Road Initiative (BRI) in Cambodia. In Sintusingha et al. (Eds.). *International Perspectives on the Belt and Road Initiative*, p. 176.

Alongside literature examining the contributions of select BRI projects on sustainability, research has also identified instances of environmental damage and harm. Some studies have found that BRI projects have contributed to increasing global emissions through support of environmentally damaging coal-powered and hydropower projects with relatively less stringent investment standards,[22] resulting in detrimental impacts on sustainable development.[23] The absence of robust environmental governance mechanisms consisting largely of voluntary initiatives[24] has limited carbon control efforts. One area of concern has been the over USD20 billion of financing for BRI-funded coal-powered plants between 2014 and 2017.[25]

Specific cases of environmental degradation have been studied in the context of existing BRI projects. In Pakistan, concerns have been raised about diminishing forest populations[26] and that the majority of power projects are coal-powered.[27] It is estimated that the demand created by power plants in Pakistan will increase climate change-induced water stress by 36–92% by 2055.[28] In Cambodia, BRI railway projects have been constructed through protected forests and projects have been initiated without prior environmental diligence.[29] In Brazil, of the six BRI-funded energy projects, one focused on renewable energy. At the same time, new partnerships have emerged focusing on rainforest protection.[30] The China–Myanmar Economic Corridor was found to contribute to an increased risk of natural disasters, water pollution, wildlife mortality and

22 Saha, S. (2020). The climate risks of China's Belt and Road Initiative. *Bulletin of the Atomic Scientists, 76*(5), 249–255. https://doi.org/10.1080/00963402.2020.1806584.

23 Lorenzo, J. A. (2021). A path toward Sustainable Development along the Belt and Road. *Journal of International Economic Law, 24*(3), 591–608. https://doi.org/10.1093/jiel/jgab032.

24 Coenen, J., et al. (2020). Environmental governance of China's Belt and Road Initiative. *Environmental Policy and Governance, 31*(1), 3–17. https://doi.org/10.1002/eet.1901.

25 Lewis, D. J., Yang, X., Moise, D., & Roddy, S. J. (2021). Dynamic synergies between China's Belt and Road Initiative and the UN's Sustainable Development Goals. *Journal of International Business Policy*, 4(1), 69. https://doi.org/10.1057/s42214-020-00082-6.

26 Imran, Ali & Janjua, Urban development challenges, p. 95.

27 Ibid.

28 Alkon, M., He, X., Paris, A. R., et al. (2019). Water security implications of coal-fired power plants financed through China's Belt and Road Initiative. *Energy Policy, 132*, 1101–1109. https://doi.org/10.1016/j.enpol.2019.06.044.

29 Han & Lim, China's Belt and Road Initiative, p. 181.

30 Hearn, A. H. (2021). Strengthening Brazil's food system: Can China's Belt and Road help?'. In Sintusingha et al. (Eds.). *International Perspectives on the Belt and Road Initiative* (pp. 271–272).

ecosystem degradation.[31] Coal-powered plants in Indonesia funded by BRI were found to be using low-end non-carbon-capturing technology,[32] while heavily polluting cement production in Tajikistan[33] has expanded following a five-fold increase in BRI outbound investment.[34]

Some efforts to remediate environmental harms have been introduced. For example, Huaxin Cement Corporation Ltd now produces an annual report on sustainable development practices,[35] while the Colombo International Container Terminals-operated Colombo Port uses electrical cranes.[36]

In addition to ecological sustainability, scholarship has examined financial sustainability challenges. For example, in Sri Lanka, control of the Hambantota Port was handed over to external funders for ninety-nine years after the Sri Lankans failed to keep up with debt payments.[37] In Malaysia, the new government in 2018 cancelled several BRI projects due to ballooning debt.[38] However, other scholars argue that Sri Lanka's and Malaysia's debt problems were caused by other systemic issues beyond BRI project funding.[39]

In Pakistan, given that the debt–equity ratio of BRI projects has reached 80:20, concerns have been raised about financial liquidity and dependency. Countries facing greater risk of default may be subject to

[31] Taidong, Z. (2019). Aligning the Belt and Road Initiative with Myanmar's Sustainable Development Plan: Opportunities and challenges. *The Belt and Road Initiative and the SDGs: Towards Equitable, Sustainable Development*, 50(4), 81–82.

[32] Tritto, A. (2021). China's Belt and Road Initiative: From perceptions to realities in Indonesia's coal power sector. *Energy Strategy Reviews, 34*, 100624. https://doi.org/10.1016/j.esr.2021.100624.

[33] Nedopil, C. (2021). Green finance for soft power: An analysis of China's Green Policy signals and investments in the Belt and Road Initiative. *Environmental Policy and Governance, 32*(2), 87. https://doi.org/10.1002/eet.1965.

[34] Lewis et al., Dynamic synergies, p. 70.

[35] Ibid, p. 70.

[36] Ibid.

[37] Stacey, K. (2017, 11 December). China signs 99-year lease on Sri Lanka's Hambantota Port. *Financial Times*. www.ft.com/content/e150ef0c-de37-11e7-a8a4-0a1e63a52f9c.

[38] Siu, R. C. (2019). China's Belt and Road Initiative: Reducing or increasing the world uncertainties? *Journal of Economic Issues, 53*(2), 576. https://doi.org/10.1080/00213624.2019.1603774.

[39] Li, L. C., Tjia, L. Y., Yan, X., & Hung, J. S. Y. (2021). The Belt and Road Initiative in Sri Lanka: Challenges for debt-led development. *China and the World, 4*(4), 2150018. https://doi.org/10.1142/s2591729321500188; Ciborowski, R., Oziewicz, E., & Pangsy-Kania, S. (2021). The Belt and Road Initiative: Shared development or a threat for the world economy? *European Research Studies Journal, 24*(1), 373. https://doi.org/10.35808/ersj/1967.

strategic leverage.[40] At the same time, project administrators see these projects as viable given the substantial anticipated revenue they aim to generate.[41] Cambodia is said to be following a similar trajectory as Sri Lanka when it comes to debt sustainability.[42] Similar concerns have been raised in relation to some projects in Myanmar.[43] This has raised concerns that such projects might need to be handed over if a default occurs,[44] while others emphasise that the BRI's objective is supporting self-reliance and alternative non-loan debt mechanisms.[45]

Local and Global Risks in BRI Project Implementation

Given that many BRI projects are implemented in regions that have long been avoided by traditional financing mechanisms due to high levels of risk, scholars have noted four key risk factors facing project implementation. These include corruption, security risks, political uncertainty and supply chain disruptions.

The first category of risk concerns corruption.[46] Research has found that kickbacks from contractors has inflated contract pricing leading to increased debt accrual[47] and posing a significant challenge to growth.[48] In Myanmar, corruption contributed to land disputes following the theft of funds allocated for compensation.[49] In Cambodia, research has found that the selection of BRI investment projects has fuelled an elite patronage

40 Łasak, P., & van der Linden René, W. H. (2019). *The Financial Implications of China's Belt and Road Initiative: A Route to More Sustainable Economic Growth*. Cham: Palgrave Pivot, p. 104.

41 Imran, Ali & Janjua, Urban development challenges, p. 92.

42 Han & Lim, China's Belt and Road Initiative, pp. 184–185.

43 Mark, S., Overland, I., & Vakulchuk, R. (2020). Sharing the spoils: Winners and losers in the Belt and Road Initiative in Myanmar. *Journal of Current Southeast Asian Affairs, 39* (3), 387. https://doi.org/10.1177/1868103420962116.

44 Ibid.

45 Lai, K. P., Lin, S., & Sidaway, J. D. (2020). Financing the Belt and Road Initiative (BRI): Research agendas beyond the 'debt-trap' discourse. *Eurasian Geography and Economics, 61*(2), 114. https://doi.org/10.1080/15387216.2020.1726787.

46 Gu, J., Corbett, H., & Leach, M. (2019). Introduction: The Belt and Road Initiative and the Sustainable Development Goals: Opportunities and challenges. *IDS Bulletin, 50*(4). https://doi.org/10.19088/1968-2019.136.

47 Ciborowski, Oziewicz & Pangsy-Kania, The Belt and Road Initiative, p. 373.

48 van Twillert, N., & Halleck Vega, S. (2023). Risk or opportunity? The Belt and Road Initiative and the role of debt in the China-Central Asia-West Asia Economic Corridor. *Eurasian Geography and Economics*, 64(3), 365–377. https://doi.org/10.1080/15387216.2021.2012816.

49 Taidong, Aligning the Belt and Road Initiative, p. 81.

system sustaining an authoritative regime.[50] Similar challenges have been found in Central Asian states.[51] Allegations of project corruption have provided political ammunition toppling governments as was the case in Malaysia.[52] Scholars have suggested that corrupt practices give rise to corresponding illicit activities such as tax evasion and money laundering, reducing investor confidence and increasing the cost of doing business.[53]

Security-related risks have further threatened the safety of such projects.[54] In Myanmar, many BRI projects are initiated in ongoing ethnic conflict zones, creating risks for project-implementing teams.[55] In Pakistan, there has been a number of recent unfortunate incidents targeting project workers.[56] Similar risks have been identified in Central Asia.[57]

Supply chain disruptions have presented additional risks to project implementation. For example, during the Covid-19 pandemic, similar to many other cross-border projects throughout the world, a number of energy projects were suspended.[58] Such disruptions have correspondingly increased debt levels, posing additional risks to financial sustainability[59] without uniform debt service suspension arrangements.[60]

Further challenges including political uncertainty in host countries, inefficiency, limited transparency and accountability have exacerbated risk.[61]

[50] Loughlin, N., & Grimsditch, M. (2021). How local political economy dynamics are shaping the Belt and Road Initiative. *Third World Quarterly*, *42*(10), 2334–2352. https://doi.org/10.1080/01436597.2021.1950528.

[51] Costa Buranelli, F. (2017). One Belt, One Road and Central Asia: Challenges and opportunities. In L. Huang, Y. Cheng & L. Song (Eds.). *The Belt & Road Initiative in the Global Arena*. London: Palgrave Macmillan, p.224. https://doi.org/10.1007/978-981-10-5921-6_12.

[52] Cai, Y. (2022). Indigenous interpretations and engagement of China's Belt and Road Initiative in Peninsular Malaysia. *Singapore Journal of Tropical Geography*, 43(3), 234–249. https://doi.org/10.1111/sjtg.12437.

[53] Łasak & René, The financial implications, p. 33.

[54] Ciborowski, Oziewicz & Pangsy-Kania, The Belt and Road Initiative, p. 377.

[55] Taidong, Aligning the Belt and Road Initiative, p. 80.

[56] Pakistan: Are attacks on Chinese workers jeopardizing Beijing's CPEC projects? *DW*. www.dw.com/en/pakistan-are-attacks-on-chinese-workers-jeopardizing-beijings-cpec-projects/a-61618631.

[57] Jian, China in Central Asia and the Balkans, p. 243.

[58] Geng, The Belt and Road Initiative, p. 47.

[59] Deng, Y. (2021). How China Builds the Credibility of the Belt and Road Initiative. *The Journal of Contemporary China*, *30*(131), 749. https://doi.org/10.1080/10670564.2021.1884958.

[60] Ibid.

[61] Geng, The Belt and Road Initiative, p. 46.

Local Community Engagement along the BRI

A growing body of scholarship has examined the relationship between local communities and infrastructure project teams. While several studies have documented fractured relations, some successful community dynamics are also evident.

Community–investor relations continue to be challenging along the BRI. In Pakistan, the Gwadar Port project contributed to grievances amongst the local population arising from issues regarding land acquisition and changing demographics.[62] Ongoing litigation in Pakistani Courts involving the Lahore Metro and coal-powered plants have contributed to tensions.[63] In Bangladesh, civil society has raised issues regarding power projects in the region.[64] In Malaysia, importation of foreign workers from China has caused tensions with the local labour force.[65] Orang Seletar villagers in Malaysia filed a class action against developers of BRI projects, resulting in the validation of their land rights.[66] Local communities in Cambodia raised complaints when their trees and crops were bulldozed following aggressive land clearing without proper compensation.[67] Other issues include increasing land prices following labour immigration into Cambodia.[68] Local communities in Myanmar have also expressed concerns regarding the loss of Indigenous lands[69] and increased military and private security presence surrounding project sites.[70]

While ongoing challenges exist, empirical research has also revealed a more nuanced picture. The Asia Foundation conducted a study of the local population near BRI projects in Cambodia and Pakistan[71] and found that in Cambodia, although the majority of the population did

[62] Imran, Ali & Janjua, Urban development challenges, pp. 93–94.

[63] Ibid, p. 86.

[64] Bogojević, S., & Zou, M. (2020). Making infrastructure 'visible' in environmental law: The Belt and Road Initiative and climate change friction. *Transnational Environmental Law*, *10*(1), 55. https://doi.org/10.1017/s2047102520000278.

[65] Chan, T. K. (2021). Malaysia: Chinese participation in infrastructure from contractor to conspirator?', in Sintusingha et al., *International Perspectives on the Belt and Road Initiative*, p. 154.

[66] Cai, Indigenous interpretations.

[67] Han & Lim, China's Belt and Road Initiative, p. 182.

[68] Ibid.

[69] Ibid.

[70] Ibid, p. 80.

[71] The Asia Foundation. (2020). *Community Engagement Along the Belt and Road: Findings from Cambodia and Pakistan: Summary Report*. https://adbiwebportal.widen.net/content/zijjifashk/original.

not know of the BRI project, and expressed some issues regarding land rights, several agreed that surrounding infrastructure projects would contribute to employment opportunities.[72] In Myanmar, Chinese investors were able to negotiate a settlement between warring factions.[73]

Given the complexity of community-infrastructure dynamics in general, BRI projects like all major infrastructure projects globally, require significant attention to engagement with local communities, particularly through strengthened public consultation.[74] While much of the literature has focused on post-dispute litigation and arbitration mechanisms, limited attention has been given to informal community consultation processes or direct accountability mechanisms (AMs) through funding bodies. Given that most projects make reference to host country due diligence and redress mechanisms with varying levels of access,[75] few avenues of early resolution are currently available and therefore most disputes end up in the courts.[76] Some scholarship has suggested that China can play a constructive role in supporting access to justice in host countries.[77]

Insights from Practitioners on BRI Dispute Prevention and Resolution Mechanisms

In a series of conversations with individuals working in dispute prevention in the greater China region, a number of insights were shared regarding approaches to dispute mitigation.

According to the general legal counsel for a large port holding company, he noted that profit was not the primary driver in partnerships, rather 'we seek to make friends instead of a profit of 10% we may go for 6%'.[78] This emphasis on building relationships influences how challenges are addressed. When disputes arise, a key requirement for assessing dispute resolution options is 'structural neutrality' and 'how the secretariat is working, how it vets arbitrators and its credibility'. Chinese businesses do not necessarily insist on Chinese law

[72] Ibid, pp. 4–5.
[73] Mark, Overland & Vakulchuk, Sharing the spoils, p. 388.
[74] Cheng, Y. (2017). Public Opinions on the Belt and Road Initiative: A cross-cultural study. In Huang, Cheng & Song, *The Belt & Road Initiative in the Global Arena.*
[75] Ferguson, *Greening China's New Silk Roads*, 100.
[76] Bogojević & Zou, Making infrastructure; Cai, Indigenous interpretations.
[77] Ferguson, *Greening China's New Silk Roads*, 100.
[78] BRI Conversation 1, General Legal Counsel of Large Port Holding Company.

for the development of contracts and resolution of disputes.[79] Often, a third-country law is selected.

The business case for the development of grievance mechanisms including mitigating risks, reducing the number of stranded assets and partially opened mines has been the focus of recent attention. China's EXIM Bank is the first institution implementing the Organisation for Economic Co-operation and Development (OECD) guidelines on access to grievance redress mechanisms. A recent case in Mongolia saw the successful resolution of a community grievance involving a mining site. These experiences have contributed to the formalisation of guidelines for community redress established under the Ministry of Ecology and the Environment, as will be explored here.

Mediation and Consultation Mechanism for the Mining Industry

As noted already, China has introduced a mechanism to preventatively address community complaints in relation to environmental and social impacts of mining projects. The Mediation and Consultation Mechanism is overseen by the China Chamber of Commerce of Metals, Minerals & Chemicals Importers & Exporters[80] and Responsible Critical Mineral Initiative.[81]

The Mediation and Consultation Mechanism is a voluntary,[82] consensus-based[83] approach designed to facilitate dispute resolution among stakeholders involved in or affected by mining and mineral value chain projects.[84] It addresses complaints about alleged environmental pollution through dialogue and mediation. The initiative was set up to enhance compliance with applicable environmental and social standards,[85] including: the UN Guiding Principles on Business and Human Rights, the International Labour Organisation Tripartite Declaration of Principles Concerning

[79] BRI Conversation 1, General Legal Counsel of Large Port Holding Company.

[80] Inclusive Development (2023). *A Guide to a New Grievance Mechanism for the Mining Industry, with Emphasis on Chinese Corporations*, p. 3, Section 1. www.inclusivedevelopment.net/wp-content/uploads/2023/06/A-Guide-to-a-New-Grievance-Mechanism-for-the-Mining-Industry-with-Emphasis-on-Chinese-Corporations.pdf.

[81] Ibid, p. 3, Section 1.

[82] Ibid, p. 2, para. 4.

[83] Ibid, p. 2, para. 4.

[84] Ibid, p. 2, para. 2.

[85] Accountability Counsel (2023). *Mediation and Consultation Mechanism for the Mining Industry and Mineral Value Chain Procedure Document*, p. 7, section 2.2. www.accountabilitycounsel.org/wp-content/uploads/may-2023-final-procedures.pdf#page=7.

Multinational Enterprises and Social Policy, the OECD Guidelines for Multinational Enterprises, and the OECD Due Diligence Guidance for Responsible Supply Chains of Minerals from Conflict-Affected and High-Risk Areas, as well as the Guidelines for Social Responsibility in Outbound Mining Investments, the Chinese Due Diligence Guidelines for Mineral Supply Chain, the Cobalt Refiner Supply Chain Due Diligence Standard and the Artisanal and Small-Scale Mining Cobalt ESG Management Framework. It aims to provide a redress platform for negative impacts[86] suffered by stakeholders in the mining industry and mineral value chains through communication, consultation and mediation. It is established on the basis of 'lawful and compliant, neutral and professional, inclusive and balanced, equal and voluntary, and transparent and open'[87] principles.

The mechanism accepts applications from a wide range of stakeholders, including[88] individuals and communities whose rights and interests have been or are likely to be adversely affected by a company's business operations, stakeholders who are concerned with the due diligence process, upstream and downstream companies in the mineral supply chain and external assessors.[89] Applicants can file an application against any upstream or downstream company in the mineral supply chain.[90]

The application and procedures are handled by a secretariat.[91] Stakeholders or their agents, may fill in an application and submit it through e-mail, post or an online portal.[92] Anonymous applications are not accepted.[93] Companies may request confidentiality during the mediation and consultation process.[94] Next, a pro forma review is conducted by the secretariat,[95] involving a two-stage test. The first limb is to consider whether the dispute falls within the scope of the mechanism. The second limb examines if sufficient evidence has been submitted to prove the existence of a dispute.[96] If both criteria are satisfied, the application is accepted.[97]

86 Inclusive Development, A Guide to a New Grievance Mechanism for the Mining Industry, p. 2, para. 3.
87 Ibid, p. 8, section 3.
88 Ibid, pp. 6–7, section 2.1.
89 Ibid, pp. 6–7, section 2.1.
90 Ibid, p. 5, section 6.
91 Ibid, p. 3, section 3.
92 Ibid, p. 6, section 8.
93 Ibid, p. 6, section 8.
94 Ibid, p. 8, section 13.
95 Ibid, p. 6, section 7.
96 Ibid, p. 5, section 7.
97 Ibid, p. 6, section 7.

Within ten days of the acceptance, an 'Invitation to Mediation and Consultation' will be issued by the secretariat to the respondent. Since the mechanism is operated on a voluntary basis, there is no legal obligation for the respondent to take action. It can accept or reject the invitation, or not respond.[98]

If the invitation is accepted, both parties will receive a 'Notice of Activating the Mediation and Consultation Procedure'.[99] Depending on the gravity of the dispute, a variety of approaches may be initiated. Bilateral dialogue (conducted by internal professionals) for relatively minor disputes[100] may be suggested; second, internal mediation may be offered for mid-sized disputes;[101] and finally, external expert mediation will be offered for major complex cases.[102] Independent fact finding is available for external expert mediation and upon request.[103]

As the mechanism operates on a voluntary basis, corporations can freely choose whether to participate or not. The lack of enforcement power may potentially limit access, though may be a useful first step to develop experience. Given the novelty of the mechanism, no case studies are yet available for reference.[104]

Belt and Road Dispute Resolution Regimes in Greater China

When community-infrastructure disputes do emerge and cannot be mitigated through pre-project consultation, reference to local courts or AMs, they generally proceed to formalised dispute resolution channels. Such mechanisms have multiplied in recent years. This next section examines the formal dispute resolution policy framework within China including the dispute resolution mechanism for the BRI and the development of international commercial courts established to handle BRI-related disputes,[105] the China Council for the Promotion of International Trade (CCPIT) 'Belt

98 Ibid, p. 9, section 14.
99 Ibid, p. 9, section 15.
100 Ibid, p. 7, section 8.
101 Ibid, p. 7, section 8.
102 Ibid, p. 7, section 8.
103 Ibid, p. 7, section 10.
104 Ibid, p. 1, para. 6.
105 Jones, W. (2018). Belt and Road insights: China announces new courts for resolving belt and road disputes. www.lexology.com/library/detail.aspx?g=9b2a23d2-a461-4e89-96a4-adeb3ecf7e20; Siddiqui, S. (2018, 7 February). Beijing plans new mechanism for Belt and Road arbitration. *Asia Times*. www.bilaterals.org/?beijing-plans-new-mechanism-for&lang=en.

and Road International Dispute Management Center', an online system called the 'Belt and Road Service Connections', and an online service in Hong Kong, eBRAM.hk.

Existing BRI dispute resolution policy research has examined the legal framework for BRI disputes;[106] the diversity of legal systems within participating countries of the BRI, including common law, civil law and hybrid systems;[107] the diversity of dispute types, including commercial, international trade and investment disputes;[108] the need for revision and development of new investor–state investment dispute (ISDS) mechanisms, including the possibility of developing an ISDS centre;[109] the prospects and challenges associated with the development of an international commercial court within China[110] and the development of 'east Asian legal hubs' to address gaps in existing BRI rule coverage through Memorandum of Understandings, complimentary recognition of judgments and choice of law rules.

In an effort to provide an overarching BRI dispute resolution policy framework, the International Academy of the Belt and Road authored a document entitled, the *Dispute Resolution Mechanism for the Belt and Road* ('Blue Book') in October 2016.[111] It puts forwards a new set of rules covering alternative dispute resolution and arbitration with the requirement that mediation be a pre-condition for initiation of proceedings and

106 Han, X. L., & Zhai, Y. M. (2017). Investor–state arbitration mechanism in Sino foreign investment agreement under the 'Belt and Road' initiative. *Chinese Review of International Law*, *5*, 32; Lu, Y. (2018). The establishment of 'Belt and Road' international investment disputes settlement institution. *Journal of Law & Commerce*, *37*(1), 1–28. http://doi.org/10.5195/jlc.2018.151; Dahlan, M. (2018). Dimensions of the new Belt & Road international order: An analysis of the emerging legal norms and a conceptionalisation of the regulation of disputes. *Beijing Law Review*, *9*(1), 87–112. http://doi.org/10.4236/blr.2018.91007.

107 Dahlan, Dimensions of the new Belt & Road international order; Onishi, N., & Moyo, J. (2017, 21 November). Robert Mugabe resigns as Zimbabwe's president, ending 37-year rule. *The New York Times*. www.nytimes.com/2017/11/21/world/africa/zimbabwe-mugabe-mnangagwa.html.

108 Wang, G. (2017). The Belt and Road Initiative in quest for a dispute resolution mechanism. *Asia Pacific Law Review*, *25*(1), 1–16.

109 Ali, S., Teramura, N., Nottage, L., & Jetin, B. (2020). *Frontiers in Asia-Pacific International Arbitration and Dispute Resolution*. Alphen aan den Rijn: Wolters Kluwer; Han & Zhai, Investor–state arbitration mechanism in Sino foreign investment agreement under the 'Belt and Road' Initiative; Lu, The establishment of 'Belt and Road' international investment disputes settlement institution.

110 Zhou, 2018; Halliday, T. (2018). China, international law, and development. LSA Panel, Moderators Comments. Could not find any LSA panel with Zhou and Halliday (2018).

111 International Academy of the Belt and Road (October 2016). *Dispute Resolution Mechanism for the Belt and Road* ('Blue Book'). http://interbeltandroad.org/en/.

recommends the development of procedures for conciliation and appeal, a code of conduct, transparency rules and the possible development of an investment court.[112]

As part of an overarching proposal to establish a 'BRI Dispute Resolution Mechanism' integrating legal services from domestic and international markets and combining litigation, arbitration and mediation to resolve trade and investment disputes arising from the BRI,[113] the CCPIT established a 'Belt and Road International Dispute Management Center' (the 'Center') in Qianhai and Chengdu in January 2018. The Qianhai Center collaborates with domestic and foreign organisations including the Shenzhen International Court of Arbitration and the Qianhai BRI legal services association to support cross-jurisdictional dispute resolution and engages with mediators from diverse jurisdictions.[114]

Most established arbitral institutions have also taken the initiative to assist parties to settle their disputes relating to BRI projects through their services. For instance, the International Chamber of Commerce (ICC) has set up its own Belt and Road Commission to promote its mediation and arbitration services by engaging with corporations and governments across BRI countries and territories. The Hong Kong International Arbitration Centre (HKIAC) also convened its Belt and Road Advisory Committee consisting of independent experts across sectors of finance, infrastructure and construction.

In addition to in-person mechanisms, a proliferation of online BRI dispute resolution programmes have emerged to address the challenge of overcoming inherent logistical issues posed where parties are located in numerous jurisdictions[115] made all the more acute in light of migration trends[116] and pandemic-related travel restrictions. Examples include the Belt and Road Service Connections.[117] Hong Kong has taken steps to provide BRI-related dispute resolution services through the Department

[112] Ibid.

[113] Dahlan, Dimensions of the new Belt & Road international order.

[114] 张玲 (8 January 2018).前海'一带一路'国际商事诉调对接中心1月7日揭牌. *Qianhai News.*

[115] Grimmer, S., & Charemi, C. (2017). Dispute resolution along the Belt and Road. *The Asia-Pacific Arbitration Review 2018.*

[116] Ahl, B., & Czoske, P. P. (2016). Migration, the law and 'One Belt, One Road'. In L. Wolff, C. Xi & J. Chan (Eds.). *Legal Dimensions of China's Belt and Road Initiative* (pp. 448–471). Hong Kong: Wolters Kluwer.

[117] State Council Information Office, 2016.

of Justice's eBRAM.hk,[118] an online dispute resolution tool tailored to major infrastructure projects under the BRI that provides for secure online arbitration and mediation.

Within the Greater Bay Area, several cooperative arrangements have been put in place between the HKSAR and Mainland entities to provide for legal cooperation on BRI and related legal matters. On 12 October 2017, the Secretary for Justice on behalf of HKSAR and the Vice Mayor of Shenzhen renewed a five-year 'Co-operative Arrangement on Legal Matters'[119] (the 'Arrangement'). Similarly, in 2011, the State Council approved the development of the Shenzhen Qianhai Modern Service Cooperation Zone, 'to further cooperate with Hong Kong lawyers'.[120]

Existing Challenges Facing BRI Dispute Settlement Mechanisms

Scholars have assessed the challenges facing existing dispute settlement mechanisms for BRI disputes. From a policy perspective, Huang[121] views challenges to host-country public interest regulation in the context of ISDS claims as requiring further innovation in light of sustainable development principles. Tao[122] finds that existing mechanisms generally have limited scope and incomplete coverage. Zhang and Li[123] examine the inconsistent rulings, regulatory fears and narrow selection of arbitrators under the International Centre for Settlement of Investment Disputes (ICSID) arbitration mechanism in relation to BRI disputes. They suggest that China participate in existing ICSID reform efforts and consider developing an investment dispute settlement mechanism. Wang and Shi[124] examine 'fork in the road' clauses in bilateral investment treaties (BITs) providing for claims against the State to be addressed either

118 Henderson, A., Tai, M., Waldek, D., & Philips, A. (2017). The role of mediation in the resolution of belt and road disputes. *HSF Notes*.

119 Constitutional and Mainland Affairs Bureau (25 November 2011). 深圳市人民政府 香港特別行政區律政司法律合作安排. www.cmab.gov.hk/upload/LegCoPaper/Annex_20120319.pdf.

120 张玮, 2015.

121 Huang, S. (2016). Innovation of international investment dispute settlement mechanism from the perspective of sustainable development. *Contemporary Law Review*, *30*, 24.

122 Tao, L. (2019). The reform and development of investor state dispute settlement mechanism and China's choice. *Contemporary Law Review*, *33*, 37.

123 Zhang, X., & Li, W. (2020). Dilemma and transformation of international investment rule of law from global governance vision. *Law Science Magazine*, *41*, 30.

124 Wang, J., & Shi, L. (2018). Discussion on the path and mechanism of dispute settlement between the investing countries and the host country of the Belt and Road Initiative. *Journal of Southwest University (Natural Science Edition)*, *39*, 99.

through ISDS or local courts. They propose that such treaties should be amended to restrict the application of host-country remedies and that mediation and arbitration should be the main focus. Wang[125] further notes challenges in the enforcement of arbitral awards, particularly in the case where counties with strong economic leverage simply refuse to fulfil treaty obligations.

Varying Reform Approaches Addressing Perceived Limits of ISDS for BRI Disputes

While there has been agreement on the necessity of dispute settlement mechanisms for BRI disputes, scholars have differed in their reform recommendations. Perspectives have ranged from establishing a distinct BRI investment dispute settlement mechanisms reforming existing ISDS mechanisms.

Among the first category of scholars, G. Wang[126] argues that the existing dispute settlement mechanisms for commercial, economic, trade and investment disputes have their own shortcomings including the fact that common law litigation procedures largely do not reflect the legal systems of most participating BRI countries. Therefore, Wang suggests that BRI countries establish new dispute resolution institutions providing mediation, conciliation and arbitration services, reflecting traditional Chinese culture. Such institutions could be mandated to resolve trade and investment disputes, thereby helping host countries to integrate into the world economy. Chu[127] likewise proposes creating a dispute settlement centre for BRI countries focused on building an arbitration-centred, mediation focused and judicially guaranteed system of resolution.

Some scholars have advocated for the development of a BRI-oriented dispute resolution institution in conjunction with the Asian Development Bank (ADB). Zhang and Xu[128] suggest that the World Bank's ICSID be used as a model for establishing an investment dispute resolution centre based on ADB and BRI cooperation. Such a mechanism would need to

[125] Ibid.

[126] Wang, G. (2017). Discussion on the mechanism of dispute settlement of the Belt and Road Initiative. *Science China Life Sciences, 56.*

[127] Chu, B. (2017). The present and future one of the Belt and Road Initiative multi-dispute settlement center. *Science China Life Sciences, 26*(6), 72.

[128] Zhang, W., & Xu, J. (2017). 'The Belt and Road' and innovation of investment dispute settlement mechanism: The role and effect of AIIB. *Southeast Asian Affairs, 71.*

consider the judicial systems of host countries and focus on the resolution of investment disputes between Chinese state-owned enterprises (SOEs) and BRI host countries. Huang[129] likewise addressed the idea of establishing a dispute resolution centre connected with the ADB with mediation as the main mechanism, followed by arbitration and litigation, and supplemented by consultation.

Other scholars such as Hu and Huang[130] have suggested establishing a formal dispute settlement body in conjunction with the AIIB to resolve trade, investment and finance disputes. The proposed mechanism could embody the principles of consensus, cooperation and mutual understanding based on a two-tiered review system with ad hoc arbitration forming the first tier followed by appellate review similar to the World Trade Organisation (WTO) Appellate Body.

In order to formalise any newly developed mechanism, Zhang[131] proposes a Convention on the Establishment of an International Center for Belt and Road Investment Dispute Resolution. She suggests that the newly established institution forge business links with the ADB, World Bank and other organisations to seek their opinions and suggestions on dispute resolution matters.

Shan and Feng[132] put forward an integrated dispute resolution framework as a 'one-stop' platform where litigation, arbitration and mediation operate concurrently. This approach aims to incorporate the merits of diverse dispute settlement mechanism. Similarly, Hu[133] proposes that BRI countries jointly establish a new, unified, diversified permanent institution to supervise case performance and improve dispute resolution efficiency.

[129] Huang, C. *Constructing a Diversified 'One Belt, One Road' International Investment Dispute Settlement Mechanism with Mediation as the Main Force: Research on Comprehensive Reform of Judicial System and Criminal Trial (Part A)*. Beijing: People's Court Press, 2019.

[130] Hu, J., & Huang, J. (2018). Dispute resolution mechanisms and organizations in the implementation of 'One Belt, One Road' Initiative: Whence and whither. *Journal of World Trade, 52*, 815–837.

[131] Zhang, L. (2018). Research on improvement of the international investment disputes settlement mechanism under 'One Belt One Road' Initiative. *Law Science Magazine, 32*.

[132] Shan, W., & Feng, Y. (2021). The China International Commercial Court: Towards an integrated dispute resolution system. *Asia Pacific Law Review, 29*, 1.

[133] Hu, X. (2018). Research on dispute settlement mechanism in the context of the implementation of the Belt and Road Initiative and discussion on the training of international legal professionals. *Law Forum, 33*, 35.

Khan[134] suggests establishing a permanent investment court specifically for the CPEC initiative. The structure of such a court, he suggests, may be modelled on similar tribunals formed under the Comprehensive Economic and Trade Agreement between Canada and the European Union, which includes a court of first instance and an appellate tribunal. To reduce conflicts of interest, the appointment of permanent, tenured judges in place of arbitrators is proposed. Khan further suggests that the court should have jurisdiction to hear claims against investors brought by local communities and companies that are adversely affected by investor activities.

The possibility of establishing a standing investment court has likewise been put forward by Yee.[135] However, the sheer volume of BRI-related cases may render case administration burdensome. A unified appellate system with jurisdiction over appeals from first instance decisions rendered by local courts and tribunals, it has been suggested, could also improve consistency and harmonisation.

A second category of scholars advocate reforming existing ISDS mechanisms to provide for greater input from the diverse cross-section of global users. Zhang and Zhang[136] advance the idea of developing 'a new model of international cooperation and global governance'. They suggest that investment dispute settlement mechanisms be based on an international platform with distinctive regional input rather than creating a separate system within the ADB. Zhang and Chen[137] similarly suggest that host countries should enhance their awareness of existing international instruments and contribute experience. Common ground may be sought through constructing a set of regional investment dispute settlement mechanisms that are compatible with both international and Asia Pacific countries. This research reflects insights regarding the important role of regional institutions in contributing to global law-making bodies.[138] Contributing to further understanding of existing

[134] Khan, R. Q. A. (2018). CPEC investment court: An investment protection and dispute resolution mechanism for the China Pakistan economic corridor. https://ssrn.com/abstract=3148731.

[135] Yee, S. (2018). Dispute settlement on the Belt and Road: Ideas on system, spirit and style. *Chinese Journal of International Law, 17*, 907.

[136] Zhang, C., & Zhang, X. (2017). Study on international dispute settlement mechanism of One Belt One Road Strategy. *Southeast Asian Affairs, 24*.

[137] Zhang, X., & Chen, Z. (2017). Construction of the Road and Belt regional investment dispute settlement mechanism. *Academic Forum, 40*, 50.

[138] Ali, S. F. (2021). *Forming Transnational Dispute Settlement Norms: Soft Law and the Role of UNCITRAL's Regional Centre for Asia and the Pacific*. Cheltenham: Edward Elgar Publishing.

dynamics, the Beijing Arbitration Commission released a *Research Report on the Dispute Resolution Mechanism of Belt and Road Engineering Projects* analysing resolution practices in the construction of infrastructure projects.[139]

Scholarship concerning improving BRI dispute settlement mechanisms has included discussion on emphasis on mediation, while others have suggested primary use of arbitration. Ming[140] highlights the unique advantages of investment mediation for the resolution of BRI investment disputes that can be encouraged through inclusion in BITs between China and BRI countries. Liu[141] similarly encourages mediation alongside arbitration and litigation. He also suggests developing a team of specialised mediators for investment disputes. Dahlan[142] likewise views mediation as an important mechanism since it accommodates diverse sensitivities, complexities, political and legal variations. Mediation has the capacity to encourage mutual compromise and preserve commercial relationships and is compatible with the value of restoration of harmony.

According to Shi and Dong,[143] not all disputes can be resolved through consultation, and therefore investment arbitration remains important. The authors suggest that ICSID arbitration under the UN Commission on International Trade Law (UNCITRAL) arbitration rules provides a global framework for resolution. Additionally, access to in-country litigation may be appropriate in some cases. As such, ISDS dispute settlement should be pluralistic with consultation, voluntary mediation, arbitration and litigation as options.

Jiang[144] proposes a flexible format adopting arbitration as the primary dispute settlement mechanism complemented by diplomatic measures. According to this view, arbitration provides a reliable guarantee of

[139] BAC (Beijing Arbitration Commission) (2021). www.bjac.org.cn/news/view?id=3919.

[140] Ming, Y. (2018). Research on 'One Belt One Road' investment dispute resolution mechanism of mediation. *Journal of Nantong University (Social Science Edition)*, *34*, 62.

[141] Liu, G. (2018). The improvement of solutions to international investment disputes under the 'Belt and Road' initiative: Concurrently discussing the status and institutional construction of mediation system under the background of multiple dispute resolution. *Journal of Jining University*, *39*, 46.

[142] Dahlan, M. (2020). Envisioning foundations for the law of the Belt and Road Initiative: Rule of law and dispute resolution challenges. *Harvard International Law Journal*, *62*.

[143] Shi, J., & Dong, N. (2018). "Yidaiyilu Changyi" Xia Towzi Zhengduan Jiejue Jizhi de Goujian. [The construction of the investment dispute resolution mechanism under the "Belt and Road Initiative Proposal"]. *Wuda Guojifa Pinglun [Wuhan University International Law Review]*, *2*, 1.

[144] Jiang, S. (2018). Establishment of an international trade dispute settlement mechanism under the Belt and Road Initiative. In Y. Zhao (Ed.). *International Governance and the*

legitimate rights, thereby promoting the smooth operation of the trading system. Diplomatic measures, in the form of consultative dialogue, also plays an important role in mitigating political risks among less economically developed countries.

For many scholars, international commercial arbitration is considered an important recourse mechanism for BRI disputes. However, Chu[145] argues that the current international commercial arbitration system is incompatible with the BRI due to cultural and legal differences. Therefore, Chu suggests that a specialised arbitration cooperation alliance promote regional participation in international commercial arbitration. McLaughlin[146] similarly finds that the current model of arbitration is unable to preserve ongoing business relationships and that investor–state mediation offers a viable non-adversarial means of dispute settlement.

While a number of proposals have been put forward, overall, strengthening global systems to be more reflective and responsive to the needs of diverse users remains critical. Likewise, experimenting with new approaches to resolution, including investor–state mediation, may provide new avenues of resolution alongside existing arbitration mechanisms.

China-Related Global ISDS Investment Arbitration Cases

Investors of the BRI may bring claims against host governments through existing global ISDS channels. The Convention on the Settlement of Investment Disputes between States and Nationals of Other States (the 'Washington Convention') provides a mechanism for the settlement of foreign investor–state investment dispute and is currently the most important international convention for the settlement of ISIDs, with 155 ratifications. China signed the Washington Convention on 9 February 1990, and ratified it on 1 July 1992, and it entered into force for China on 6 February 1993.[147] The Washington Convention established the ICSID, the world's first specialised arbitration body for

Rule of Law in China under the Belt and Road Initiative (pp. 295–311). Cambridge: Cambridge University Press.

[145] Chu, B. (2019). Study on the establishment of the international arbitration cooperation alliance of the Belt & Road initiative. *Modern Law Science*, *41*, 181.

[146] McLaughlin, M. (2021). Investor–state mediation and the Belt and Road initiative: Examining the conditions for settlement. *Journal of International Economic Law*, *24* (3), 609. https://doi.org/10.1093/jiel/jgab028.

[147] International Centre for the Settlement of Investment Disputes (ICSID) list of contracting states and other signatories of the convention. *SICE*. www.sice.oas.org/dispute/comarb/icsid/w_csig.asp.

handling investment disputes between investors and host countries. In addition to ICSID, the main investor–states arbitration institutions include the Permanent Court of International Arbitration (PCA), Arbitration Institute of the Stockholm Chamber of Commerce in Sweden, London Court of International Arbitration, ICC and HKIAC.

According to the UN Conference on Trade and Development (UNCTAD), the key measures a foreign investor can leverage against a host country are those for alleged acquisition, expropriation or nationalisation of investments; measures for alleged breach of, non-performance of, or interference with contracts or concession agreements; measures for termination, nonrenewal or suspension of contracts or concession agreements; measures for the revocation or refusal to grant permits or licenses; measures for compulsory liquidation or winding up; and measures related to taxation, such as the imposition of capital gains taxes or back taxes.[148] According to recent case information, roughly half of filed disputes are related to decisions made by local governments, such as provinces and municipalities, or state agencies regarding issues such as the revocation of concessions or the conduct of privatisation programmes.

In recent years, China has become involved in ISDS investment arbitrations, both in cases where Chinese overseas investors have brought arbitration claims against foreign governments and in cases where China, as the host country, has been subject to arbitration claims by foreign investors.[149] As of the end of January 2022, of the cases handled by ICSID and PCA involving China that have been made public, nineteen of them were filed by Chinese investors (including Hong Kong and Australian investors) against foreign governments and seven were filed by foreign investors against the Chinese government, all seven of which were filed under BITs signed by China.[150] None were filed under investment contracts or host-country laws, nor were any cases filed under China's foreign free trade agreements (including investment chapters). The main legal issues involved in China-related investment arbitration cases have been blocked work, project suspension, equity acquisition, license cancellation, tax freezes and forced demolition.

[148] UNCTAD (2001). *Host Country Operational Measures.* https://unctad.org/system/files/official-document/psiteiitd26.en.pdf.

[149] Gong, B. H., & Wu, S. L. (2020). *Shehua Touzizhe: Dongdaoguo Zhongcaian Pingshu [Study on Investor–State Arbitration Cases Related to China].* Shanghai: Shanghai Renmin Chubanshe.

[150] Lexology. Year in review: International arbitration in China. www.lexology.com/library/detail.aspx?g=d26ffcec-b97d-45f4-9eba-4001dc0c09c1.

Among the known China-related cases, the controversies have centred on issues such as the appropriateness of the BITs invoked by investors, and the scope of the BITs submitted for dispute resolution. One recent issue is the status of Chinese SOEs given their deep involvement in overseas investment projects, and whether SOEs may be considered an agent of the Chinese government and therefore not an appropriate party for investment arbitration.

The case of *Beijing Urban Construction* v. *Yemen* (2014) involved Chinese investors suing a foreign government participating in the BRI.[151] In this case, the Yemeni Government argued that Beijing Urban Construction (BUC) was not a private investor. The tribunal opined that as long as SOEs maintain a competitive neutral position in the outbound investment process and perform their commercial functions in the investment process, they will likely be deemed qualified private investors and thus be regarded as nationals of a country within the meaning of the Washington Convention. Chinese SOEs therefore need to be concerned about whether the relevant BIT mandates registering as an investor under the host country's law. The arbitral tribunal in this case applied the Broches standard, analysing the Chinese SOE's conduct by separate considerations of (1) whether it acted as an agent of the government and (2) whether it performed governmental functions. The tribunal concluded that BUC was not acting as an agent of the Chinese government and that, on the facts, BUC performed commercial functions. Although the tribunal in this case ruled in favour of the Chinese SOE, its decision is not a binding precedent. This question has been raised in other venues, including the WTO where the question of whether Chinese SOEs are ipso facto 'public bodies' has been examined.

In another case involving China, *China Heilongjiang* v. *Mongolia* (2010),[152] the Mongolian Government adopted a similar strategy to Yemen, arguing that Heilongjiang International Economic and Technical Cooperative and Beijing Shougang Mining Investment Company Ltd ought to be considered public bodies rather than commercial entities; they did not have sufficient independence. Additionally, their activities in Mongolia were not economic in nature; therefore, the firms did not meet the three criteria to be deemed an 'economic entity' under Article 1 of the 1993 China–Mongolia

[151] Tian, H. (2018). Beijing Chengjian Jituan Su Yemen Zhengfu an Guanxiaquan Caiding Pingshu [Comments on the ruling of jurisdiction in *Beijing Urban Construction Group Co. Ltd.* v. *Republic of Yemen* (ICSID Case No. ARB/14/30)]. *Journal of Heilongjiang Administrative Cadre College of Politics and Law*, (2), 128–131.

[152] *Beijing Shougang & Others* v. *Mongolia*, UNCITRAL PCA Case No. 2010-20, Award (30 June 2017).

BIT. The tribunal found that the definition of economic entity in this provision was broad and did not differentiate on the basis of organisational purpose, commercial form, or ownership or control, and that there was no indication that the drafters of the BIT intended to restrict the concept of the economic entity through these criteria. The tribunal took the position that the term economic entity in the BIT was a reference to any type of legal entity engaged in economic or commercial activities; in this light, the Chinese SOEs met the requirements of Article 1(2) of the China–Mongolia BIT.

As can be seen from these cases, BRI host countries often face issues of geopolitical instability, economic imbalance, environmental degradation and ethnic and cultural conflicts, contributing to an increase in disputes.[153] A dispute prevention mechanism facilitating communications between host governments and investors may not completely prevent conflicts, and disputes but may facilitate improved information collection and early warning systems in order to avoid the considerable costs of international investment arbitration. Several countries with the support of UNCTAD have established prevention and coordination systems to help governments identify investment obstacles and challenges by obtaining relevant information through surveys and meetings with investors, and following up on such challenges.[154]

Conclusion

This chapter has reviewed the role of the BRI in infrastructure development alongside efforts at engagement with local communities. When referencing host-country standards, gaps in diligence may give rise to disputes. A number of approaches to addressing BRI disputes have emerged at the pre- and post-dispute stage. These include both formal and informal dispute mitigation and resolution mechanisms including China's mediation and consultation mechanism for the mining industry. Conversations with project coordinators highlight the importance of neutrality and relationship preservation in selecting between resolution options. During the post-dispute phase, formal mechanisms have likewise evolved to expand options available for resolving investment-related disputes.

[153] Chen, J., & Li, Z. (2018). Zhongguo dui 'Yidaiyilu' Yanxian Guojia Zhijie Touzi de Fengxian ji Qi Fangfan [China's risks and prevention of outward foreign direct investment in countries along 'the Belt and Road']. *Economic Geography*, *12*, 11.

[154] 'Unctad', UNCTAD. https://unctad.org/.

8

Conclusions and Policy Recommendations

Drawing on a qualitative triangulating approach that compares public facilitation policy with case-based practice, the book drew on project statistics, case studies and interviews with and surveys of dispute resolution professionals to better understand the dynamics of community-investor dispute prevention and resolution in practice and conditions for successful community engagement. Both positive and negative case studies, as explored in this book, help to elucidate the prerequisites necessary to move towards the aspiration of genuine shared ownership of pre-project consultative decision-making processes such that communities and stakeholders collectively benefit from the fruits of such projects.

The key empirical findings of this study confirm the adage that an ounce of prevention is in fact worth a pound of cure in the context of infrastructure development, yet challenges remain in facilitating effective preventative measures. Project data, survey findings and comparative case studies suggested that the introduction of heightened pre-project community consultation and grievance mechanisms within global multilateral development banks (MDBs) in the mid-2010–2020s have corresponded with a drop in the percentage of grievances per project from 15.4% in 2019 to 7.1% in 2021. While this downward trend was followed by a slight resurgence[1] simultaneously after 2021, the lack of consultation, disclosure or due diligence was no longer the single most cited cause of grievances amongst project-affected communities.[2] Greater attention to pre-project due diligence and community awareness of grievance channels appeared to account for these findings. Survey findings of fifty-five practitioners engaged in infrastructure-related dispute prevention in the Asia Pacific region likewise found that prior community consultation was considered the most effective approach to preventing infrastructure disputes. Overall,

[1] See Accountability Council Report: A new decade of complaints. www.accountabilityconsole.com/newsletter/articles/a-new-decade-of-complaints/.

[2] Ibid.

most disputes arose because of lack of adequate consultation with members of the community. Similarly, the twelve community–investor dispute case studies showed that in circumstances of increasingly heightened standards for pre-project community consultation compared with ad hoc discretionary consultation practices, the number of stalled/cancelled and litigated case declined by 33%, the percentages of cases referred to local courts declined by 16%, and the number of cases pursuing party agreement through mediation or negotiation increased by 50%. Overall, these findings provided measured evidence supporting the development of increasingly robust community consultative engagement channels, particularly for multilateral and national banks that have not yet implemented such policies. Such engagement channels, far from aggregating complaints, conversely correlate with a reduction in the overall proportion of project disputes.

The findings of this study have theoretical significance demonstrating the importance of community engagement in the Asia Pacific infrastructure development context. While infrastructure development theory has largely moved beyond an emphasis on top-down approaches to planning and implementation with growing recognition of the importance of community engagement for project sustainability, legitimacy and responsiveness, limited evidence of impacts of community-based engagement in dispute prevention has been available in the Asia Pacific region. This study has demonstrated that where attention to consultation, information sharing, grievance mechanisms and accountability are robust, a higher rate of project completion and dispute mitigation is reported. These findings confirm prior research regarding the efficiency gains of cohesive, inclusive and meaningful local partnerships.[3]

In addition, the findings demonstrated the important role of independent accountability professionals within multilateral and national banking institutions, non-governmental organisations (NGOs) and community groups in both advancing the quality of community engagement and contributing to increasingly harmonised legal and policy innovations for expanded accountability through decentralised transnational knowledge generation.[4]

Historically, in the several decades since the first multilateral community-investor dispute resolution and accountability mechanisms (AMs) were

[3] Ali, S. (2016). *Governing Disasters: Engaging Local Populations in Humanitarian Relief*, Cambridge: Cambridge University Press.

[4] Ali, S. (2021). *Forming Transnational Dispute Settlement Norms: Soft Law and the Role of UNCITRAL's Regional Centre for Asia and the Pacific*. Cheltenham: Edward Elgar.

introduced, much has been learned about public facilitation, community engagement and dispute prevention during the early stages of infrastructure development programmes. Part I of this book examined these historical developments. Knowledge sharing between banks supported a robust process of collective norm development. Multilateral community–investor dispute resolution and AMs were forged in response to past crises. Through a decentralized process, MDBs, NGOs and community groups generated knowledge through lessons learnt, resulting in legal and policy innovations. These changes ultimately expanded community protections and enhanced accountability for funding institutions. The creation of shared learning spaces such as the International Financial Institution Meetings, hosted by the world's MDBs on a rotating basis on themes such as information disclosure and stakeholder engagement, resulted in growing agreement on the relevance of underlying principles and good practices in community engagement in the context of infrastructure planning including open communication, accountability, redress and information disclosure.

The emergence of global principles of community engagement in infrastructure development through a process of global norm development were explored. Agreement on the parameters of community engagement have been crystalised in global policy documents including the Equator Principles, the United Nations (UN) Guiding Principles on Business and Human Rights, the Organisation for Economic Co-operation and Development Due Diligence Guidelines for Meaningful Stakeholder Engagement in the Extractive Sector, the Principles for Responsible Investment, and the International Labour Organisation Convention advancing the need for consultation between project finance institutions and host communities to arrive at shared understanding and agreement on matters that affect community well-being and prosperity.

Multilateral development bank-funded project data, survey research and case studies on the achievements, challenges and lessons learned in community–investor dispute prevention and resolution mechanisms amongst MDBs operating in the Asia Pacific region were examined. This included aggregate comparative data tracking the development and impact of dispute prevention mechanisms in MDBs on subsequent claims. The research found that prior to the mid-2010s, MDBs investor–community consultation was largely conducted on an ad hoc basis, usually after grievances occurred. Since then, greater attention has been placed on facilitating early-stage consultation, information disclosure and mechanisms for communities and investors to collectively address grievances.[5] Internal bank policies have likewise converged towards requiring increasingly higher levels of accountability and responsiveness for project-affected communities including transparent disclosure of prior complaints and outcomes. In some cases, broad community support is required for project initiation while for projects in the highest-risk categories, community consent is necessary.

The aim of the survey and follow-up conversations was to provide insights into the dynamics, challenges and lessons learned in engaging with communities to prevent and manage disputes in the context of infrastructure projects. Respondents offered suggestions as to how community–investor dispute resolution systems could be improved, including the need for more public education of community consultation and grievance mechanisms, a clear framework for the consultation process and more efforts to educate the community so that they 'understand . . . the risk of investment'. Follow-up conversations between 2021 and 2023 with practitioners working in dispute mitigation offered additional insights regarding the emerging duty of consultation and social license to operate, the development of hybrid forms of resolution and an emphasis on long-term contracting models and multi-tiered approaches to resolution. Given the small size of the survey sample, the findings cannot be considered generalisable. Likewise self-reported perceptions are subject to bias so statements may not always reflect actual practice.[6] However, the survey findings, together with the statistical analysis in Chapter 3 and subsequent case studies, point to a common finding underscoring the significance of prior community consultation and effective grievance mechanisms in mitigating infrastructure disputes.

Chapters 5 and 6 presented twelve case studies of community–investor dispute cases arising from projects either solely financed by the World Bank/International Finance Corporation or collaboratively financed with the Asian Development Bank, Asian Infrastructure Investment Bank and European Investment Bank in the Asia Pacific region in the transport, extractive and special economic zone development sectors. The first six cases presented in Chapter 5 were selected from disputes occurring prior to 2013 when pre-project consultation processes were largely discretionary. The second set of six cases presented in Chapter 6 occurred after 2013 when consultation processes became increasingly mandated and a higher

[5] Ali, S., Davis, W. E., & Lee, J. (2011). Multi-stakeholder dispute resolution: Building social capital through access to justice at the community level. *Pepperdine Dispute Resolution Law Journal, 11*(2), 181–206.

[6] Wall, J. A., & Kressel, K. (2012). Research on mediator style: A summary and some research suggestions. *Negotiation and Conflict Management Research, 5*(4), 403–421.

threshold for ascertaining community consent was introduced. During the first discretionary consultation phase prior to 2013, of the six cases, four were cancelled or stalled, one proceeded to court litigation and one was closed. For the second post-2013 phase characterised by heightened consultation standards, of the six cases, two were stalled/cancelled, zero proceeded to litigation, one was closed and three underwent a process of mediation or negotiation.

The case studies highlighted the risks of insufficient attention to community consultation, the necessity of maintaining relationships with decision makers that emerge over the course of a project life cycle, the need for genuine multi-directional rather than 'uni-directional' consultation, and the importance of thorough prior environmental and social impact assessment. Prior to 2013, standards for pre-project community engagement were relatively lax. The primary issues raised in project complaints included insufficient community consultation, lack of environmental planning, inadequate compensation for relocation, damage to local resources including water and farmland, economic harm, forced land transfer, undue influence, lack of consent and limited external monitoring.

After increasingly mandated community engagement practices emerged starting in 2013, a number of continuities and advancements were identified. These cases broadly demonstrate a number of key improvements including greater rigour in consultation and diligence mechanisms, heightened precision in identifying issues of community concern, higher pre-project diligence and screening standards, ongoing environmental and technical monitoring, the presence of locally trained mediators, capacity building for consultation participants, a longer-term view of community welfare and responsive grievance remedies. Shortcomings persisted in some cases, including instances of duress, lack of information disclosure, fraud, limited access to grievance mechanisms and environmental harm leading to project cessation in two cases.

The key comparative finding of the cases is that in circumstances of increasingly heightened standards for mandated community consultation with higher thresholds for ascertaining community consent, the number of stalled/cancelled and litigated case declined by 33%, the percentages of cases proceeding to court declined by 16%, and the number of cases pursuing party agreement through mediation or negotiation increased by 50% compared with ad hoc discretionary consultation practices prior to 2013.

Part III examined community engagement developments in the Belt and Road initiative (BRI) region and beyond. Chapter 7 explored the contributions and challenges in advancing sustainable development along the BRI and efforts at engagement with local communities. Through analysis of selected case studies, it found that when project funders referenced relatively robust host-country environmental, social and governance standards with higher pre-project diligence and accountability requirements, disputes tend to be avoided, while conversely when referencing lax host-country standards, gaps in diligence often give rise to disputes. A number of approaches have emerged to address resulting claims. These include the development of both formal and informal dispute mitigation and resolution mechanisms including the introduction of China's mediation and consultation mechanism for the mining industry, as well as post-dispute mediation and arbitration. Conversations with project coordinators highlighted the importance of neutrality and relationship preservation in the selection of resolution forums.

Future Directions and Recommendations

Drawing on case studies and survey data, this book explored the achievements, challenges and lessons learned in community–investor dispute prevention and resolution in infrastructure projects. Given the widescale impact of multi-jurisdictional infrastructure development initiatives in the Asia Pacific region, understanding how to advance a practice of shared ownership with local communities is necessary in order to realise the benefits of sustainable growth. The key finding of the book – that community consultation channels, far from aggregating complaints, conversely are correlated with a reduction in the overall proportion of project disputes – support the exploration of a number of relevant recommendations as follows.

First, given that the majority of funding support for infrastructure development projects in the Asia Pacific region come from national banks, engaging in joint knowledge generation with MDBs to advance effective pre-project due diligence policy in the region is recommended. This includes exploring the development of increasingly robust transparency, accountability and pre-project consultation standards. Systematic and regular shared learning spaces between independent AMs and national banking institutions to explore best practices will be helpful in supporting this effort.

Second, within the context of UN Commission on International Trade Law's WG III and relevant global bodies, specialised learning spaces can be arranged to advance shared understanding regarding the interface between policies advancing sustainability and the resolution of cross-border infrastructure investment disputes to ensure that such mechanisms account for public welfare and private interests drawing on the broad diversity and experience of users.

Third, the development of shared screening standards for infrastructure funding bodies at the national level will be useful further to filter out projects that present unjustifiable risks to communities in terms of social and environmental impact. Ongoing monitoring and evaluation of such standards will ensure that they reflect existing experience. Such standards can be reinforced over time through regional and multilateral instruments and agreements.

Fourth, while attention to the necessity and reach of community consultation has expanded over time, advancing the quality of consultation can be further strengthened through deeper exploration of relevant consultation principles that can guide the processes in diverse cultural settings including accountability and truthfulness, diversity, gender equity and justice;[7] the forms of community representation that result in manageably sized groups to advance high-quality consultative decision making;[8] exploring the type of preparation necessary to ensure that individuals have the requisite skills and capabilities to constructively engage in the consultation process; exploring the safeguards needed to protect the integrity and objectivity of the consultation process from coercive practices and examining the type of systems that can track effective follow-up implementation of decisions. Ongoing learning amongst members of the infrastructure development community to advance genuine consultative engagement for community prosperity will strengthen the beneficial impact of such projects.

[7] Ali, S. (2010). Measuring success in devolved collaboration. *Journal of Land Use & Environmental Law*, *26*(1), 93–112.

[8] See: George Soraya, World Bank. https://blogs.worldbank.org/en/eastasiapacific/indonesia-turning-unity-rebuilding-communities-after-natural-disasters.

SELECT BIBLIOGRAPHY

Ahl, B., & Czoske, P. P. (2016). Migration, the law and 'One Belt, One Road'. In L. Wolff, C. Xi & J. Chan (Eds.). *Legal Dimensions of China's Belt and Road Initiative*. Hong Kong: Wolters Kluwer, pp. 448–471.

Alexander, N., & Chong, S. (2019). *The Singapore Convention on Mediation: A Commentary*. Alphen aan den Rijn: Wolters Kluwer.

Ali, S. (2010). Measuring success in devolved collaboration. *Journal of Land Use & Environmental Law, 26*(1), 93–112.

Ali, S. (2011). *Resolving Disputes in the Asia Pacific Region: International Mediation and Arbitration in East Asia and the West*. New York: Routledge.

Ali, S. (2013). *Consumer Financial Dispute Resolution in a Comparative Context: Principles, Systems and Practice*. Cambridge: Cambridge University Press.

Ali, S. (2016). *Governing Disasters: Engaging Local Populations in Humanitarian Relief*. Cambridge: Cambridge University Press.

Ali, S. (2018). *Court Mediation Reform: Efficiency, Confidence and Perceptions of Justice*. Cheltenham: Edward Elgar Publishing.

Ali, S. (2018). The power of reflection: Advancing governance and dispute resolution systems through devolved reflection and shared knowledge generation. *The Journal of Baha'i Studies, 28*(4), 23–89.

Ali, S. (2021). *Forming Transnational Dispute Settlement Norms: Soft Law and the Role of UNCITRAL's Regional Centre for Asia and the Pacific*. Cheltenham: Edward Elgar Publishing.

Ali, S. (2023). Advancing research and practice in the governance of dispute resolution institutions through inclusive devolved reflection. In *Comparative and Transnational Dispute Resolution* (pp. 59–79). Abingdon: Routledge.

Ali, S. (Ed.). (2023). *Comparative and Transnational Dispute Resolution*. Abingdon: Taylor & Francis.

Ali, S. (2023). Decentralized global legal ordering. *Michigan State Law Review, 2023*(2), 319–376. https://ssrn.com/abstract=4047456.

Ali, S. (2024). Comparative international arbitration law. In Mathias Siems & Po Jen Yap (Eds.). *Cambridge Handbook of Comparative Law* (pp. 610–624). Cambridge: Cambridge University Press.

Ali, S. (2024). The seeming paradox of prevention: Dispute mitigation by multilateral development banks. *Civil Justice Quarterly*, *43*, 142–168.

Ali, S. F., Balcerzak, F., Colombo, G. F., & Karton, J. (2022). *Diversity in International Arbitration: Why It Matters and How to Sustain It*. Cheltenham: Edward Elgar Publishing.

Ali, S., Davis, W. E., & Lee, J. (2011). Multi-stakeholder dispute resolution: Building social capital through access to justice at the community level. *Pepperdine Dispute Resolution Law Journal*, *11*(2), 181–206.

Ali, S. F., & Ginsburg, T. B. (2013). *International Commercial Arbitration in Asia* (3rd ed.). Huntington, NY: Juris Publishers.

Ali, S., Teramura, N., Nottage, L., & Jetin, B. (2020). *New Frontiers in Asia-Pacific International Arbitration and Dispute Resolution*. Alphen aan den Rijn: Wolters Kluwer.

Arnstein, S. R. (1969). A ladder of citizen participation. *Journal of the American Institute of Planners*, *35*(4), 216–224. https://doi.org/10.1080/01944366908977225.

Balaton-Chrimes, S., & Haines, F. (2015). The depoliticisation of accountability processes for land-based grievances, and the IFC CAO. *Global Policy*, *6*(4), 446–454. https://doi.org/10.1111/1758-5899.12275.

Bath, V., & Nottage, L. (2011). Foreign investment and dispute resolution law and practice in Asia: An overview. In V. Bath & L. Nottage (Eds.). *Foreign Investment and Dispute Resolution Law and Practice in Asia*. Abingdon: Routledge.

Boulle, L. (2014). International enforceability of mediated settlement agreements: Developing the conceptual framework. *Contemporary Asia Arbitration Journal*, *7*(1), 35–68.

Buckley, A. (2012). Best practice community engagement for infrastructure projects: Building community ties that dig deeper. *Public Infrastructure Bulletin*, *1* (8), 1–2.

Campbell, C., Nottage, L. R., & Nappert, S. (2013). Assessing treaty-based investor–state dispute settlement: Abandon, retain or reform? *Transnational Dispute Management*, *11*(1), i–iv.

Chambers, R. (2002). *Participatory Workshops: A Sourcebook of 21 Sets of Ideas and Activities*. London: Earthscan.

Chu, B. (2017). The present and future one of the Belt and Road Initiative Multi-dispute Settlement Center. *China Legal Science*, 26(6), 72.

Chu, B. (2019). Study on the establishment of the International Arbitration Cooperation Alliance of the Belt & Road Initiative. *Modern Legal Science*, *41*, 181.

Coe, J. J. (2008). Transparency in the resolution of investor–state disputes: Adoption, adaption, and NAFTA leadership. *Kansas Law Review*, *54*, 1339–1385.

Connor, D. M. (1988). A new ladder of citizen participation. *National Civic Review*, *77*(3), 249–257. https://doi.org/10.1002/ncr.4100770309.

Cuppen, E., Bosch-Rekveldt, M. G., Pikaar, E., & Mehos, D. C. (2016). Stakeholder engagement in large scale energy infrastructure projects: Revealing perspectives using Q methodology. *International Journal of Project Management, 34*(7), 1347–1359. https://doi.org/10.1016/j.ijproman.2016.01.003.

Dahlan, M. R. (2018). Dimensions of the new Belt & Road international order: An analysis of the emerging legal norms and a conceptionalisation of the regulation of disputes. *Beijing Law Review, 9*(1), 87–112. https://doi.org/10.4236/blr.2018.91007.

Das, R., Laishram, B., & Mohammad, J. (2019). Public participation in urban water supply projects: The case of south-west Guwahati, India. *Water Research, 165*, 114989. https://doi.org/10.1016/j.watres.2019.114989.

De Sousa Santos, B. (2006). Globalizations. *Theory, Culture & Society, 23*(2–3), 393–399. https://doi.org/10.1177%2F0263276406023002 68.

Denzin, N. K. (1978). *The Research Act: A Theoretical Introduction to Sociological Methods*. New York: McGraw-Hill.

Deva, S. (2021). The UN Guiding Principles on Business and Human Rights and its predecessors. In I. Bantekas, M. A. Stein, & F. Seatzu (Eds.). *The Cambridge Companion to Business and Human Rights Law* (pp. 145–171). Cambridge: Cambridge University Press.

Diessner, R. (2020). Action research. *Converging Realities, 1*(1). Retrieved from https://bahai-library.com/diessner_action_research.

Erie, M. (2018). Dispute resolution, law and development, and legal elites in China's outbound investment. Law and Society Association talk on Panel 'China, International Law, and Development', CRN 33.

Erkul, M., Yitmen, I., & Çelik, T. (2016). Stakeholder engagement in mega transport infrastructure projects. *Procedia Engineering, 161*, 704–710. https://doi.org/10.1016/j.proeng.2016.08.745.

Errico, S. (2019). ILO Convention No. 169 in Asia: Progress and challenges. *The International Journal of Human Rights, 24*(2–3), 156–169. https://doi.org/10.1080/13642987.2019.1677611.

Feldman, E. A. (2015). Compensating the victims of Japan's 3-11 Fukushima disaster. *Asian-Pacific Law & Policy, 16*, 127.

Felstiner, W. L. F., Abel, R. L., & Sarat, A. (1980). The emergence and transformation of disputes: Naming, blaming, claiming ... *Law & Society Review, 15*(3–4), 631–654.

Foster, S. R. (2002). Environmental justice in an era of devolved collaboration. *The Harvard Environmental Law Review, 26*, 459–498.

Gallagher, K. P., & Yuan, F. (2017). Standardizing sustainable development: A comparison of development banks in Latin America. *Journal of Environment and Development, 26*(3), 243–271.

Garnett, R. (2017). Arbitration of cross-border consumer transactions in Australia: A way forward? *Sydney Law Review, 39*(4), 569–599.

Ginsburg, T., & Shaffer, G. (2012). The empirical turn in international legal scholarship. *American Journal of International Law, 106*(1), 1–46. https://doi.org/10.5305/amerjintelaw.106.1.0001.

Gulliver, P. H., & Greenhouse, C. (1978). *The Disputing Process: Law in Ten Societies*. New York: Columbia University Press.

Guo, Y. (2020). Construction strategy of China–Central Asia regional international Investment Dispute Settlement Mechanism in the context of the Belt and Road Initiative. *Practice in Foreign Economic Relations and Trade, 45.*

Halliday, T. C., & Shaffer, G. (Eds.). (2015). *Transnational Legal Order*. Cambridge: Cambridge University Press.

Han, X. L., & Zhai, Y. M. (2017). Investor–state arbitration mechanism in Sino-foreign investment agreement under the 'Belt and Road' Initiative. *Chinese Review of International Law, 5*, 32.

Hu, J. (2019). Arbitration mechanism to solve the tax problem of the Road and Belt Initiative. China National Cond Strength, *67*.

Hu, X. (2018). Research on dispute settlement mechanism in the context of the implementation of the Belt and Road Initiative and discussion on the training of international legal professionals. *Law Forum, 33*, 35.

Huan, H., & Zhang, S. (2019). A study of innovative legal system for arbitrators in China under the Belt and Road Initiative. *International Business Research, 40*, 79.

Huang, S. (2016). Innovation of international investment dispute settlement mechanism from the perspective of sustainable development. *Contemporary Law Review, 30*, 24.

Irwin, A., & Gallagher, K. P. (2013). Chinese mining in Latin America: A comparative perspective. *The Journal of Environment & Development, 22* (2), 207–234.

Jin, C. (2019). Coordination between international commercial arbitration and bankruptcy law in the context of the Initiative and Road: On judicial interpretation of Enterprise Bankruptcy Law (3). *People's Judicature, 16.*

Jin, R., & Sun, Y. (2019). Research on legal risks and countermeasures of Chinese enterprises' investment along the Belt and Road. *Intertrade, 70.*

Kang, N. (2019). Contractuality and judicialization: Enlightenment from the generating logic of international commercial arbitration to the Belt and Road Initiative. *Tribune of Political Science and Law, 37*, 167.

Kanosue, Y. (2015). When land is taken away: States' obligations under international human rights law concerning large-scale projects impacting local communities. *Human Rights Law Review, 15*(4), 643–667. https://doi.org/10.1093/hrlr/ngv026.

Larsen, P. B. (2019). Contextualising ratification and implementation: A critical appraisal of ILO Convention 169 from a social justice perspective. *The*

International Journal of Human Rights, *24*(2–3), 94–111. https://doi.org/10.1080/13642987.2019.1677613.

Lee, J., & Quek Anderson, D. (2016). The Global Pound Conference: A conversation on the future of dispute resolution. *Asian Journal on Mediation, 70.*

Levine, J., & Castles, S. (2021). The use of international arbitration tribunals for business and human rights disputes. In I. Bantekas, M. A. Stein & F. Seatzu (Eds.). *The Cambridge Companion to Business and Human Rights Law* (pp. 428–452). Cambridge: Cambridge University Press.

Levitt, P., & Merry, S. (2009). Vernacularization on the ground: Local uses of global women's rights in Peru, China, India, and the United States. *Global Networks*, *9*(4), 441–461. https://doi.org/10.1111/j.1471-0374.2009.00263.x.

Li, M. (2019). Online arbitration system of Hainan Free Trade Port. *Journal of Qiongzhou University*, *26*, 43.

Li, T. H. Y., Ng, S. T., & Skitmore, M. (2011). Conflict or consensus: An investigation of stakeholder concerns during the participation process of major infrastructure and construction projects in Hong Kong. *Habitat International*, *36*(2), 333–342. https://doi.org/10.1016/j.habitatint.2011.10.012.

Li, Y., & Panizza, U. (2012). The economic rationale for the principles on promoting responsible sovereign lending and borrowing. In C. Espósito, Y. Li & J. P. Bohoslavsky (Eds.). *Sovereign Financing and International Law: The UNCTAD Principles on Responsible Sovereign Lending and Borrowing* (pp. 15–37). Oxford: Oxford University Press.

Li, J., & Shaffer, G. (2024). China and the international legal order: Introduction to the Symposium. *UC Irvine Journal of International, Transnational, and Comparative Law*, *9*(1). https://escholarship.org/uc/item/3mq3p93m.

Li, Y., & Wang, L. (2017). Construction, legal risk identification and coping strategies of the Belt and Road Initiative. *Journal of Chinese Academy of Governance, 77.*

Liu, G. (2018). The improvement of solutions to international investment disputes under the 'Belt and Road' Initiative: Concurrently discussing the status and institutional construction of mediation system under the background of multiple dispute resolution. *Journal of Jining University*, *39*, 46.

Lo, C. W., & Tang, S. (2014). *Institutions, Regulatory Styles, Society, and Environmental Governance in China*. Abingdon: Routledge.

Lu, Y. (2018). The establishment of 'Belt and Road' international investment disputes settlement institution. *Journal of Law & Commerce*, *37*(1), 1–28. https://doi.org/10.5195/jlc.2018.151.

Luke, E. (2019). Environment and human rights in an investment law frame. In J. E. Viñuales & K. Miles (Eds.). *Research Handbook on Environment and Investment Law* (pp. 150–173). Cheltenham: Edward Elgar Publishing.

Mahmoudi, H., Roe, J., & Seaman, K. (Eds.). (2022). *Infrastructure, Wellbeing and the Measurement of Happiness*. Abingdon: Taylor & Francis.

McIntyre, O., & Nanwani, S. (Eds.). (2020). *The Practice of Independent Accountability Mechanisms (IAMS): Towards Good Governance in Development Finance*. Leiden: Brill-Nijhoff.

Menkel-Meadow, C. J. (2011). Why and how to study 'transnational' law. *UC Irvine Law Review*, *1*(1), 97–129.

Merry, S. E. (2011). Measuring the world. *Current Anthropology*, *52*(S3). https://doi.org/10.1086/657241.

Merry, S. E. (2012). Transnational human rights and local activism: Mapping the middle. In *Dialogues on Human Rights and Legal Pluralism* (pp. 207–228). New York: Springer.

Merry, S. E., & Levitt, P. (2018). The vernacularization of women's human rights. In S. Hopgood, J. L. Snyder & L. Vinjamuri (Eds.). *Human Rights Futures* (pp. 213–236). Cambridge: Cambridge University Press.

Min, J. H., Jang, W., Han, S. H., Kim, D., & Kwak, Y. H. (2018). How conflict occurs and what causes conflict: Conflict analysis framework for public infrastructure projects. *Journal of Management in Engineering*, *34*(4). https://doi.org/10.1061/(ASCE)ME.1943-5479.0000625.

Ming, Y. (2018). Research on "One Belt One Road" investment dispute resolution mechanism of mediation. *Journal of Nantong University: Social Sciences Education*, *34*, 62.

Ministry of Commerce of the People's Republic of China, National Bureau of Statistics, and State Administration of Foreign Exchange. (2018). *2017 Statistical Bulletin of China's Outward Foreign Direct Investment*. Beijing: China Statistics Press.

Mistelis, L. A., Stavros, L. B., & Lew, J. D. M. (Eds.). (2016). *The Evolution and Future of International Arbitration*. Alphen aan den Rijn: Kluwer Law International.

Muñoz Cabré, M., Gallagher, K. P., & Li, Z. (2018). Renewable energy: The trillion-dollar opportunity for Chinese overseas investment. *China & World Economy*, *26*(6), 27–49. https://doi.org/10.1111/cwe.12260.

Naudé Fourie, A. (2015). Expounding the place of legal doctrinal methods in legal-interdisciplinary research: Experiences with studying the practice of independent accountability mechanisms at multilateral development banks. *Erasmus Law Review*, (3), 95–110. https://doi.org/10.5553/elr.000045.

Ng, S., Skitmore, M., Tam, K., & Li, T. (2014). Public engagement in major projects: The Hong Kong experience. *Proceedings of the Institution of Civil Engineers: Municipal Engineer*, *167*(ME1), 22–31. https://doi.org/10.1680/muen.13.00009.

Ng, S. T., Wong, J. M. W., & Wong, K. K. W. (2010). Public participation in public private partnership projects: The way forward. *WIT Transactions on Ecology and the Environment*, *142*, 79–87. http://dx.doi.org/10.2495/SW100081.

Nickelsburg, S. M. (1998). Mere volunteers? The promise and limits of community-based environmental protection. *Virginia Law Review, 84*(7), 1371–1409. https://doi.org/10.2307/1073675.

Nonet, P., & Selznick, P. (1978). *Law and Society in Transition: Toward Responsive Law* (1st ed.). Piscataway, NJ: Transaction Publishers.

Nottage, L., Ali, S., Jetin, B., & Teramura, N. (2021). *New Frontiers in Asia-Pacific International Arbitration and Dispute Resolution.* Alphen aan den Rijn: Kluwer Law International.

Oi, J. C., Walder, A. G., & Kuik, C. C. (2024). *China's Global Economic Footprint: The Belt and Road Initiative and Beyond.* ASIANSTUDIES.

Pretty, J. N., Guijt, I., Thompson, J., & Scoones, I. (1995). *Participatory Learning and Action: A Trainer's Guide.* London: International Institute for Environment and Development.

Ramraj, V. V., & Tengaumnuay, T. (2022). Privatization of constitutional law: Thailand. In *Constitutionalism in Context* (pp. 517–540). Cambridge: Cambridge University Press. https://doi.org/10.1017/9781108699068.024.

Rasche, A. (2021). The UN Global Compact and the OECD guidelines for multinational enterprises and their enforcement mechanisms. In I. Bantekas, M. A. Stein, & F. Seatzu (Eds.). *The Cambridge Companion to Business and Human Rights Law* (pp. 195–213). Cambridge: Cambridge University Press.

Saper, B. M. (2012). The International Finance Corporation's Compliance Advisor Ombudsman (CAO): An examination of accountability and effectiveness from a global administrative perspective. *New York University Journal of International Law and Politics, 44*, 1279–1329.

Seck, S. L. (2016). Indigenous rights, environmental rights, or stakeholder engagement: Comparing IFC and OECD approaches to implementation of the business responsibility to respect human rights. *McGill International Journal of Sustainable Development Law and Policy, 12*(1), 57–97.

Shaffer, G. (2016). Theorizing transnational legal ordering. *Annual Review of Law and Social Science, 12*, 231–253.

Shi, J., & Dong, N. (2018). The construction of investor–state dispute settlement mechanism under 'the Belt and Road' initiative. *International Law Review of Wuhan University, 2*, 1.

Siddiqui, J., & Uddin, S. (2016). Human rights disasters, corporate accountability and the state. *Accounting, Auditing & Accountability Journal, 29*(4), 679–704. https://doi.org/10.1108/aaaj-07-2015-2140.

Sirajuddin, Z., & Grudens-Schuck, N. (2017). Public participation in agriculture and natural resource management projects in south and southeast Asia: A literature review. *Asian Journal of Agriculture and Development, 14*(1), 107–118.

Steininger, S. (2021). The Cambridge Companion to business and human rights law. In I. Bantekas, M. A. Stein & F. Seatzu (Eds.). *The Cambridge Companion to*

Business & Human Rights Law (pp. 406–426). Cambridge: Cambridge University Press.

Stipanowich, T., & Lamare, J. R. (2013). Living with 'ADR': Evolving perceptions and use of mediation, arbitration and conflict management in Fortune 1,000 corporations. *Harvard Negotiation Law Review, 19*. http://dx.doi.org/10.2139/ssrn.2221471.

Suárez Santos, R. (2019). Three decades since the ILO's Convention 169: Reflections in light of the experience of the private sector with prior consultation. *The International Journal of Human Rights, 24*(2–3), 272–278. https://doi.org/10.1080/13642987.2019.1677618.

Tan, J., & Yao, M. (2019). On China-Asean free trade area food trade disputes: Perfection of arbitration settlement mechanism. *Innovation, 13*, 73.

Tao, L. (2019). The reform and development of investor state dispute settlement mechanism and China's choice. *Contemporary Law Review, 33*, 37.

Teubner, G. (2002). Hybrid laws: Constitutionalizing private governance networks. In P. Selznick, R. A. Kagan, M. Krygier & K. I. Winston (Eds.). *Legality and Community: On the Intellectual Legacy of Philip Selznick* (pp. 311–331). Lanham, MD: Rowman & Littlefield.

Teubner, G. (2006). The anonymous matrix: Human rights violations by 'private' transnational actors. *Modern Law Review, 69*(3), 327–346. https://doi.org/10.1111/j.1468-2230.2005.00587.x.

Teubner, G. (2006). In the blind spot: The hybridization of contracting. *Theoretical Inquiries in Law, 8*(1), 51–71. https://doi.org/10.2202/1565-3404.1143.

Teubner, G. (2011). Self-constitutionalizing TNCs? On the linkage of 'private' and 'public' corporate codes of conduct. *Indiana Journal of Global Legal Studies, 18* (2), 617–638. https://doi.org/10.2979/indjglolegstu.18.2.617.

Teubner, G. (2014). *Constitutional Fragments: Societal Constitutionalism and Globalization*. (G. Norbury, trans.). Oxford: Oxford University Press.

Teubner, G. (2017). Corporate codes in the varieties of capitalism: How their enforcement depends on the differences among production regimes. *Indiana Journal of Global Legal Studies, 24*(1), 81–97. https://doi.org/10.2979/indjglolegstu.24.1.0081.

Tomaselli, A. (2019). Political participation, the International Labour Organization, and Indigenous peoples: Convention 169 'participatory' rights. *The International Journal of Human Rights, 24*(2–3), 127–143. https://doi.org/10.1080/13642987.2019.1677612.

Wang, G. (2017). The Belt and Road initiative in quest for a dispute resolution mechanism. *Asia Pacific Law Review, 25*(1), 1–16. https://doi.org/10.1080/10192557.2017.1321731.

Wang, G. (2017). Discussion on the mechanism of dispute settlement of the Belt and Road initiative. *China Legal Science, 56*.

Wang, C. (2019). Analysis on the construction of the amicable arbitration within Qianhai Free Trade Zone: Theory and the three-layered construction. *Hebei Legal Science, 37*, 52.

Wang, J., & Shi, L. (2018). Discussion on the path and mechanism of dispute settlement between the investing countries and the host country of the Belt and Road initiative. *Journal of Southwest University National, 39*, 99.

Wang, Q. (2020). ADR system construction for economic disputes settlement in the Belt and Road. *Hebei Legal Science, 38*, 115.

Wang, X. (2017). Construction of investment dispute settlement mechanism in the context of the Road and Belt initiative. *Northeast Asia Forum, 40*, 50.

White, M. (2021). Does the slipper fit? National action plans on business and human rights in South East Asia. In R. Ramcharan & J. Gomez (Eds.). *Business and Human Rights in Asia: Duty of the State to Protect* (pp. 21–34). Singapore: Palgrave Macmillan.

Xie, Y. (2020). China's foreign financial investment risks and countermeasures in the context of the Belt and Road initiative. *Modern Marketing, 6*.

Zhang, C., & Zhang, X. (2017). Study on international dispute settlement mechanism of One Belt One Road strategy. *Southeast Asian Affairs, 24*.

Zhang, L. (2018). Research on improvement of the international investment disputes settlement mechanism under 'One Belt One Road' initiative. *Law Science Magazine, 8*, 32–42.

Zhang, W., & Xu, J. (2017). 'The Belt and Road' and innovation of investment dispute settlement mechanism: The role and effect of AIIB. *Southeast Asian Affairs*, 71.

Zhang, X., & Chen, X. (2017). Construction of the Road and Belt regional investment dispute settlement mechanism. *Academic Forum, 40*, 50.

Zhang, X., & Li, W. (2020). Dilemma and transformation of international investment rule of law from global governance vision. *Legal Science Magazine, 41*, 30.

Zumbansen, Peer. (2023). Law as critical cartography: Global value chains, borders, and the spatialisation of vulnerability. *Transnational Legal Theory, 14*(1), 1–45. https://doi.org/10.1080/20414005.2023.2206760.

INDEX

Printed in the United Kingdom by TJ Clays Ltd.